COLLINS
WORDPOWER

Vocabulary Expander
Graham King

TED SMART

This edition produced for The Book People Ltd, Hall Wood Avenue, Haydock, St Helens WA11 9UL

HarperCollins*Publishers*
Westerhill Road, Bishopbriggs, Glasgow G64

www.**fire**and**water**.com

First published 2000

Reprint 10 9 8 7 6 5 4 3 2 1 0

© 2000 Estate of Graham King

Cartoons by Bill Tidy. Bill Tidy's website is at www.broadband.co.uk/billtidy/

HarperCollins Publishers would like to thank Bob Coole for reading and commenting on the text of this book.

ISBN 0 00 765988 1

A catalogue record for this book is available from the British Library

Typeset by Davidson Pre-Press Graphics Ltd, Glasgow G3

Printed and bound by Bookmarque

Contents

Dictionaries

Answers, Definitions and Meanings

Graham King (1930-1999)

Graham King was born in Adelaide on October 16, 1930.
He trained as a cartographer and draughtsman before joining Rupert
Murdoch's burgeoning media empire in the 1960s, where he became one
of Murdoch's leading marketing figures during the hard-fought Australian
newspaper circulation wars of that decade. Graham King moved to
London in 1969, where his marketing strategy transformed the *Sun*
newspaper into the United Kingdom's bestselling tabloid; subsequently,
after 1986, he successfully promoted the reconstruction of *The Sunday
Times* as a large multi-section newspaper.

A poet, watercolourist, landscape gardener and book collector,
Graham King also wrote a biography of Zola, *Garden of Zola* (1978) and
several thrillers such as *Killtest* (1978). Other works include the novel *The
Pandora Valley* (1973), a semi-autobiographical account of the hardships
endured by the Australian unemployed and their families set in the 1930s.

In the early 1990s, inspired by the unreadability and impracticality
of many of the guides to English usage in bookshops, Graham King
developed the concept of a series of reference guides called The One-Hour
Wordpower series: accessible, friendly books designed to guide the reader
through the maze of English usage. He later expanded and revised the
texts to create an innovative series of English usage guides that would
break new ground in their accessibility and usefulness. The new range of
reference books became the Collins Wordpower series (see page 227), the
first four titles being published in March 2000, the second four in May
2000. Graham King died in May 1999, shortly after completing the Collins
Wordpower series.

Introduction

A vocabulary with a purpose

Here is London art critic William Feaver describing an exhibition of paintings:

> Allen Jones gives recitals of body-language (the jut of the silken
> bottom, the parting of the lips) and colour code (1,000-watt yellows,
> ice-maiden blue), tracing erotic lines that slither down the thigh
> and die away in drips and stains.

That verbal communication must surely be as vivid and exhilarating as the paintings it describes. In it, the writer has obviously had at his elbow a formidable palette of words, none of them, incidentally, rare or quaint or outlandish, but words selected and blended to create a crystal-clear word-picture and a raw feeling of high excitement.

That is what communication, spoken or written, is fundamentally about – *clarity* and emotion: clarity to get your thoughts across unambiguously, and *emotion* to attract attention and convey feeling.

To help you achieve this you have the immeasurable advantages of the English language, which many regard as England's supreme gift to the world – a glittering emporium stocked with half a million words. Some 350 million people speak and write it exclusively, while a further *billion* use it as a second, official or dialect language. And these numbers are growing and will continue to grow as English becomes – as seems likely – the world's lingua franca.

The words are there; it's up to us to use them. The choice is mindboggling. And if there is anything – an object, an experience, a feeling or thought – for which there is no existing word, then the English language will promptly invent one (and does, at the rate of several thousand new words a year).

How many of them, though, do we need to know?

The answer is that we need a vocabulary sufficient to express ourselves clearly and confidently, and to enable us to understand any communication – from tax forms to travel brochures, newspapers to novels – with ease and enjoyment.

How large is your lexicon?

How large is your lexicon – your vocabulary, your stock of words that you can rattle off intuitively in your speech and writing? Ten thousand? Twenty thousand?

For the average person, estimates vary wildly. But first it's important to understand that everyone possesses *two* vocabularies. The smaller of these is what's called your *active vocabulary*, consisting of words you use from day to day. Then there is your *retentive vocabulary* – a rather larger hoard of words that you carry in your memory, words which you may not use regularly or even at all, but whose meanings are more or less familiar to you. This is the vocabulary you use when listening to someone speaking, or reading what someone else has written.

Recent research suggests that our vocabularies are far more extensive than we ever thought they were. A 1986 project studying children's vocabularies in Britain indicated that an average 11-year old understood more than 10,000 words and that an average 14-year old had a vocabulary of at least 20,000 words. To achieve these vocabularies, the kids must have learned four new words every day since birth!

These high levels are reflected in a similar US study of adult vocabularies, which revealed that a secretary, for example, had an active vocabulary of 30,000 words and a retentive or passive vocabulary of nearly 40,000. For a college lecturer, or a person who was a voracious reader, these levels soared to 60,000 and 75,000 respectively.

Yet the King James version of the Bible (1611) has a vocabulary of just 8,000 words, and John Milton, perhaps the leading writer and poet of the 17th century, made do with a similarly modest stock of words. Shakespeare's works have also been subjected to lexicographical examination: and that master of the English language commanded the use of a mere 15,000 or so root words plus a similar number of variants – and of these 1,500 were his own inventions!

However we must remember that in Shakespeare's time the lexicon of English was probably only a tenth of the size it is today. As consumers of an ever-expanding communications and media network we are increasingly challenged by words, expressions and names that are unfamiliar to us. There is a growing trend for newspaper and magazine reviewers and columnists to pepper their prose with words that (if we are conscientious) send us scuttling for our dictionaries. Contemporary novelists take delight in provoking in us feelings of ignorance, intellectual laziness or guilt by insinuating into their fiction passages cunningly counterpoised on words that elude understanding, the only key to which is a good dictionary. Here are just a few hard words plucked from the pages of a best-selling novel* of the 80s ostensibly aimed at ordinary readers:

> *cachexy, chrestomathy, frowardness, nacreous, peccant,*
> *raparee, scend, scrovies, syzygy, tramontane, tumblehome.*

All those words are justified in the context of the narrative, but can your vocabulary cope with that sort of lexical assault – words that to some people are simply irritating obstacles to understanding?

Nowadays, it's not just broadsheets and 'clever' novelists who challenge our understanding. Popular television shows, inspired by the intellectual audacity of *The Simpsons*, now frequently challenge the viewer's comprehension: ten years ago, who would have expected a 'teen' show such as *Buffy the Vampire Slayer* to demand that its audience become acquainted with words such as 'unconscionable'? Aside from merely showing off, every writer and speaker is duty bound to search out and use words that convey his or her thoughts and intentions *precisely*, just as the caring reader and listener is obliged to find out what they mean. If this entails a trip to the dictionary now and then, so be it. Anyway, that's how much of our individual vocabularies are shaped and enlarged.

There is, however, a far more direct method of developing a vocabulary to meet the challenge of today's verbal onslaught.

Collins Wordpower Vocabulary Expander is specifically designed to boost your vocabulary – and with it your understanding and mastery of the English language – efficiently, enjoyably, and in a remarkably short time.

*The Ionian Mission, a Napoleonic seafaring novel by the great Patrick O'Brian (HarperCollins).

But far from being merely a list of words and meanings (for which you can easily consult a dictionary) it is a road-tested method that will help you increase and, more importantly, *retain*, the valuable knowledge you acquire. Your vocabulary will become a word bank in which the words you deposit in your expanding account can be withdrawn when you need them. With interest.

How to use this book

Collins Wordpower Vocabulary Expander is a workbook – but a workbook you will find not only instructive but fun. Its purpose is twofold: to introduce you to an extensive range of words in the English language that may be unfamiliar to you but which you will find useful, even essential; and to help you *memorise* them so that they can be safely tucked away in your vocabulary for future use.

The words are arranged alphabetically in sections from A to WXYZ. Each entry is presented as a mini-test. You may be asked to assign the meaning of a word from a choice of two or three definitions, or you may be given the meaning and asked to come up with the word. You may be asked whether the usage of a word in a statement is correct or not, or challenged to use a word in a sentence. Answers and meanings can be checked quickly and easily and scoring guides will give you some clues to your progress. All the way from A to Z, this method is designed to be the most stimulating and engaging, as well as an exceptionally efficient, way with which to expand your vocabulary and knowledge of the language.

If you are serious about building your vocabulary you will inevitably become interested in words themselves – their power and elegance, their history and even their contrariness – so each alphabetical section includes short articles on usage; new, rare and unusual words; word elements and derivations; and specialist vocabularies – those to do with our bodies, food and drink, literature, the arts and science, and so on.

How long will the course take? The answer is very much up to you, the time you spend on the book, and, of course, your powers of concentration and your capabilities. During the 'road-testing' of *Collins WordPower Vocabulary Expander*, many trial readers found it convenient and ultimately rewarding to tackle a different letter group each week, taking about 20 weeks in all (they didn't require a week to tackle all the word groups – those beginning with *k, q* and *wxyz* were a doddle in a day!)

It can take a lot less time, of course. Several trial readers stormed through the entire vocabulary from A to WXYZ in just two weeks while still retaining a large proportion of what they'd learnt, but it's vitally important not to rush things. There is little point in learning the meanings of, say, 20 words that are new to you, and then promptly forgetting them. Throughout the book you are encouraged to revise, and there are various quizzes and games to help make revision as painless as possible.

You are also urged to acquire a really good dictionary (if you don't already own one) and guidance on choosing and using a dictionary will be found on page 40.

By the time you reach WXYZ there is every possibility that your vocabulary will have expanded by a thousand or two thousand words which you can call into play at any time – in your reading, speech or writing. That would be a very worthwhile attainment. And one which, in due course, should result in your regarding a well-stocked vocabulary as one of your most precious possessions.

Acknowledgements

Much of the source material for this book came from the following works, which the author and publisher gratefully acknowledge:

The New Shorter Oxford English Dictionary (OUP); *The New Oxford Dictionary of English* (OUP); *The Collins Softback English Dictionary* (HarperCollins); *Collins English Dictionary, Millennium Edition* (HarperCollins); *The Chambers 21st Century Dictionary* (Chambers); *Cambridge International Dictionary of English* (CUP); *David Crystal: The Cambridge Encyclopaedia of the English Language,* (CUP); *Dictionary of Contemporary English* (Longman); *Cassell Dictionary and Thesaurus* (Cassell); *BBC English Dictionary* (BBC and HarperCollins); *Roget's International Thesaurus* (HarperCollins); *Webster's New Twentieth Century Dictionary; Funk and Wagnalls Standard College Dictionary; The Encyclopedia Britannica; The New Fowler's Modern English Usage* (Clarendon Press, Oxford); *The Concise Dictionary of English Etymology* (Clarendon Press, Oxford); *David Grambs: Literary Companion Dictionary* (Routledge & Kegan Paul); *J A Cuddon: A Dictionary of Literary Terms* (Doubleday & Co, New York); *Chambers Science and Technology Dictionary* (Chambers); *The Times Guide to English Style and Usage* (Times Books); *The Economist Style Guide* (Hamish Hamilton); *Steven Pinker: The Language Instinct; Richard P Brennan: Dictionary of Scientific Literacy* (John Wiley & Sons).

A

Choose the Correct Meaning

Which one of the three alternatives, a, b or c, most accurately fits the meaning of the word? Circle your choices (while trying not to make wild guesses!) and then check the answers on page 212.

aberration **a.** excessive sneezing **b.** a departure from the normal **c.** airline navigators' allowance for polar magnetism.

abeyance **a.** a state of being suspended **b.** the Muslim law of parental respect **c.** humiliation.

abnegation **a.** to be resigned to one's fate **b.** to renounce upon oath **c.** renouncing or denying oneself a privilege.

abrogate **a.** to coarsely insult someone **b.** to formally revoke or abolish **c.** to condense or abridge a text.

abstruse **a.** to be argumentative **b.** hard to understand **c.** hopeless.

accede **a.** agree **b.** abandon **c.** the steepest part of a slope.

accolade **a.** a meritorious award **b.** the plumage on a governor's ceremonial headgear **c.** a fizzy yoghurt-style drink.

accrue **a.** to turn sour **b.** to attack bitterly **c.** to increase by addition or growth.

accretion **a.** to increase by external growth **b.** the components of concrete **c.** residue left by high tides.

Achilles heel **a.** an athlete's complaint **b.** fashionable shoes by a Greek designer **c.** a vulnerable spot

acolyte
a. a devoted attendant **b.** ancient Egyptian hand-held oil lamp **c.** a pinkish gemstone.

acquiesce
a. a wine-making process reducing sweetness **b.** to agree without protest **c.** to motivate unconsciously.

acrid
a. a bluish hair colouring **b.** excessively solemn **c.** unpleasant pungent smell.

acrimonious
a. caustic or bitter in manner **b.** inclined to drunkenness **c.** following bad advice.

actuary
a. a hospital volunteer helper **b.** part of a library where religious books are kept **c.** an insurance statistician.

acuity
a. keenness or sharpness in thinking b. brilliance with maths and numbers **c.** the pain experienced by gout sufferers.

acumen
a. a pepper-like substance from S America **b.** penetrating insight **c.** the ability to tolerate giddy heights.

adamant
a. easily adaptable **b.** hard and inflexible **c.** ant-like.

ad hoc
a. for a particular purpose **b.** very occasionally **c.** a last-minute invitation.

adjunct
a. a fracture of the wrist **b.** something incidental or not essential added to something else **c.** a cancelled advertisement.

adroit
a. left-handed **b.** very skillful **c.** easily manipulated.

adventitious
a. appearing accidentally or unexpectedly **b.** prone to take extreme risks **c.** reluctance to take risks.

aegis
a. giving protection or sponsorship **b.** the overuse of commas and other punctuation marks **c.** racial harmony.

affidavit
a. a solicitor's instruction **b.** a written statement made on oath **c.** a judge's direction to the jury.

aficionado
a. the sword thrust that kills in a bullfight **b.** a large wine barrel for aging sherry **c.** a keen devotee or follower.

aggrandize
a. to withhold information from an official enquiry **b.** to increase one's wealth or power **c.** to marry late in life.

agnostic
a. a religious hermit **b.** a severe sinus irritation **c.** someone who holds that knowledge of the existence of God is impossible.

agronomy   **a.** the study of grasses **b.** the study of river pollution **c.** the study of soil and cultivation.

akimbo   **a.** sitting with legs crossed **b.** standing with hands on hips, elbows pointing away **c.** standing with legs wide apart.

alacrity   **a.** liveliness and cheerful briskness **b.** withdrawn and uncommunicative **c.** argumentative.

alfresco   **a.** famous New York salad containing walnuts **b.** a refreshing wine-based drink **c.** in the open air.

allude   **a.** a composition for the harp **b.** to refer to something indirectly **c.** the first stage of drug rehabilitation.

alter ego   **a.** a mind-bending drug **b.** one's other or second self **c.** an overwhelming desire to be someone else.

altruism   **a.** unselfish concern for and generosity towards others **b.** in horses a tendency to lameness **c.** an inability to form conclusions from overwhelming evidence.

ALTRUISM (**c**)

amalgam **a.** a compound of different metals **b.** ash left from burnt ivory **c.** fool's gold.

amanuensis **a.** a nurse specialising in tubercular care **b.** a secretary **c.** a sewing machine attachment that makes buttonholes.

ambidextrous **a.** the ability to juggle with hands and feet **b.** the ability to jump long distances **c.** the ability to use both hands with equal facility.

ambience **a.** the glow from a fire **b.** the natural warmth of a human body **c.** the feeling or atmosphere of a place.

ambivalent **a.** not complete **b.** exhibiting conflicting or contradictory attitudes **c.** inability to walk although physically capable.

ameliorate **a.** to blend oil and water **b.** to improve or make better **c.** to initiate a person into a religious order.

amenable **a.** open to suggestion **b..** easily succumbing to temptation **c.** keen to apologise, even when unnecessary.

amoral **a.** overly prone to sexual excitation **b.** lacking normal moral standards **c.** sleeping with two partners simultaneously.

amortise **a.** to reduce or pay off a debt **b.** to fix two pieces of wood together without nails or screws **c.** to die leaving two or more wills.

anachronism **a.** type of lobster **b.** passion for collecting old clocks **c.** a person or event misplaced in time.

analgesic **a.** a non-mercuric dental filling **b.** a substance that reduces pain **c.** a family of drugs that reduces inflammation.

analogous **a.** capable of being analysed **b.** similar in some respect **c.** process for waterproofing leather.

anathema **a.** something detested **b.** a love-hate relationship **c.** a diagnostic technique for lung diseases.

ancillary **a.** doubtful in meaning **b.** shapeless **c.** subsidiary.

angst **a.** fleeting mental instability **b.** unfounded sense of anxiety or remorse **c.** obsessional need to seek revenge.

annuity   **a.** the period between Christmas and New Year **b.** a
stipend paid each year to C of E vicars **c.** a fixed sum
paid annually.

If, after checking the answers, you find that you failed to identify
the correct meanings of all these 50 words beginning with A, you'll find it
worthwhile revisiting those that caused you to stumble and to commit
them to memory. If you scored 40 correct you did well – and in the process
you will add a further 10 words to your growing vocabulary. Now for
another 50 A words . . .

Identify the word

From the meanings given, fill in the gaps and identify the words:

1. To abolish, or cancel the validity of something.   *a _ _ u l*
2. Deviating from the norm or usual   *ano _al _us*
3. Obsessional fear of becoming fat by refusing
   food   *a _ _ r _ xia*
4. A collection of literary works, excerpts or
   passages   *anth _ _ _ gy*
5. A course of *hors d'oeuvres* in an Italian meal   *an _ ip _ sto*
6. A feeling of intense dislike or hatred   *ant _ pa _ _ y*
7. Something that's the exact opposite   *ant _ tht_ s _ s*
8. A word that means the opposite of another
   word   *an _ o _ ym.*
9. A laxative   *aper _ _ nt*
10. A short pithy saying expressing a general
    truth   *aph _ r _ sm*
11. Someone who keeps bees   *api _ _ ian*
12. Extreme self-confidence or self-possession   *ap _ _ mb*
13. A prophetic revelation or disclosure   *apo _ _ lyp _ e*
14. Something of questionable authenticity   *apo _ _ _ phal*
15. The highest point   *ap _ _ ee*
16. Abandonment of one's faith or religion   *ap _ sta _ y*
17. A short cryptic remark containing an accepted
    truth   *apo _ _ egm*
18. The elevation of a person to the status of a god   *ap _ theo _ _ s*
19. Ideally suited for the purpose   *app _ _ ite*

20. Worthy of praise and commendation — *app _ _bation*
21. A less significant part or thing — *app _ _ ten _ nce*
22. Appropriate or pertinent — *apr _ _ os*
23. The domed or vaulted recess at one end of a church — *a _se*
24. Having the curved shape of an eagle's beak — *aq _ _ line*
25. Land capable of being cultivated for crops — *ar _ _ le*
26. The scientific group name for spiders — *ar _ ch _ id*
27. Subject to personal whims and prejudices — *arb _ _ r _ ry*
28. Requiring secret knowledge to be understood — *a _ cane*
29. The jargon peculiar to a group, often thieves — *a _ _ ot*
30. A catastrophic conflict; a war to end all wars — *Arma _ _ ddon*
31. A large French-style chest or cabinet — *ar _ _ ire*
32. To bring a prisoner before a court to answer an indictment — *ar _ a _ gn*
33. Someone unscrupulously ambitious — *arr _ vi _ te*
34. Someone who abstains from worldly pleasures — *as _ _ tic*
35. Someone who acts obstinate or stupid — *as _ _ine*
36. A malicious or disparaging remark — *as _ _ r _ ion*
37. A sharp temper — *asp _ r _ ty*
38. Persevering and hard-working — *ass _ _ uous*
39. To soothe and relieve pain or grief — *ass _ _ ge*
40. The wasting away of part of the body — *atro _ h _*
41. To extend and make thin, or to weaken — *att _ _ u _ te*
42. Wearing away to weaken or destroy — *att _ i _ ion*
43. Not conforming to type; not typical — *at _ _ i _ al*
44. In touch and fully informed — *au f _ _ t*
45. A situation that's favourable — *aus _ _ c _ ous*
46. Independent of others — *auton _ _ ous*
47. A person's job or career — *a _ oc _ tion*
48. Resembling or concerning a helpful uncle — *av _ _ cular*
49. Something askew or twisted — *aw _ y*
50. A fact or a truth that is self-evident — *ax _ _ _ tic*

A few spaces unfilled? With the aid of the answers on page 212 fill in the gaps and your knowledge at the same time. If you scored 35 or more, well done.

30-Sec Quickpick: Spot the Misfits

With a minimum of hesitation, underline or circle the misfits in each word group:

abase, degrade, demean, coarsen
abettor, urger, eager, demagogue
abrogate, abrupt, rash, precipitate
accentuate, emphasise, contend, stress
ameliorate, antedate, improve, rectify
anneal, proclaim, declare, promulgate
aphorism, proverb, epigram, antithesis
argot, whim, cant, dialect
asinine, ascetic, foolish, fatuous
attest, witness, audition, vouch for

Answers on page 212. Snap tests like this one will feature throughout this book and are designed to reveal weaknesses in your grasp of word meanings. With such tests you should be aiming for scores of 9+.

Androphobia and other Fears and Obsessions

There are hundreds of recognised phobias and manias. Most are extremely exotic (*theophobia* = fear of God's wrath; *phobophobia* = fear of fear?) but many crop up in our everyday reading and are worth knowing about. Here is a selection:

Fears and Phobias

Fear of confined spaces	*claustrophobia*
high places	*acrophobia*
men	*androphobia*
women	*gynophobia*
water	*hydrophobia*
work	*ergophobia*
animals	*zoophobia*
crossing a street	*agyrophobia*
death and corpses	*necrophobia*
open spaces	*agoraphobia*
spiders	*arachnephobia*

7

the number 13	*triskaidekaphobia*
foreigners or strangers	*xenophobia*

Obsessions and Manias

A craze for alcoholic drink	*dipsomania*
books	*bibliomania*
death and corpses	*necromania*
faeces	*coprophilia*
lighting fires	*pyromania*
sex with a man (by women)	*nymphomania*
sex with a woman (by men)	*satyromania*
grandeur, self-importance	*megalomania*
one's self	*egomania*
stealing	*kleptomania*

Clues to meaning: Recognising word elements

A vast number of English words have been built from Greek and Latin roots and other elements: prefixes, suffixes and combining forms. Recognising these can provide instant clues to the meanings of thousands of otherwise unfamiliar words. Here is a selection of '*a*' words.

Word, Element	Origin	Meaning	English words
amor, am, amat	Latin	love	*amour, amorous, enamoured. amicable*
annus, annu, enni	Latin	year	*annual, annuity, annals, perennial*
audire, audi, audit	Latin	to hear	*audio, audible, audience, audition, audit, auditor, auditorium, auditory*
arkhaio, archae	Greek	beginning	*archaeology, archaic, archaism. Archaeozoic*
autos, aut, auto	Greek	self	*autobiography, autograph,*

			autocrat, autocracy, autologous
ante-	Latin	before	*antecedent, antechamber, antedate, antebellum, antenatal, antediluvian, anterior, ante (stake)*
-able, -ible	Latin	capable of suitable for	*watchable, eatable, forcible, edible, payable*

Astronomy, Space and The Universe

Now let's train a telescope on your knowledge of the heavens. No, you're not expected to be on intimate terms with the Doppler effect, Hubble constants or syzygy, merely *au fait* with a few basic terms and concepts. Just answer *true* or *false* to these 10 questions. Then check the answers on page 212.

	True	**False**
1. A *satellite* is a man-made orbiting structure	___	___
2. An event that occurs on the hour is called *diurnal*	___	___
3. A *meteor* is a mass that glows on entering the earth's atmosphere	___	___
4. The time light takes to reach the sun from the earth is a *light year*	___	___
5. The *'big bang'* is the theoretical explosion that gave birth to the universe	___	___
6. A *corona* is the bright ring surrounding a celestial body	___	___
7. An *eclipse* occurs when one celestial body moves in front of and blocks the light from another	___	___
8. An *aurora* is the brightest part of a sunspot	___	___
9. A *supernova* is a mass of millions of stars bonded by gravity	___	___
10. The *cosmos* is a synonym for the *universe*	___	___

A little light revision

No doubt by now you've had your fill of A words. But before we leave them, how sure are you that your vocabulary's digestive system is in good working order? Hand on heart, do you remember the meanings of these words?

acolyte, ad hoc, adventitious, angst, approbation, avuncular, asinine, adamant, agnostic, anathema.

Animal Droppings

A news item reported recently that a Government Environment Agency officer "had found *spraints* on a river bank near Reading", and from these deduced that after an absence of many years otters had returned to the area. Spraints? Indeed,

ANIMAL DROPPINGS

spraints are otter droppings, the term being a relic from the time when humans were much closer to animals than they are now. The ability to identify the faeces of animals could make the difference between catching a meal and going hungry. Droppings weren't merely droppings. They had character, along with distinctive names: *waggyings* (fox); *friants* (boar); *crotels* (hare); *fumets* (deer) and *werderobes* (badger) – all now extinct, of course (the names, not the animals).

Another scatological curiosity is the old word for dried, bleached dog excrement, which up until the early 19th century used to be collected from the streets and sold for use in the preparation of fine leather. The word for this noisome product was *pure*.

B

Right or Wrong?

Knowing the meanings of a lot of words can be very useful. But knowing how to *use* words in their proper context, expressively and precisely, can be even more rewarding and profitable. Here's an exercise to test your knowledge of certain words.

Are they being used correctly? Answer right/wrong and then check the answers on page 212.

	Right	**Wrong**
1. The rave ended on a distinct **bacchanalian** note, for those who could remember the next morning.	—	—
2. Senior surgical nurses had to undergo a stiff examination in **badinage** before graduating.	—	—
3. For Rockefeller, the $16 million donation was a mere **bagatelle**.	—	—
4. The giant fixed a **baleful** eye on the two children.	—	—
5. They leaned on the **balustrade**, watching the crowd beneath.	—	—
6. In his finest ceremonial robes the chief led the solemn **banal** to the sacrificial temple.	—	—
7. The **barmitzvah** holiday is the one enjoyed most by Jews.	—	—
8. Kitty's designs exhibited all the extravagance of the **baroque**.	—	—

9. The director's interpretation of *Uncle Tom's Cabin* was spoiled by the **bathos** of the final scene. ___ ___

10. The rustlers rode cautiously through the parched **bayou**. ___ ___

11. Edith returned from her visit to the cathedral in a state of **beatitude**. ___ ___

12. The **behemoth** spread her pretty wings and flew from his hand. ___ ___

13. They listened in silence as the church team rang the **bel canto**. ___ ___

14. The document **belied** the sister's claim to the estate. ___ ___

15. The red-faced driver assumed a **bellicose** manner and refused to allow them on the bus. ___ ___

16. They decided to sail, as the **bellwether** indicated good conditions. ___ ___

17. The comedian from Manchester left them **bemused** and rolling in the aisles. ___ ___

18. Mr and Mrs Drayton were the most gentle and **benign** couple you could ever hope to meet. ___ ___

19. Left mostly to themselves in the decrepit orphanage, the children were **bereft** of all hope. ___ ___

20. The factory was immensely profitable, turning out millions of **bespoke** garments every month. ___ ___

You've made 20 choices, but are you absolutely sure about all of them? You'll find the correct meanings of those words used incorrectly in this exercise on page 000. If you are in doubt about any of the others, be smart and look them up in your dictionary.

Choose the Correct Meaning

Which of the alternatives, *a* or *b*, most accurately defines the meaning of the word? Circle your choices (wild guesses should count as a blank!) and then check your answers on page 213.

bête noire   **a.** a liquorice-based sweetmeat from southern France;
                b. someone or something regarded with fear and loathing.

bibelot **a.** a trinket; **b.** a French sailor.

biennial **a.** twice a year; **b.** every two years.

bifurcate **a.** forking or dividing into two parts or branches; **b.** making an iron bar with two flat, parallel surfaces.

bijou **a.** an object that is small and elegant; **b.** a style of two-piece swimsuit fashionable in the 1960s.

bilateral **a.** an underground stream that surfaces as a spring; **b.** involving two sides or parties.

billabong **a.** An Australian bushman's cooking gear; **b.** a branch of a river that forms a separate lagoon or pool.

billet-doux **a.** a love letter; **b.** a small Parisian apartment for two.

binary **a.** a mathematical system based on two numbers **b.** a machine that renders corn into flakes.

biodegradable **a.** the breakdown of biological mechanisms in the human body; **b.** capable of being decomposed by bacteria.

biopsy **a.** a state of giddiness and nausea caused by sudden change of temperature; **b.** removal of tissue from a body for examination.

bisque **a.** a French game played on a court with rope rings; **b.** a soup made from crustaceans and shellfish.

Black Maria **a.** a police van for transporting prisoners; **b.** a type of highly destructive typhoon generated in the Caribbean.

blag **a.** to wheedle or con a favour or advantage from someone; **b.** to boast, especially about one's sexual prowess.

blandishments **a.** violent threats; **b.** flattery intended to acquire something.

blasé **a.** the glaze on fine porcelain; **b.** indifferent and bored.

blench **a.** to flinch or shrink back; **b.** to feel suddenly ill.

blithe **a.** outwardly friendly, but with the purpose of cheating; **b.**. casual, happy and cheerful.

bombastic **a.** using pompous, boastful language; **b.** using sarcastic, hurtful language.

Bombay duck **a.** Indian duck dish reputed to generate enormous amounts of wind; **b.** Indian fish curry dish.

bona fide   **a.** real or genuine; **b.** the law governing sworn oaths in court.

bonhomie   **a.** contents of Christmas crackers; **b.** exuberant friendliness.

bon vivant   **a.** have a pleasant voyage; **b.** one who loves food and drink.

boondocks   **a.** remote rural areas; **b.** deserted, former wharves.

boreal   **a.** an evening sky flushed with red; **b.** relating to the north.

bourgeois   **a.** middleclass **b.** radical working class.

bowdlerise   **a.** to cut words and passages from a book on prudish grounds; **b.** to force women to cover their legs and ankles.

boycot   **a.** a handkerchief with knotted corners used as a makeshift head covering for sun protection; **b.** to protest by refusing to deal with or buy from a person or organisation.

braggadocio   **a.** bragging and boasting **b.** an Italian veal and onion dish.

braise   **a.** to cook lightly in a closed pan; **b.** a bruise caused by subcutaneous inflammation.

brasserie   **a.** a bar serving drinks and cheap food; **b.** a foundry specialising in making pewter and brassware.

bravura   **a.** The automatic cry from a Spanish crowd after the killing of a bull in the ring; **b.** a display of artistic boldness and brilliance.

breccia   **a.** a style of mosaic with blue shades predominating; **b.** a rock with angular fragments embedded in it.

breviary   **a.** the closed-off part of some churches devoted to reverence for royalty; **b.** a book of psalms, hymns and prayers.

bric-a-brac   **a.** small collectable objects and curios; **b.** discarded half-bricks.

brioche   **a.** a woman's hairstyle with a bun; **b.** a light yeasty roll or loaf.

Brobdingnagian **a.** huge **b.** tiny.

brouhaha	**a.** a commotion or uproar **b.** the fancy decoration on a gable.
brusque	**a.** blunt or abrupt in manner or speech; **b.** a ballet movement in which the male dancer spins his female partner..
bucolic	**a.** a viral disease in cattle; **b.** relating to the countryside.
bulimia	**a.** chronic boils on the neck; **b.** compulsive over-eating followed by self-induced vomiting.
bum steer	**a.** misleading information; **b.** a deformed male calf.
bumptious	**a.** extremely clumsy; **b.** unpleasantly self-assertive.
burgeoning	**a.** vigorously sprouting and growing; **b.** overflowing.
burgher	**a.** an upright, respectable citizen; **b.** a disgraced parson.
burlap	**a.** a prickly bush, originally from South Africa; **b.** a coarse canvas or sacking.
burnish	**a.** to polish and make smooth and shiny; **b.** a deep gold colour that displays iridescence in certain light.
buttress	**a.** a wooden press that squeezes whey from curds in butter- making; **b.** a construction that supports a masonry wall.
Byronic	**a.** romantically melancholic; **b.** the birth defect of a shrunken foot, after Lord Byron's disability.
Byzantine	**a.** inflexible, complex and baffling; **b.** uniquely bizarre.

If, after checking the answers on page 213 you find you've scored 40 correct, then you've done well. Those you missed out on are worth checking, too, in your dictionary, and committing to memory.

Bones and Ligaments

In these days of health consciousness it helps to know a bit about your body. Surprisingly, many people haven't a clue as to what a *hernia* is. And many more have heard the term *carpal tunnel syndrome* but have never bothered to find out what it is and how it affects the body. So here's some bone and body language in common usage. Simply choose the correct definition, *a* or *b*. Answers on page 213.

1. When a bone breaks it is called: **a.** a fracture; **b.** a perforation.
2. The substance found in bone cavities that helps produce blood is called **a.** spinal fluid; **b.** marrow.
3. The bone that forms the lower jaw is **a.** the ilium; **b.** the mandible.
4. A hernia is **a.** damage to the cardiac (heart) muscles; **b.** a rupture or tear in a muscle wall.
5. 'Tennis elbow' is **a.** an imaginary complaint to explain poor form during a tennis match; **b.** inflammation of the tendon of the outer elbow.
6. When a bone separates from the joint and ligaments it is called **a.** a dislocation; **b.** a stress fracture.
7. Carpal tunnel syndrome is a complaint caused by **a.** progressive degeneration of the spine; **b.** pressure on a nerve between a ligament and one of the wrist bones.
8. Lumbago is **a.** lower back pain; **b.** painful weakening of bones caused by lack of calcium.
9 When a surgeon views a joint through small incisions ('keyhole surgery') it is called **a.** a subcutaneous observation; **b.** arthroscopy.
10. The two bones of the lower leg are called **a.** the tibia and fibula; **b.** the femur and patella.

If eight of your choices were correct then you are reasonably informed about your body – or at least about your bones and muscles. You probably also know that the'tailbone' at the bottom of your spine is called the *coccyx* (pronounced *kok-six*); that your collar bone is the *clavicle*; that the muscle around the anus is the anal *sphincter*; and that inflammation of a joint is the dreaded *arthritis*. But watch out – there's a lot more body language ahead!

30-Sec Quickpick: Name the synonym

Underline or circle the synonym of the given word – the alternative that most accurately matches it in meaning. Answers on page 000.

bribe	signal, backhander, warning
ballpark	approximate, juggle, throw
beau	hatband, cape, sweetheart
bemuse	joke, bamboozle, tease

bedraggled	soaked, damp, untidy
bland	uninteresting, lukewarm, shady
boisterous	noisy, irritating, argumentative
bosh	flattery, nonsense, deceit
brazen	shameless, sunburnt, statuesque
broach	untangle, initiate, peel

Can you give it a name?

How many times in conversation do we accurately describe something but can't remember its name? Here are some definitions of fairly common things; see if you can supply their names. Clue: they all begin with *b*. Answers on page 000.

1. The raised-dot alphabet used by blind people.

2. The long French loaf of bread.

3. The leaf or nut chewed as a stimulant in South-East Asia.

4. The Spanish shops that sell wine.

5. The two-humped camel.

6. The drink that combines vodka and tomato juice.

7. The type of birth in which the buttocks or feet appear first.

8. The full name for the cattle disease BSE.

9. The Russian or Polish soup made primarily from beetroot.

10. The heavy metal or wooden posts on kerbs intended to protect buildings and pedestrians from vehicular traffic.

A spot of revision

Revision is a chore, but it's really worthwhile checking to see if you've absorbed and can remember the majority of the *B* words you've learned. Can you correctly define the following?

*baroque, bemused, biopsy, bulimia, burgeoning, brazen,
behemoth, biennial, bonhomie, brouhaha.*

Biggest, longest, shortest, oldest, . . .

There are thousands of uncommon words in the English language: words the average person will never use and probably never come across in a lifetime's reading; underemployed words on the cusp of abandonment. There are also many thousands of words such as *byke* (a wasp's nest); *blashy* (insipid, thin); *blonke* (a very large horse) and *brabble* (to quarrel) that were in daily use a couple of centuries ago but are now *benothinged* (vanquished or annihilated), never likely to grace the pages of an English dictionary again.

There are some exceedingly common words, too. In written English, based on a study of newspapers, the most commonly used words are, perhaps unsurprisingly, *the, of, to, in, and, a, for, was, if* and *that*. Or, perhaps surprisingly, in that the ubiquitous single-letter determiner *a* is relegated to sixth place.

Our vocabulary-building *'B'* word list included *blag* – a coinage of the 1990s and one of the few thousand new words that become respectable dictionary entries each decade, along with dweeb, scuzz, ocker, grunge and alcopop. How long they will keep their place in the leading dictionaries is moot. On the other hand some words have been around for a very long time. *The Oxford English Dictionary* cites the words *town, priest, theft, worth, church* and *thing* as being in regular use from the 7th century.

Words that hang around for a few centuries tend to attract a multitude of meanings. Why bother to invent a word when you can simply (and lazily) attach a fresh meaning to a secondhand one? So we find that words such as *strike, get, put, fall* and *turn* have well over 200 different meanings in *The Oxford English Dictionary*. The word *go* has over 300 meanings, *run* has nearly 400 but *set* takes the honours with a record 464 meanings – to *set* a prisoner free; to *set* a trap; to *set* a broken limb; to buy a *set* of coins; to *set* eyes on someone; to watch the sun *set*; to be *set* in your ways; to *set* off; to *set* aside; to *set* upon and 454 more.

I and *a* are among the ten most common words in the language, and are also the shortest. Fortunately, and probably for good reason, the longest words are fairly uncommon; we have little cause to use such words as *honorificabilitudinitatibus* (Shakespeare used it in *Love's Labour's Lost*), *floccinaucinihilipilification* (the habitual estimation of the worthlessness of something) and *supercalifragilisticexpialidocious* (a nonce word from the *Mary Poppins* stories). The longest word in the Oxford is the 45-letter *pneumonoultramicroscopicsilicovolcanoconiosis*, a lung disease, but that pales beside the names of some chemical compounds. There exists an 8,000-letter behemoth that describes the components of a protein derivative, but the usually accepted longest word in the language (actually published in the American Chemical Society's *Abstracts*, identifying a tobacco virus) is a 1,185-letter jumbo beginning *acetylseryltyrosylserylisol* . . . . and ending . . . . *lanylprolylalanylserine*.

Seasoned players of Scrabble will be familiar with a range of very short words; having a few of these tucked away in the memory can whip a game away from a less knowledgeable opponent. We all know two-letter words such as *an, at, ah, be, is, go, he, me* and *us*. But did you know that an *ai* is a three-toed sloth; that *ko* is a type of Chinese porcelain; that *se* is a Japanese unit of area, and that a *zo* is a Asian cattle breed? These are just a few of the 139 two-letter words recognised by *The Official Scrabble Player's Dictionary* but not necessarily by many others.

C

What's the appropriate word?

From the description given in brackets, substitute the appropriate word in each sentence. For example, in the sentence *The intention of the [group of plotters] was to bring down the government* the word that fits the description closest is *cabal*. Although some might claim that *gang* is just as good a fit, the smarter among you will realise that *gang* doesn't begin with *c* and therefore won't score. Answers page 213.

1. They both admired the 18th century chair with the [*gracefully curved and tapering*] legs.
2. Mark was delighted when he came across the [*hidden store*] of ancient coins.
3. She did everything to [*wheedle or persuade by flattery*] him into buying her the oriental carpet she coveted.
4. Apart from the strict diet, he also embarked on a course of [*light exercises designed to promote fitness, strength and beauty*].
5. The poor professor was a victim of [*malicious and defamatory utterance of false statements*] put about by his departmental enemies.
6. It was delightful to observe the [*spirit of familiarity and loyalty between friends*] among the new officers.
7. In Venice they managed to climb the 275 steps to the top of the [*bell tower*].
8. The village church was noted for its excellent training in [*the art of bell ringing*].
9. Dr Phillips energetically refuted the [*rumour or false report*] that he had

faked his medical credentials.

10. Although the board was deeply disappointed by his financial report, they all thanked him for his [*honesty, openness and frankness*].

11. Now in his late 70s, Mr Needham was a kindly, incredibly knowledgeable but [*irascible, disagreeable and crotchety*] old man.

12. Priscilla hated walking in the city on the grounds that the traffic fumes were [*liable to produce cancer*].

13. The selectors believed that the inclusion of a spin bowler in the team was of [*fundamental, principal, prime*] importance.

14. The company decided to give their chief executive [*complete discretion and authority*] in the forthcoming merger negotiations.

15. The Consumer Council accused the oil companies of operating a [*collusive association intended to monopolise distribution and pricing*].

16. The house was rather pretentious, with a [*having battlements, like a castle*] facade and a fake turret.

17. Jeremy felt outraged at being [*severely rebuked and criticised*] by Mr Peters in front of all the staff.

18. Annabel's presence no doubt acted as a [*a substance, object or person that causes change*] in the love affair between Joe and Margaret.

19. The young man's confessions obviously acted as a much needed [*the bringing of repressed and buried experiences into consciousness*].

20. The injured driver was tethered to his bed by a mass of drip tubes and a [*tube inserted into the bladder for draining fluid*].

There are no apologies for the aforegoing 20 vocabulary posers. They are designed to make you think a little harder about words and their meanings, and to enhance their memorability. A score of 10 or more is passable; 15 or more correct is excellent. But the point of the exercise is to cement 20 useful words into your vocabulary.

Complete the word

From the meanings given, fill in the missing letters and complete the words.

1. Universal, liberal, all-inclusive.   *cath _ _ ic*
2. A closed meeting or committee of members of a political party.   *c _ _ cus*

3. To carp and quibble and raise petty objections.   *ca _ il*
4. Involving intelligence rather than emotions
   or instinct.   *cereb _ _ l*
5. Ceasing or stopping.   *ce _ _ ation*
6. The area around the altar of a church reserved
   for the clergy   *chan _ _ l*
7. Having exceptional personal qualities and
   power to influence and inspire many others.   *char _ _ matic*
8. A person falsely claiming to have knowledge
   and expertise   *charl _ tan*
9. Smug, aggressive belief in the superiority of
   one's country, sex, race or cause   *ch _ _ vinism*
10. Dishonest or sharp practice.   *chican _ _ y*
11. A sideboard, often with shelves and mirror
    above   *chi _ _ onier*
12. An imagined monster or horror   *c _ imera*
13. Bad-tempered, irascible, touchy   *ch _ leric*
14. Audacity and impudence (from the Yiddish)   *chut _ pah*
15. A serious movie enthusiast.   *cin _ aste*
16. Prudent, cautious, discreet.   *c _ _ cumspect*
17. To outwit, evade or bypass   *circum _ _ nt*
18. Activity which is furtive, secretive, concealed.   *clandest _ _ e*
19. A team of people hired to applaud a
    performance   *cla _ ue*
20. Weather that's mild and gentle   *clem _ _ t*
21. An event causing or involving a climax   *clim _ _ tic*
22. To merge, blend, come together in one body
    or mass   *c _ _ lesce*
23. An addition revoking or modifying a will   *c _ dicil*
24. To compel or restrain, disregarding individual
    wishes or rights.   *co _ rce*
25. Forcefully convincing, authoritative, to the
    point.   *cog _ _ t*
26. Connoisseurs with informed appreciation of
    the fine arts   *c _ _ noscenti*
27. Security pledged for the repayment of a loan.   *coll _ _ eral*
28. Conversational, informal speech or vocabulary   *collo _ _ ial*
29. Stupefied, sluggish, lethargic   *com _ tose*
30. Proportionate, or corresponding in amount,
    degree or size   *commen _ _ rate*

31. Able to exist harmoniously together   *c _ _ patible*
32. Easy-going, careless self-satisfaction   *c _ _ placent*
33. Eagerness to comply, oblige and be polite   *compl _ _ sant*
34. Being an accomplice in an intrigue or criminal
     act   *complic _ _ y*
35. Occurring or existing together   *conc _ _ itant*
36. The quality of being brief and concise   *conc _ sion*
37. Extremely lustful erotic desire   *concupi _ cence*
38. Parallel or taking place at the same time and
     location   *concu _ _ ent*
39. Fitting and well-deserved (e.g., punishment)   *condi _ n*
40. Combining or blending two things to form
     a whole   *con _ lation*

Check the answers on page 213. A score of 30 for this round would indicate that you already possess a serviceable vocabulary. Still, the exercise will help you enlarge it by a further ten new words. Now for a final assault on *c* words:

Choose the Correct Meaning

Which, of the two definitions given for each word, *a* or *b*, is correct? Circle your choices (and once again, try not to make wild stabs) and then check the answers on page 214.

congenital	**a.** an abnormal condition existing at birth; **b.** a hereditary disease or disability.
congeries	**a.** an accumulation or collection; **b.** The area of a town or city once reserved for a fish market.
congruence	**a.** the state of marital disharmony; **b.** the state of agreeing or corresponding.
connotation	**a.** an idea or association suggested by a word or phrase; **b.** the ability of human and animal tissue to heal naturally.
consanguinity	**a.** unlawful acts between humans and animals; **b.** related by birth or blood.
construe	**a.** To draw out or lengthen; **b.** to interpret or deduce the meaning of something.

24

consummate	**a.** To bring to completion or perfection; **b.** to achieve an orgasm.
contiguous	**a.** joining or adjacent; **b.** every alternate page of a book.
contrapuntal	**a.** contradicting expectations; **b.** music that combines two or more melodic lines.
contretemps	**a.** an embarrassing mistake or situation; **b.** a situation in which two sides at first disagree, then find agreement.
contrite	**a.** unlawful severing of a contract; **b.** full of remorse.
contumacious	**a.** readily submitting to flattery; **b.** stubborn and obstinate and resistant to authority.
contusion	**a.** a bruise or injury where the skin is unbroken; **b.** a wound in which bone or bone fragments break through the skin.
convoluted	**a.** spiral shaped; **b.** twisted, involved, hard to comprehend.
corollary	**a.** a deduction or result; **b.** the angle formed by the meeting of two converging lines or surfaces.
corroborate	**a.** to be eaten away; **b.** to confirm or prove correct.
corrugated	**a.** any material formed into alternate curved furrows and ridges; **b.** cardboard made from recycled pulp.
coruscate	**a.** To fiercely admonish; **b.** to sparkle and flash.
costive	**a.** cheating by altering prices; **b.** sluggish and constipated.
coterie	**a.** an exclusive group of people sharing common interests; **b.** a Caribbean dance performed by four people.
crapulous	**a.** grossly and repulsively untidy; **b.** given to overindulgence in eating and drinking.
credo	**a.** a formal statement of beliefs; **b.** the decorative strip on a wall parallel to floor and ceiling.
credulity	**a.** readiness to believe anything; **b.** lack of financial creditworthiness.
crepuscular	**a.** relating to dimness and twilight; **b.** knobbly and lumpy.
criterion	**a.** an army flag-bearer; **b.** a standard by which something can be judged or decided.
cruciform	**a.** a deep clay pot for smelting metal alloys; **b.** shaped like a cross.

culpable	**a.** blameworthy, deserving censure; **b.** left-handed.
cupidity	**a.** eagerness to please; **b.** greed for money and possessions.
curmudgeon	**a.** a surly, crabby, miserable person; **b.** a person who avoids any form of work and leaves chores to others.
cursory	**a.** hasty and superficial; **b.** bad-tempered.
cynosure	**a.** a distrust of people and ideas; **b.** someone or something that attracts unusual interest and attention.

It's worth pointing out that all the *c* words in these vocabulary-building exercises, far from being esoteric examples, were chosen from two national British newspapers, where they appeared over a two-month period. How did you fare? A score of 25 or more would be a result to be proud of. But if yours fell below that you have all the more reason to increase and sharpen your vocabulary.

Clues to meaning: Recognising word elements

We've already noted that an awareness of Greek and Latin roots and elements such as prefixes and suffixes can often help identify the meanings of words that are unfamiliar to you. Here is a selection of *C's*.

Word; Element	Origin	Meaning	English words
caro, carn	Latin	flesh	*carnal, carnivorous, carnivore, carnage, carnival*
cognitio, cogn	Latin	to know	*cognisant, cognisance, cognitive, recognise, incognito*
corpus, corp	Latin	body	*corpse, corporation, corporate, corps, corporal, corpulent,*

			corporeal,
			corpuscle, corpus
creditum, cred,	Latin	to trust,	*credible,*
			credibility, credit,
credo	Latin	believe	*credentials,*
			incredulous,
			creed, discredit,
			credulous
circum-	Latin	around, on	*circumnavigate,*
		all sides,	*circumference,*
		surrounding	*circumlocution,*
			circumvent,
			circumcise,
			circumstance
contra-	Latin	opposite,	*contradict,*
			contravene,
			contraband,
			contraception,
counter-	Latin	against	*counteract,*
			counterattack,
			counterfeit,
			countermand
centum, cent-	Latin	hundred	*century,*
			centenary,
			centimetre,
			centipede,
			centigrade
chroma, chrom-	Greek	colour	*chromatic,*
			chrome,
			chromosome
chronos, chron-	Greek	time	*chronology,*
			chronicity,
			chronic,
			chronometer,
			synchronise
cosmos, cosmo-	Greek	universal	*cosmic,*
			cosmopolitan,
			cosmology
-krates, -crat,-cracy	Greek	ruler	*democrat,*
			autocrat,
			bureaucracy

30-Sec Quickpick: Identify the antonym

In 30 seconds, try to identify the antonym of each of these ten *c* words – i.e., the word with the opposite meaning. Answers on page 214.

1. **calm**   *imperturbable, agitated, serene.*
2. **captious**   *easygoing, petulant, critical.*
3. **curb**   *impede, restrain, encourage.*
4. **circumscribe**   *distend, confine, limit.*
5. **compromise**   *accommodate, dispute, agree.*
6. **circumlocution**   *brevity, verbosity, prolixity.*
7. **cheerful**   *contented, genial, forlorn.*
8. **condemn**   *denounce, absolve, censure.*
9. **confess**   *dissemble, disclose, acknowledge.*
10. **conquer**   *capitulate, overpower, vanquish.*

Chemical Competence

We live in a chemical world. The food we eat, the clothes we wear, the air we breathe are all composed of chemicals. One way or another we manage to acquire a basic vocabulary about this aspect of the physical world, but perhaps we should know more. How does your knowledge of chemistry stack up? Here are ten statements. Are they true or false? Circle your choices. You'll find the answers on page 214.

		True	False
1.	Water boils at a temperature of 212 Celsius.	___	___
2.	A substance that neutralises acids is an alkali.	___	___
3.	Alcohol is produced by evaporation.	___	___
4.	A kilogram is equivalent to 100 grams.	___	___
5.	An element is matter composed of just one type of atom.	___	___
6.	Dry ice is the solid, frozen form of oxygen	___	___
7.	24-carat gold is the purest form of this metal.	___	___
8.	Hydrochloric acid is found in the human stomach.	___	___
9.	Neon is the element used to make glass tubing.	___	___
10.	Acetylsalicylic acid is the chemical name for aspirin.	___	___

Well? Check the answers and if you scored 8 (without guesses) you have a useful knowledge of chemistry in everyday life.

Revision Time

A sure test of your understanding of a word's meaning is: can you use the word in the context of a sentence? For example, one of our '*c*' words was *chutzpah*. If you knew, or learned, the meaning of this word (and of all the others), don't just file it away in your memory – make an attempt to use it:

> *Emily had the necessary* **chutzpah** *to talk the radio station into giving her a job as a programme director.*

Now try your hand at putting the following words into sentences. If you're in any doubt about the appropriateness or accuracy of your usage, check your dictionary.

> *cerebral, charismatic, clandestine, compatible, complaisant, connotation, contiguous, contretemps, coterie, cynosure.*

Collective Nouns : Two or More of a Kind

Everyone knows that 'a lot of sheep' is a *flock* and that 'a lot of cows' is a *herd*. But difficulty can arise when other creatures get together. For example, do you know the collective nouns for:

1. *A _ _ _ _ _ _ _ of crows*   5. *A _ _ _ _ of squirrels*

2. *A _ _ _ _ _ of lions*   6. *A _ _ _ _ _ of partridges*

3. *A _ _ _ _ _ _ _ _ of ferrets*   7. *A _ _ _ _ of whales*

4. *An _ _ _ _ _ _ _ _ _ _ of larks*   8. *A _ _ _ _ _ _ of swallows*

The answers are on page 214. You will, of course, be familiar with a *school* of fish, a *parliament* of owls and a *gaggle* of geese. But how about these:

A *piteousness* of doves.   A *convocation* of eagles.

A *skulk* of foxes.

A *smack* of jellyfish.

A *watch* of nightingales.

A *crash* of rhinoceroses.

A *murmuration* of starlings.

A *charm* of finches.

A *leap* of leopards.

An *unkindness* of ravens.

A *clamour* of rooks.

An *ostentation* of peacocks.

They are all bona fide collective names for animals. But note also these more recent, whimsical offerings: a *rash* of dermatologists; A *piddle* of puppies; an *overcharge* of plumbers; a *failing* of students; a *slew* of dragons; a *descent* of in-laws; an *innuendo* of gossips, and an *afraid* of ghosts.

D

Correct the Confusables

Many words in the English language look alike and sound alike, so it isn't surprising that they are often used incorrectly. We call these verbal tripwires *confusables*, and as you add to your vocabulary you'll need to be on the lookout for them. Here's a small selection chosen from words beginning with *d*, used in sentences. Do you know which of the usages are correct, and which are not?

Your choice

1. The associate members were *disbarred* / *debarred* from entering the clubhouse. _____
2. They noted with dismay his *descent* / *decent* into alcoholism. _____
3. The crowd watched from a respectful distance as the Army team *diffused* / *defused* the bomb. _____
4. The man claimed he had eleven *dependents* / *dependants* to support _____
5. We were all secretly pleased that Sam finally got his just *desserts* / *deserts* _____
6. Her rudeness *detracted* / *distracted* from the otherwise good impression we'd made of her. _____
7. The lecturer emphasised that the two subjects were quite *discrete* / *discreet*. _____
8. George confessed that he was totally *disinterested* / *uninterested* in Barbara's romantic affairs. _____

9. The accident happened on a *duel* / *dual* carriageway. _____

10. He *decried* / *descried* the use of force in getting
the prisoners to cooperate. _____

Now check your choices with the answers on page 214.
A score of 8 would indicate that you have a keen awareness of difficult
'lookalikes' and chronically misused words.

Now for a further round of vocabulary building.

Choose the Correct Meaning

Which one of the three alternatives, a, b or c, most accurately fits
the meaning of the word? Circle your choices and then check the answers
on page 214.

dado   **a.** early 20th century surrealist movement; **b.** the
decorated or panelled lower part of a room; **c.** a drink
made from almonds.

dalliance **a.** flirting **b.** sparkling **c.** long-winded oratory.

dearth **a.** a plague; **b.** scarcity; **c.** frightening appearance.

debacle **a.** an ornamental silver buckle; **b.** a large garden party; **c.** a complete rout and collapse.

debilitate **a.** to nourish; **b.** to wound; **c.** to weaken.

decant **a.** to pour from one receptacle to another; **b.** to confess one's sins; **c.** to sing in a monotone voice.

déclassé **a.** to lose social status; **b.** to act superior to one's status; **c.** to offer wine in the wrong glass.

declivity **a.** an abrupt drop; **b.** a gradual slope downwards; **c.** a sudden drop in barometric pressure.

décolletage **a.** a decorative fringe on curtains; **b.** sediment sometimes found in red wine; **c.** a woman's revealing neckline.

decrepitude **a.** persistent drunkenness; **b.** enfeebled and worn out; **c.** old age.

de facto **a.** existing, though perhaps not legally; **b.** in defiance of the law; **c.** with the permission of the court.

deferential **a.** showing respect; **b.** sullen; **c.** habitually careless.

déjà vu **a.** old fashioned; **b.** a person acquainted with witchcraft; **c.** the illusion of having previously experienced a present event.

deleterious **a.** noxious; **b.** extremely sweet; **c.** wholesome.

deliquescent **a.** a substance that dissolves in moisture absorbed from the air ; **b.** a substance capable of burning the skin; **c.** a substance that can explode on contact.

Delphic **a.** of dark appearance; **b.** always smiling; **c.** ambiguous

demagogue **a.** a person who hates religion; **b.** a person with an urge to degrade others; **c.** an agitator who plays on the passions and prejudices of the mob.

demeanour **a.** manner of behaviour and appearance; **b.** the art of arguing a cause; **c.** prone to easy seduction.

demimonde **a.** objects and clothing made in the 1920s; **b.** women of dubious character; **c.** a jewelled cloche hat.

demotic **a.** relating to the common people; **b.** staring wildly; **c.** a student of the black arts.

demurrer **a.** an objection; **b.** a writ; **c.** a demand for payment.

denigrate **a.** to use cosmetics excessively; **b.** to belittle or defame; **c.** to remove teeth unnecessarily.

denouement **a.** a foiled elopement; **b.** a military surrender; **c.** the unravelling and solution of a mystery.

depilatory	**a.** for preventing bleeding; **b.** for removing hair; **c.** for controlling perspiration.
deprecate	**a.** to attack someone in a cowardly way; **b.** to express disapproval of someone or something; **c.** to harass someone.
depreciate	**a.** to reduce the value of someone or something; **b.** to cause a false alarm; **c.** to lose one's social position.
derogatory	**a.** the part of a church tower that contains the bells; **b.** a church service for the sick; **c.** offensively disparaging.
deshabille	**a.** only partly dressed; **b.** wanton; **c.** in mourning.
desiccated	**a.** chopped finely; **b.** dried or dehydrated; **c.** bleached.
desuetude	**a.** unused or abandoned; **b.** relaxation; **c.** tiredness.
desultory	**a.** fish able to live in fresh and sea water; **b.** casual and unmethodical; **c.** to feel inferior.
determinism	**a.** belief that determination will solve all problems; **b.** belief that the father more than the mother determines a child's features; **c.** belief that all events and human actions are predetermined.
devolution	**a.** the transfer of powers from central to regional authority; **b.** the process of one state being absorbed by another; **c.** the political aftermath of a revolution.
dextral	**a.** left-handed; **b.** right-handed; **c.** colour-blind.
dharma	**a.** Indian cooking based on lamb and hot spices; **b.** Hindu religious and moral duty; **c.** silk sash worn with a sari.
dialectic	**a.** a debate intended to resolve differences; **b.** a religious belief based on self-analysis; **c.** relief through electrolysis.
Diaspora	**a.** The circlet of rubies in the British royal crown; **b.** the dispersal of the Jews; **c.** The Russian Orthodox hierarchy.
diatribe	**a.** cross-breeding between communities; **b.** a bitter verbal denunciation; **c.** folk medicine.
dichotomy	**a.** the second hymn in a church service; **b.** an operation on the joints of the foot; **c.** divided into two parts.
didactic	**a.** inclined to teach; **b.** inclined to avoid problems; **c.** inclined to depend on others.

Check your choices against the answers on page 214. There are some toughies in this round so don't be too disappointed if your score is around or below 30. The really important point in vocabulary building is *follow-up* – double-check your wrong choices in a dictionary and commit the words and their meanings to memory.

Now for a second round . . .

What's the word?

From the definitions given, fill in the missing letters and identify the words:

1. Shy, timid, and lacking in self-confidence.   *diff _ dent*
2. Wasting time and putting off tasks until later   *dil _ tory*
3. An art-loving person whose interests are
    rather superficial   *dile _ _ ante*
4. The philosophy of spontaneity and
    irrationality   *Dion _ sian*
5. A person with an uncontrollable desire for
    alcohol   *_ _ _ somaniac*
6. To rid someone of a misguided idea   *dis _ buse*
7. To cause inconvenience to someone   *disco _ _ ode*
8. To disturb the composure of someone   *disconc _ _ t*
9. Disappointed, dejected, sad beyond
    comforting   *discons _ _ ate*
10. An inconsistency between facts or figures   *discr _ _ ancy*
11. Consisting of quite distinct or separate parts   *discr _ te*
12. Speech or writing that jumps from one
    subject to another   *discur _ ive*
13. Insincere and lacking in frankness   *dis _ ngenuous*
14. To be objective and impartial   *disinter _ _ ted*
15. Utterly different and distinct   *dis _ ara _ e*
16. To conceal by pretence, to hide one's
    intentions   *di _ semble*
17. Discordant combination of sounds   *dissona _ ce*
18. A daily event, or happening during the day   *d _ urnal*
19. A prima donna; a world class female singer   *d _ v _*
20. A brief entertainment, usually between acts
    of a play   *div _ _ tissement*
21. Stubbornly theoretical, with no regard for
    practicality   *doctrin _ _ re*

35

22. Humorous verse	*do _ _ erel*
23. Causing or involving pain or sorrow	*dolor _ us*
24. One's dwelling place or legal residenced	*_ _ icile*
25. A word or phrase that can be interpreted in two ways	*dou _ le entend _ e*
26. Tough and resolute	*doug _ _ y*
27. The senior member of a group, profession or society	*do _ en*
28. Extremely harsh	*Drac _ nian*
29. A coarsely woven mat	*drug _ et*
30. Doubtful and uncertain	*dubi _ _ s*
31. A metal that can be beaten or stretched very thinly	*du _ tile*
32. Sullen anger and resentment, often 'high'	*dud _ eon*
33. Pleasant and soothing music or sounds	*d _ lcet*
34. The first section of the small intestine	*duod _ num*
35. A market shared by only two producers or suppliers	*du _ poly*
36. Deceptive double-dealing	*duplici _ _*
37. Compulsion by the use of force or threats	*d _ _ ess*
38. A sequence of hereditary leaders, rulers or heads of a family	*dy _ asty*
39. The impaired ability to read	*d _ slexia*
40. Suffering from indigestion or upset stomach	*dyspe _ tic*

The completed words in this final set of words beginning with *d* are on page 215. A score of 30 or more correct would confirm that you have an above-average vocabulary and one well worth improving. Use your dictionary to check the meanings of those words that stumped you.

60-Sec Quickpick: Same, Opposite or Different?

Here are 15 pairs of words. Some pairs are synonyms (the meanings are the same); some are antonyms (opposite meanings) and some are jokers in the pack – words which have no relationship or connection with each other. Your task is to indicate which pairs are the same, opposite or different – in just 60 seconds! Simply place a tick in the appropriate column to indicate your choice. Then check the answers on page 215.

	Same	Opposite	Different
1. *daft, smart*	___	___	___
2. *damning, condemnatory*	___	___	___
3. *daunted, dismayed*	___	___	___
4. *deathless, timeless*	___	___	___
5. *debauch, decease*	___	___	___
6. *deceptive, trustworthy*	___	___	___
7. *decorum, propriety*	___	___	___
8. *deem, deduct*	___	___	___
9. *deleterious, wholesome*	___	___	___
10. *diffusion, dispersion*	___	___	___
11. *diocese, funereal*	___	___	___
12. *discountenance, embarrass*	___	___	___
13. *digressive, terse*	___	___	___
14. *deviant, aberrant*	___	___	___
15. *designate, ambassador*	___	___	___

Have you marked seven the same, four opposite and four different? Just to be sure of your ground, check the answers on page 215.

Digestion and the Digestive System

Here are some words to read, mark, learn and inwardly digest, as *The Book of Common Prayer* advises. So, which of these statements are true or false?

	True	False
1. The *kidneys* are the pair of organs that filter unwanted substances from the blood.	___	___
2. *Hepatitis* is a viral infection of the liver.	___	___
3. *Salmonella* is a bacteria in food causing severe vomiting.	___	___
4. A *colostomy* is a surgically created opening for the colon.	___	___
5. Removal of all or part of the stomach is called a *gastrectomy.*	___	___
6. A laxative designed to melt in the colon is an *enema.*	___	___
7. *Cirrhosis* is the progressive scarring and destruction of the liver.	___	___

37

8. The passage in the throat through which food
   passes into the stomach is the gullet or *oesophagus*.   ___ ___
9. Abnormally enlarged veins in the anus are
   haemorrhoids.   ___ ___
10. *Dialysis* is the artificial removal of impurities from
    the blood.   ___ ___

You'll find the answers on page 215.

Have you Understood? Time for Revision

Before we depart from *D* territory it would be wise to test your
understanding of some of the more unfamiliar words, but words you may
nevertheless find useful in your everyday conversation and reading. In
your mind, try using each of the following words, appropriately and
accurately, in a sentence:

> *disinterested, debilitate, déjà vu, denouement, desultory,*
> *disabuse, disingenuous, Draconian, desiccated, décolletage.*

Dr Johnson and the Dictionary

In 1746 a scruffy scribbler from Staffordshire rented a garret in
Gough Square, just off London's Fleet Street, and, with a bookseller's
contract for 1,500 guineas and six assistants, began compiling a dictionary
of the English language.

Existing dictionaries were primitive, shambolic affairs compared
with their counterparts on the continent. From an early effort in 1604
listing just 3,000 words, a dozen or more dictionaries were published in
the ensuing century and a half, but none could claim to be comprehensive
and authoritative. By the mid-18th century an inquisitive, educated book-
reading middle class was emerging, and the need for a systematic and
reliable guide to the language was becoming acute.

In his 36th year, Dr Samuel Johnson was an unlikely candidate for
such a gigantic and exacting task. He was half-blind, corpulent,
periodically ill, untidy, impatient, emotionally turbulent and given to
chronic fits of indolence. And lurking over his shoulder were the
achievements of his continental contemporaries – the French and Italian

dictionaries, each the product of learned academies, large teams of compilers, generous budgets and forty years of patient endeavour. Johnson had promised his backers that his dictionary would be ready in three years.

Nine weary and penurious years and 42,773 entries later, *A Dictionary of the English Language* was finally published in two folio volumes, priced at £4.50 (about £450 today). Despite the price it found sufficient buyers to warrant successive editions. By the fourth edition of 1773, which included some 15,000 alterations and additions, the dictionary had become the unquestioned authority on the English language, a position it occupied for over a century until replaced by the first of 12 volumes of what was to become the *Oxford English Dictionary*. In the US, however, Johnson's authority was challenged by Noah Webster, whose *American Dictionary of the English Language*, published in 1828 and containing 70,000 words, heralded the split from the spelling and pronunciation traditions of the mother tongue and the emergence of what is now recognised as American English.

So what made Johnson's dictionary the literary landmark it was? Why had Johnson succeeded where others had failed?

First, he recognised that English was a *living* language. Words were constantly being purloined from other languages; fresh meanings were ascribed to existing words; new words, terms and phrases were being invented daily, tumbling into the lexical lake in a never-ending stream. Unlike the French he determined not to be a guardian of the language, but a recorder of it, or, as he humbly described his role, to be "doomed only to remove rubbish and clear obstructions from the paths of Learning and Genius".

Second, Johnson trawled for his words among original sources – the streets and the populace, the trades and sciences, and, above all, works of English literature – to provide instances of actual usage. In all, the first edition of his dictionary contained no less than 114,000 quotations, or proofs of usage. And, finally, Johnson's systematic method of presenting the origin, spelling, grammar, pronunciation and usage of every word was so brilliantly logical that it served as the model for every subsequent dictionary of English, and still does.

Users of English now had a dictionary they could depend on. More than that: Johnson's unique contribution to English learning, literature and life is almost beyond estimation. It was a magnificent gift. As he wrote in the dictionary's preface, "I have devoted this book, the labour of years, to the honour of my country, that we may no longer yield the palm of philology to the nations of the continent."

Yet Johnson's dictionary was far from being a po-faced academic tome. Many of his definitions were distinctly opinionated. His definition of **patron**: *commonly a wretch who supports with insolence, and is paid with flattery* (a reflection of the lack of support he received from his own patron, Lord Chesterfield). Of **uxorious**: *submissively fond of a wife; infected with connubial dotage*. Of **cough**: *a convulsion of the lungs, vellicated by some sharp serosity: it is pronounced coff*. Of **oats**: *a grain, which in England is generally given to horses, but in Scotland supports the people* (Johnson was no lover of the Scots). And of his own trade: **lexicographer**: *a writer of dictionaries, a harmless drudge*.

Dr Johnson's *A Dictionary of the English Language* defined what a dictionary should be: descriptive, not prescriptive. His remarks on the futility of prescribing what words people should use, and how to use them, is typically Johnsonian: ". . academies have been instituted, to guard the avenues of their languages, to retain fugitives, and repulse intruders; but their vigilance and activity have hitherto been vain . . . to enchain syllables, and to lash the wind, are equally the undertakings of pride".

The first edition of Dr Johnson's dictionary is a collector's rarity costing many thousands of pounds. Later editions can be bought for a few hundred pounds and there is a facsimile edition (Longman, 1990, £195) and, more recently, a CD-ROM on which are the full texts of the first (1755) and fourth (1773) editions, plus facsimile images of the pages of both (Cambridge, 1996, £195).

How to Buy a Dictionary: ask yourself these questions before buying a dictionary

1. **Is it up to date?** Check the reverse of the title page to see when it was first published and whether it has been revised since.
2. **Does it list the words I want to look up?** It's a good idea to collect some words that you've had to look up recently. Nothing can be more irritating than owning a dictionary that lets you down – a scaled down 'bargain' dictionary that predictably lists all the words you know, but in which those you don't know are frustratingly absent.
3. **Does it contain encyclopaedic references?** If you want biographical, geographical, cultural and scientific facts, check it for such information: e.g. *Harrier* (British vertical takeoff jet aircraft); *Koran* (sacred book of Islam); *Lapsang Souchong* (variety of China tea); *Lusatian* (relating to Lusatia, a region of Central Europe); *Planck's*

ACTUALLY I WANTED ONE THAT OPENED FLAT AND STAYED OPEN!

constant (a fundamental constant equal to the energy of any quantum of radiation divided by its frequency).

4. **How comprehensively does it explain words with many meanings?** Remember that some words have a hundred or more shades of meaning and usages.

5. **Does it cover American and Commonwealth English?** Ideally, international variations of English words should be included.

6. Does it give examples of usage? These can be very useful, especially with abstract and difficult concepts. Are the examples real (ie, from existing published works) or invented? The former are preferable.

7. **Does it provide information about variations?** The average user wants information and guidance on spelling variations, plural forms, capitalisation, hyphenation, etc.

8. **Can you follow the guide to pronunciation?** Most dictionaries use the International Phonetic Alphabet (IPA) to illustrate the pronunciation of words. This alphabet, with its baffling symbols, is pretty much the standard these days, so you don't have much choice. Does the dictionary provide pronunciation variants?

9. **Does it include slang, idioms and phrases?** These are part of our everyday language and should be comprehensively listed.
10. **Has it a system of cross-referencing?** Does it provide cross-references to words with related or relevant meanings?
11. **Does it give etymological information?** It is interesting and sometimes useful to know the story or origin of the words you are looking up.
12. **Is it a well-made, practical book?** Whether hardback or softback, your dictionary should be built to withstand daily use and abuse. Will it open flat, and stay open (an important consideration)? Is the type legible? Are the entries well-laid out and appealing to the eye? Does the look and feel please you? Is it value for money?

    More than ten out of twelve? ***Then buy it!***

How to use a Dictionary

Your first thought about the word *hard* would probably be: "It's one of the earliest words I ever learned! Why should I want to look it up in a dictionary?"

But look again. Like many seemingly simple words *hard* has many meanings, shades of meanings and usages – in fact, over forty. Its entry also provides a good example of the lexicographical bounty a dictionary has to offer. Our example is from a previous edition of the *Collins English Dictionary*.

Let's analyse the entry:

1. **Headword or Main Entry**. This is typically flagged in a bold or different typeface to catch your eye.
2. **Pronunciation. This is illustrated with the symbols of the International P**honetic Alphabet and won't mean much to you until you consult the key, usually found at the front of the dictionary and sometimes at the foot of each page.
3. **Grammatical designation or part of speech.** The main part of the entry treats *hard* as an adjective (its main use) but if you look further down the entry you will see that the word is also used as an adverb and as a noun.
4. **The first of 25 definitions.** These are usually listed in order of usage. The first definition, *'firm or rigid'* is the most common; its use to describe a type of nuclear missile defence (definition **23b**) is technical and fairly rare.

42

1. *2.* *3.* *4.*

hard (hɑːd) *adj.* **1.** firm or rigid. **2.** toughened; not soft or smooth: *hard skin.* **3.** difficult to do or accomplish: *a hard task.* **4.** difficult to understand: *a hard question.* **5.** showing or requiring considerable effort or application: *hard work.* **6.** demanding: *a hard master.* **7.** harsh; cruel: *a hard fate.* **8.** inflicting pain, sorrow, or hardship: *hard times.* **9.** tough or violent: *a hard man.* **10.** forceful: *a hard knock.* **11.** cool or uncompromising: *we took a long hard look at our profit factor.* **12.** indisputable; real: *hard facts.* **13.** *Chem.* (of water) impairing the formation of a lather by soap. **14.** practical, shrewd, or calculating: *he is a hard man in business.* **15.** harsh: *hard light.* **16. a.** (of currency) in strong demand, esp. as a result of a good balance of payments situation. **b.** (of credit) difficult to obtain; tight. **17.** (of alcoholic drink) being a spirit rather than a wine, beer, etc. **18.** (of a drug) highly addictive. **19.** *Physics.* (of radiation) having high energy and the ability to penetrate solids. **20.** *Chiefly U.S.* (of goods) durable. **21.** short for **hard-core.** **22.** *Phonetics.* (not in technical usage) denoting the consonants *c* and *g* when they are pronounced as in *cat* and *got.* **23. a.** heavily fortified. **b.** (of nuclear missiles) located underground. **24.** politically extreme: *the hard left.* **25.** *Brit. & N.Z. inf.* incorrigible or disreputable (esp. in **a hard case**). **26. a hard nut to crack. a.** a person not easily won over. **b.** a thing not easily done or understood. **27. hard by.** close by. **28. hard of hearing.** slightly deaf. **29. hard up.** *Inf.* **a.** in need of money. **b.** (foll. by *for*) in great need (of): *hard up for suggestions.* ~*adv.* **30.** with great energy, force, or vigour: *the team always played hard.* **31.** as far as possible: *hard left.* **32.** earnestly or intently: *she thought hard about the formula.* **33.** with great intensity: *his son's death hit him hard.* **34.** (foll. by *on, upon, by,* or *after*) close; near: *hard on his heels.* **35.** (foll. by *at*) assiduously; devotedly. **36. a.** with effort or difficulty: *their victory was hard won.* **b.** (*in combination*): *hard-earned.* **37.** slowly: *prejudice dies hard.* **38. go hard with.** to cause pain or difficulty to (someone). **39. hard put (to it).** scarcely having the capacity (to do something). ~*n.* **40.** *Brit.* a roadway across a foreshore. **41.** *Sl.* hard labour. **42.** *Taboo sl.* an erection of the penis (esp. in **get** or **have a hard on**). [OE *heard*] —**'hardness** *n.*

5. *6.* *7.*

11. *8.* *9.* *10.*

5. **The first of 4 related phrases and idioms.** An up-to-date dictionary will include these.
6. **The first of several definitions with *hard* as an adverb.** These are illustrated with examples of usage, e.g. *hard up for suggestions; hard on his heels; prejudice dies hard*. This facility is invaluable to understanding.
7. **A definition with *hard* as a noun.**
8. **Slang form.** Up-to-date dictionaries include slang as it is irretrievably part of our everyday language.
9. **Taboo form.** Again, it is a mark of modernity to include so-called taboo applications of the headword.
10. **Etymology**. This explains the origin of the word – in the case of *hard* we are told that it derives from the Old English *heard*. More expensive dictionaries give more comprehensive details about a word's history.
11. **Cross-reference to related words and meanings.** Here we are directed, if we wish, to look up the separate entry for the noun *hardness*.

That entry isn't the last we see of *hard*, however. Following entries will typically include *hardback, hard-bitten, hardboard, hard-boiled, hardcore, hard-edge, harden* (the verb form), *hardened* (another adjectival form), *hardener* (noun), *hard hat, hard-headed, hard-hitting, hardly* (adverb), *hardness* (noun), *hard-nosed, hard rock, hard sell, hard shoulder, hardware* and many more.

While all dictionaries provide explanatory meanings to words, some include synonyms, which is useful if you have a poor memory and are forever searching for precisely the word you want yet have no wish to invest in a thesaurus or a dictionary of synonyms.

* * * * * * * * *

Having reached this far, and been diligent in your pursuit of a wider and more rounded vocabulary, you will have needed to consult a dictionary on many dozens of occasions. Now is the time to ask yourself: *Has my dictionary provided the answers to all my queries about words and meanings, spelling and pronunciation? Instantly and unambiguously? Has it relieved my doubts and hesitations about using certain words? Is it a pleasure to use?*

Or has it given you a hard time? Made you want to fling it out of the window when you can't find a word, or its meaning eludes you? Or given you the queasy feeling that you're not getting the full monty? (does it, in fact, explain the meaning of *the full monty?*).

Before you proceed any further with your vocabulary building, now's the time to decide whether to keep your dictionary or to replace it. Acquiring a new, up-to-date comprehensive dictionary could be one of the best investments you'll ever make.

Right or Wrong?

When you're truly familiar with a word you can use it confidently
in its correct context in a sentence. Are you that familiar with the
following 20 words? Are they being used correctly? Answer right/wrong
and then check the answers on page 215.

		Right	Wrong
1.	At John's stag party, Edmund was even more *ebullient* than he usually was.	___	___
2.	Lorna's *eclectic* and notorious shyness made it impossible for her to enjoy social occasions.	___	___
3.	The bishop was regarded as the most liberal and *ecumenical* of all his church colleagues.	___	___
4.	They peered in vain at the old gravestone but all the markings had been *effaced* long ago through time and weather.	___	___
5.	Shirley had always been a bright and *effervescent* girl.	___	___
6.	The sky, *effete* with crisp, billowing clouds, promised a fine day	___	___
7.	The prescribed medicine unfortunately proved to be *efficacious* and Mr Gower expired that night.	___	___
8.	The neighbours even had the *effrontery* to leave their car parked right across our drive.	___	___

9. After the meal Bernie felt distinctly bloated
   and *effulgent.*   ___   ___

10. Despite his aristocratic background and
    undoubted wealth, Lord Mayberry was
    egalitarian at heart.   ___   ___

11. The discus soared overhead in a perfect
    egocentric arc.   ___   ___

12. It was well known that Mark was an
    egregious liar and thief.   ___   ___

13. The young boy performed the piece with
    tremendous *élan.*   ___   ___

14. The *elegiac* strains of evensong drifted across
    the fields.   ___   ___

15. Because the material of the carving looked
    elephantine the expert pronounced it to be
    genuine ivory.   ___   ___

16. The investigator did his best to *elicit* the truth
    from the woman.   ___   ___

17. Harold had formerly belonged to the *élite*
    Horse Guards.   ___   ___

18. John had inherited the family's tendency to
    elliptical fits   ___   ___

19. Abigail's psychological state caused her to
    elucidate and to recall the most remarkable
    dreams.   ___   ___

20. He fondly recalled the *Elysian* days of their
    Greek holiday.   ___   ___

Having only a hazy idea of a word's meaning can lead you into error if
you use it in your speech or writing. The result can be an embarrassing
malapropism. So check your 20 responses against the answers on page
215 and double-check your dictionary to nail those words whose meanings
you didn't know or misunderstood.

Top and Tail the Words

The following round lists words with their first and last letters
missing – which you are asked to replace. As the meanings of the words
are supplied you shouldn't have too much trouble.

1. To issue or flow from. _ *manat* _
2. To free from restraint, to liberate. _ *mancipat* _
3. To weaken, to deprive of masculine properties. _ *masculat* _
4. To prohibit or restrict. _ *mbarg* _
5. The blocking of an artery or vein by a blood clot. _ *mbolis* _
6. In an early stage; undeveloped. _*mbryoni* _
7. To correct by removing errors or faults. _ *mendat* _
8. Retired from full-time work (usually academic or professional) but retaining one's title on an honorary basis. _ *meritu* _
9. A substance that causes vomiting. _ *meti* _
10. A preparation that sooths and softens the skin. _ *mollien* _
11. The quality of understanding and sympathising and sharing another person's feelings . _ *mpath* _
12. Conclusions based on experiment, experience or observation _ *mpirica* _
13. Heavenly and sublime; relating to the heavens or sky. _ *mpyrea* _
14. To equal or surpass by imitation. _ *mulat* _
15. A citation of very high praise _ *ncomiu* _
16. Found in or exclusive to a localised area. _ *ndemi* _
17. To invigorate. _ *nergis* _
18. To weaken or debilitate. _ *nervat* _
19. An embarrassing child or discomfortingly indiscreet person. _*fant terribl* _
20. To cause or bring about something. _*gende* _
21. Something unexplainable. _ *nigm* _
22. To order or instruct someone to do something. _ *njoi* _
23. A feeling of hostility or ill will. _ *nmit* _
24. A feeling of listlessness and boredom. _ *nnu* _
25. Something outrageous, of extreme wickedness. _ *normit* _
26. To implore, beg or plead. _ *ntrea* _

27. To articulate clearly   _ nunciat _
28. Something transient or short-lived.   _ phemera _
29. A person devoted to sensual pleasures,
    especially eating and drinking.   _ picur _
30. A witty or paradoxical saying or short verse   _ pigra _

The answers are on page 215. You should have had very little
trouble replacing the first letter of each word! So for this round a score of
25 or more would be appropriate for someone making good progress with
their vocabulary building.

Choose the Correct Meaning

Which of the two choices, *a* or *b*, most accurately fits the meaning
of each word? Circle your choices – the result of knowledge, not guessing!
– and then check the answers on page 216.

epitome	**a.** a typical or ideal example of something; **b.** the first volume of a three-volume set of books.
eponymous	**a.** a word or name derived from the real name of a person or place; **b.** someone who attempts to remain anonymous but fails.
equable	**a.** capable of being balanced by an equal mass or amount; **b.** placid and even-tempered.
equanimity	**a.** closeness; **b.** calmness of mind or temper.
equinox	**a.** When the orbit of the moon is furthest from the earth; **b.** The two annual occasions when day and night are of equal length.
equitable	**a.** fair and just; **b.** a desire for revenge.
equivocal	**a.** ambiguous and uncertain; **b.** loudmouthed and rude.
ergonomics	**a.** the study of the efficiency of human muscles; **b.** the study of the relationship between workers and their environment.
erogenous	**a.** sensitive to sexual stimulation; **b.** fatty tissue.
ersatz	**a.** a rare variety of mink fur; **b.** an artificial or inferior substitute.
eructation	**a.** a painful erection of the penis; **b.** belching.
erudite	**a.** well-read and well-informed; **b.** blackened.
eschatology	**a.** taboo expressions in the Bible; **b.** the branch of

	theology concerned with the end of the world.
eschew	**a.** processing nuts into a cream; **b.** to avoid or abstain from.
esoteric	**a.** obscure and restricted to an initiated minority; **b.** a style of art that blends erotic and religious subjects.
esprit de corps	**a.** sense of comradeship and shared purpose; **b.** the principle of 'fighting to the death'.
ethos	**a.** the distinctive character or spirit of a culture or era; **b.** the difference between races of humans.
etymology	**a.** the origin and history of food; **b.** the origin and history of words.
eugenics	**a.** the study of selective breeding in humans; **b.** a form of dancing for fitness introduced in the 1920s.
eulogise	**a.** to weep over the dead; **b.** to praise highly.
euphemism	**a.** a stifled sneeze or cough; **b.** an inoffensive word or phrase substituted for one considered to be hurtful or obscene.
euphonious	**a.** pleasing to the ear; **b.** feeling great joy.
euphoria	**a.** a feeling of extreme elation; **b.** goods sold in bargain stores.
Eurasian	**a.** relating to the Kingdom of Eurasia; **b.** of mixed European and Asian blood.
euthanasia	**a.** partial anaesthesia; **b.** killing someone painlessly to relieve suffering.
evanescent	**a.** fading away; **b.** saturated with the perfume of flowers.
eviscerate	**a.** to disembowel; **b.** to produce excessive saliva.
exacerbate	**a.** to abrade or roughen; **b.** to aggravate or make worse.
excoriate	**a.** to remove the core or middle of something; **b.** to severely censure or denounce.
exculpate	**a.** to free from blame or guilt; **b.** in surgery, to remove the top of the skull.
execrable	**a.** of very poor quality; **b.** of doubtful parentage.
exegesis	**a.** the last three books of the Old Testament; **b.** explanation or interpretation of a text, particularly of the Bible.
exemplary	**a.** an example fit to be imitated or to serve as a warning; **b.** severely restrictive.
exigency	**a.** an urgent or pressing demand or requirement; **b.** a state of self-inflicted poverty.
exonerate	**a.** to incriminate an innocent party; **b.** to clear or absolve from blame or criminal charges.

exorcise	**a.** to remove subcutaneous tissue; **b.** to drive out evil spirits.
expatiate	**a.** to elaborate on a subject at great length; **b.** a person living temporarily in a foreign country.
expiate	**a.** to atone for or make amends; **b.** to return stolen money.
exponentially	**a.** with great and ever-increasing rapidity; **b.** the discovery of hidden possibilities.
expropriate	**a.** to illegally transfer public property to private ownership; **b.** to seize possession of private property for public use.
expunge	**a.** to delete or obliterate; **b.** to moisten lightly.
expurgate	**a.** to threaten a defendant in court with a custodial sentence; **b.** to remove supposedly offensive passages from a book.

YOU FORGOT THE WELLINGTONS!

EXTEMPORE

extempore	**a.** outdoor classical ballet; **b.** impromptu or unprepared.
extenuating	**a.** qualifying or justifying **b.** broadening or fattening.

51

extraneous	**a.** non-essential or irrelevant; **b.** relating to the outdoors.
exuberant	**a.** rotund; **b.** abounding in vigour and high spirits.

This round contained some interesting and useful *'e'* words, and perhaps a few that prompted some head-scratching. Check the answers on page 216 and if you scored 35 or more correct you did very well.

Eyes and Sight

Few of us escape a visit to the optician during our lives. Come to think of it, what's the difference between an *optician,* an *optometrist* and an *ophthalmologist?* The one you usually meet is the *optician,* who fills out optical prescriptions and sells spectacles and contact lenses. An *optometrist* tests your eyes and vision and also prescribes, while *ophthalmologists* are medical practitioners who specialise in diseases and malfunctions of the eye. Here is some more optic terminology.

cornea	The clear, convex outer coating of the eye.
iris	The coloured muscular diaphragm that surrounds and controls the size of the pupil.
retina	The light-sensitive inner layer of the eye on which images are focused by the lens and transmitted to the brain.
pupil	The dark centre of the iris of the eye through which light enters.
myopia	Shortsightedness or nearsightedness
astigmatism	A defect of the eye's lens causing distorted images.
cataract	Clouding of the eye's lens, eventually causing blindness.
glaucoma	Pressure within the eye causing damage to the optic disc and eventual loss of vision.
conjunctivitis	Inflammation of the eye's mucous membrane.
trachoma	A chronic viral disease of the eye's mucous membrane and cornea resulting in scar tissue and possible blindness.
colour blindness	An inherited inability to distinguish some colours.
tunnel vision	Restriction of peripheral vision.
ophthalmoscope	An instrument for looking into the eye.

30-Sec quickpick: Odd Man Out

With a minimum of hesitation, underline or circle the 'odd man out' in each of these word groups:

ease, discomfort, tranquility, contentment.
entry, egress, outlet, exit.
eliminate, discard, dismiss, attract.
enigmatic, baffling, comprehensible, inscrutable.
equilibrium, symmetry, unstable, equanimity.
embrace, espouse, elect, reject.
evince, disguise, demonstrate, establish
execrable, abhorrent, pleasant, obnoxious.
expiration, beginning, termination, culmination.
extort, extract, give, wrest.

A couple of these may have caused you to think twice. The answers are on page 216 and if you finished inside 30 seconds with 8 or more correct, your knowledge of words is well above average.

Element of Words give Clues to Meanings

Let's tune in again to our serialisation about the roles played by prefixes and suffixes in word formation. You doubtless already know that when you see a word ending in *ess* it's likely to describe the female or feminine of something or someone: an *actress* is an actor, but a female one. Likewise you probably instinctively know that a word ending in *et, ette* or *let* is most likely a smaller version of someone or something: a *booklet*, for example, is a small book. But what about *trumpet,* you teasingly ask. The same principle applies, albeit disguised. The English word *trumpet* is derived from the Old French *trompette*, or 'little trompe', a diminutive version of a larger instrument. But *strumpet* – a 'little strump'? We'll never know. Although the word has been around for half a millennium its origin is unknown.

Word, Element	Origin	Meaning	English words
epi-	Greek	upon, on, over, above	*epicentre, epidermis, epitaph, epidemic, epidural*

53

ex-	Latin	out of, from	*exit, exclude, exhume, excuse, exhale, extort*
extra-	Latin	beyond, outside	*extraordinary, extramarital extraterrestrial*
-ee	Latin	involved	*addressee, employee, escapee, licencee*
-ess	Greek	female	*hostess, lioness, baroness, laundress, princess*
-et, -ette, -let	Old French	lesser, small, minor	*cigarette, islet, maisonette, flatlet, midget, droplet*

It's Revision Time Again!

Spend a few minutes brushing up on the *'e'* words you've learned. Here are a dozen words which, although you may not use them or come across them every day, are in fairly common use. Hand on heart – can you instantly and accurately define them?

eclectic, egalitarian, empirical, enormity, epitome, equivocal, ersatz, exacerbate, extempore, extraneous, effete, empathy.

Enrich Your Wordpower (it pays!)

One of the pioneering efforts to educate people about the importance of having an enhanced vocabulary is *It Pays to Enrich Your Word Power*, which is still a regular feature in *The Reader's Digest*.

It was first published in 1945, the bright idea of American lexicographer Wilfrid Funk who convinced the magazine's founder, DeWitt Wallace, that readers would enjoy a game designed to help improve their vocabularies, or 'word power'. They did, and the weekly exercises were an instant hit. Within a short time the feature settled down to a format in which readers were asked to pick, from four alternative choices, the correct meanings of 20 words.

It Pays to Enrich Your Word Power has enjoyed a continuous run in the magazine ever since. And as *The Reader's Digest* has for many years sold over 25 million copies a month in a dozen or more languages, the feature can fairly claim to address itself to "the largest classroom in the world".

IPTIYWP has changed little over half a century although now each monthly wordgame follows a theme. A typical recent game featured key words that celebrated spring, or the season of renewal: *vernal, rite, paean, burgeon, gambol, teeming* and the like. You might like to take a crack at these rather tougher examples:

- **scud**   a. to escape; b. move swiftly; c. scrape; d. disable.
- **florescence**   a. flowering; b. blaze of colour; c. gust of wind; d. prosperity.
- **farrow**   a. pasture; b. litter of pigs; c. feast; d. blacksmith's forge.
- **pullulate**   a. to swarm; b. wrench; c. return; d. throb.

The answers are, in order: **b.** (as in "clouds *scud* along in high winds"); **a.** (as in "she was entranced by the vivid *florescence* of the melon vines"); **b.** (as in "the champion sow produced a *farrow* of nine"); **a.** (as in "the hatchery *pullulated* with hundreds of young chicks").

F

Increase your Word Power!

Let's take a leaf out of the *Reader's Digest* and create our own *It Pays to Increase Your Word Power* game, similar to the thousands that have appeared in the magazine since 1945. Circle or tick the word or phrase you believe is *nearest in meaning* to the key word. The answers are on page 216.

1. *facetious*   **a.** long-winded; **b.** inclined to be secretive; **c.** to make a joke at an inappropriate time; **d.** self-pitying.

2. *facile*   **a.** superficial; **b.** rapid; **c.** sporting; **d.** left-handed.

3. *facilitate*   **a.** to hesitate; **b.** to interfere; **c.** to be sympathetic to another's troubles; **d.** to make things easier.

4. *factotum*   **a.** a bookmaker's clerk; **b.** a 'jack of all trades' servant; **c.** an undertaker's assistant; **d.** a weather summary.

5. *fait accompli*   **a.** a clueless crime; **b.** a willing accomplice to a crime; **c.** something already accomplished and beyond alteration; **d.** having faith only in practical matters.

6. *fallacy*   **a.** a false belief or argument; **b.** a Papal law; **c.** a deliberate lie; **d.** a hidden truth.

7. *Falstaffian*   **a.** argumentative; **b.** belligerent, looking for a fight; **c.** thin as a pikestaff; **d.** plump, jovial and dissolute.

8. *farcical*   **a.** painfully unfunny; **b.** funny, but hurtful to others; **c.** a 17th century comic play; **d.** ludicrous and absurd.

9. *farinaceous*   **a.** food containing starch; **b.** inclined to be sticky; **c.** any

	grain that's imported; **d.** having the appearance of corn.
10. *farrago*	**a.** invective; **b.** an overlong speech; **c.** a hotchpotch or jumble; **d.** a West African sailing vessel.
11. *fascism*	**a.** an art movement; **b.** an authoritarian and undemocratic ideology or government; **c.** a left-wing movement that preceded communism; **d.** a branch of the Italian mafia.
12. *fastidious*	**a.** smartly dressed; **b.** over-critical and hard to please; **c.** excessively tidy; **d.** punctual.
13. *fatuous*	**a.** complacently foolish; **b.** complacently overweight; **c.** complacently smug; **d.** complacently idle.
14. *fatwa.*	**a.** Muslim teacher; **b.** the shawl headdress of certain Muslim priests; **c.** one of the key Muslim holy books; **d.** a decree issued by a Muslim leader.
15. *faux pas*	**a.** cunning like a fox; **b.** a social indiscretion; **c.** a false ballet step; **d.** a doomed failure.
16. *fealty*	**a.** bravery; **b.** foolhardiness; **c.** cowardice; **d.** loyalty.
17. *febrile*	**a.** lukewarm; **b.** itching; **c.** feverish; **d.** decaying.
18. *feckless*	**a.** a person without purpose, plan or principles; **b.** a horse impossible to train; **c.** a clear skin; **d.** a young criminal.
19. *fecund*	**a.** one millionth of a minute; **b.** muddy; **c.** fertile; **d.** a natural ability for playing sport.
20. *feign*	**a.** a pretender to a royal crown; **b.** to pretend; **c.** a boxer's move to avoid a punch; **d.** to remove impurities from gold.

As with *The Reader's Digest*, there are no prizes for getting all 20 correct in this version of *It Pays to Increase Your Word Power* – merely congratulations. A score of 15 or more would be above average. But don't be discouraged if you scored less – just keep working at it and revise, revise, revise!

Fill in the Missing Letters

Each of the words in this set have a letter missing. From the meanings given, can you replace the letters to form the complete and correct words? The answers are on page 216.

1. Lively and quick-tempered — *fe _ sty*
2. Happy and agreeable — *felici _ ous*
3. Involving a criminal act — *f _ lonious*
4. An animal or plant that reverts to its wild state — *fer _ l*
5. A subversive infiltrator — *fifth col _ mnist*
6. Pertaining to sons and daughters — *f _ lial*
7. Obstructing legislation with long speeches and other delaying tactics. — *fili _ uster*
8. The ornament on top of a spire or gable — *fin _ al*
9. Flabby, soft and limp — *flac _ id*
10. Blatant and outrageous — *fla _ rant*
11. Showy and extravagant — *flambo _ ant*
12. Inappropriate frivolity — *flip _ ant*
13. Having a red or flushed complexion — *flo _ id*
14. To treat with contempt — *fl _ ut*
15. The nauseating smell of decay — *foet _ d*
16. A peculiarity or idiosyncrasy — *fo _ ble*
17. To instigate or stir up trouble — *f _ ment*
18. Trivial and silly — *fo _ tling*
19. A raid, an incursion or a first attempt — *o _ ay*
20. Self-control and patience — *forbear _ nce*
21. Relating to or connected with a court of law — *fore _ sic*
22. To anticipate or to take action to delay or stop an event — *fo _ estall*
23. Something at which a person excels — *f _ rte*
24. Accidental or unplanned — *fort _ itous*
25. A rowdy quarrel or brawl — *frac _ s*
26. Restless and irritable — *fra _ tious*
27. Someone who admires France and things French — *Franco _ hile*
28. The act of killing one's brother — *fratr _ cide*
29. Distracted and frantic — *fre _ etic*
30. Easily broken up and crumbled — *fr _ able*
31. The realisation or fulfilment of something worked for — *fr _ ition*
32. To denounce noisily and explosively — *fu _ minate*
33. Obvious and embarrassing sincerity — *ful _ ome*
34. Belief in the literal truth of sacred texts, and in their strict observance — *funda _ entalism*

35. Gloomy, mournful and suggestive of a
    funeral   *fune _ eal*
36. Showy ornamental trimming on women's
    clothing   *furbe _ ow*
37. A public protest or outburst of rage   *furor _*
38. Pompous or bombastic speech or writing   *fus _ ian*

The idea behind these 'missing letters' rounds is not so much to
allow you to gleefully reinstate the missing letters (relatively easy) but to
pause sufficiently long enough to allow the accompanying meanings to
attach themselves to your memory. So how successful were you? Check
the answers on page 216 and, as always, look in your dictionary for the
full meanings of those words that tripped you up.

Developing a really good vocabulary depends very much on the two
i's – *inquisitiveness* and *initiative*. Always be inquisitive about the words you
read and hear, especially those you don't quite understand; and have the
initiative to find out what they really mean.

Food and Drink

Perhaps we're becoming increasingly sophisticated, because
without a vocabulary covering dining, wining and the preparation of food
we might as well stay home and exist solely on beer and chips. We're
talking about a specialised vocabulary of tens of thousands of words,
terms, names and phrases, many if not most of them foreign. How
extensive is your gustatory vocabulary? Just answer **true** or **false** to the
following statements to find out. The answers are on page 216.

		True	False
1.	When we were in France we bought all our cooked meats at the *charcuterie*	__	__
2.	*Nosh* was originally the Jewish word for 'snack'.	__	__
3.	The Mexican drink of tequila and lime juice is a *spritzer*	__	__
4.	*Prosciutto* is a sausage popular in southern Italy	__	__
5.	In France, breakfast is called *petit déjeuner*	__	__
6.	We particularly liked those Spanish restaurants serving *tapas*	__	__
7.	When you wish to order wine, call the *sommelier*	__	__

8. *Pesto* sauce is made with basil, garlic, pine nuts
   and olive oil.   ___ ___
9. The Greek speciality *taramasalata* is made from
   cheese.   ___ ___
10. The traditional long French loaf is the *baguette*. ___ ___
11. To make *lasagna* always use fresh fish and
    shellfish   ___ ___
12. All Indian food lovers seem to like *biriani,* the
    dish of lamb and chicken, rice and spices.   ___ ___
13. The salad consisting of romaine lettuce, anchovies,
    croutons, Parmesan cheese, egg and lemon is called
    Niçoise.   ___ ___
14. *Kiwi fruit* is just another name for the 'Chinese
    gooseberry'.   ___ ___
15. Spicy Spanish sausages are called *zampone.*   ___ ___
16. The coffee made with steamed, foamy milk is
    cappuccino.   ___ ___
17. The famous Swiss cheeses are *Gruyere, Havarti*
    and *Gouda.*   ___ ___
18. A menu with each dish priced separately is the
    table d'hôte.   ___ ___
19. *Hollandaise sauce* is made from egg yolks and
    lemon juice.   ___ ___
20. Many people dislike *Szechuan* style Chinese
    cooking because they find it is too hot   .___ ___

A mouthwatering score would be 20 correct, but you can still count
yourself as a passable gourmet if you scored 16 or more. And while you're
checking up on those you missed are you familiar with the following?

*Angels on horseback, velouté, rijsttafel, keftédes, pain grille,
Zweiback, enchilada, mulligatawny, falafel, gefiltefish.*

60-Sec Quickpick: Spot the Misprint

Even with today's advanced word processing and printing
technology misprints are not unknown – especially in newspapers. Here
are 10 short passages, each containing a misprint. You have two tasks: (1)
spot the misprint; (2) correct it. The answers are on page 216.

1. The young lady had a farway look in her eyes.   _____

2. Of the contingent, only fourty-five returned.   _____

3. The headmaster admitted that he was quite
   phased by the experience.   _____

4. The Millenium Dome has been plagued by
   debt and doubt.   _____

5. She seems always willing to jump at his
   beckoned call.   _____

6. The two men were captured and remanded
   in custardy.   _____

7. Mr Patrick always remembered the first
   sentence of the novel *Moby Dick*: "Call me
   Fishmeal".   _____

8. The court was told how the accused ran amuck
   in the store before brandishing the knife.   _____

9. Hooping cough is a complaint hardly known
   today.   _____

10. The winner was eventually exposed as a
    transexual.   _____

All correct? Then you should apply for a job as a proofreader on *The Gruaniad*.

Word Elements: Clues to Meaning

Here are some more word elements, suffixes and prefixes derived mostly from Latin and Greek, that can often help you recognise the meanings of words. From the Latin word *ferrum*, for example, meaning iron, we get the combining form *ferro*. Once we know this we can safely assume that any word beginning with *ferro* (*ferrocyanide, ferromagnetism, ferruginous, ferrule, ferrous,* etc) has something to do with iron.

Word, Element	Origin	Meaning	English words
for-	Old English	rejection, prohibition	*forbid, forswear, forlorn, forfend*
fore-	Old English	before; in front	*foresight, forefather, foreman, forecast, forestall*

61

| -fy, -ify | Latin | making, becoming | *pacify, gratify, falsify, nullify, testify, notify* |
| -fer, -ferre | Latin | to bring | *offer, proffer, prefer, confer, refer, transfer, suffer* |

Revision, Revision, Revision!

Know your *'f'* words? Here's a ***baker's dozen**** worth revisiting. Do you know their meanings precisely?

> *facile, fastidious, faux pas, flaccid, flout, forensic, forte, fortuitous, fracas, fulsome, furore, facetious, farrago.*

> * *An interesting old term, meaning 13, and deriving from a baker's anxiety not to be accused of giving light weight; if someone ordered a dozen rolls he would pop in one extra.*

Fermat's last theorem and other theories

Every so often you're bound to come across a reference to someone's law, theory, principle or rule. Often it's a writer's attempt to be clever but to a reader it can be frustrating, not knowing what the allusion is all about. Here are a few that seem to crop up fairly regularly.

Chaos theory	Even apparent randomness and random phenomena have an underlying order.
Domino effect	When a series of similar or related events occur as a direct and inevitable result of an initial event.
Electra complex	The desire in female children for their father, and jealousy towards the mother. See *Oedipus complex*.
Fermat's last theorem	The hypothesis that the equation $x_n + y_n = z_n$ has no integral solutions for n greater than two. It was finally solved by British mathematician Professor Andrew Wiles in 1998.
Heimlich manoeuvre	A first aid technique: applying sudden upward pressure on the abdomen to dislodge a bone or foreign body stuck in a person's windpipe.

Hubble's constant	In astronomy, a measure of the rate at which the universe is expanding. By this means it is calculated that from the Big Bang until now 10-20 billion years have elapsed.
Murphy's law	If anything can go wrong, it will. To this law are attached several corollaries: Nothing is as easy as it looks. Every solution breeds new problems. Everything takes longer than you think. Nature always sides with the hidden flaw. It is impossible to make anything foolproof because fools are so ingenious.
Occam's razor	A maxim stated by 14th century philosopher William of Ockham that in explaining something, assumptions should not be unnecessarily multiplied.
Oedipus complex	The desire of a child for its parent of the opposite sex, usually a son for his mother. See *Electra complex.*
Parkinson's law	Work expands to fill the time available for its completion.
Peter principle	All members in a hierarchy tend to rise to their own level of incompetence.
Sod's law	See *Murphy's law.*
Truman's law	If you can't convince 'em, confuse 'em.

And, of course, there is ***Cole's law,*** even though it is regarded by many as a load of old shredded cabbage.

G

Replace the Missing Words

Below are ten words and ten sentences. A word is missing from each of the sentences. Can you place the appropriate words in all ten sentences?

gaffe	*galaxy*	*galleria*	*Gallic*	*galvanised*
gambit	*gamine*	*gamut*	*gangrene*	*garrulous*

1. Audrey Hepburn always played the role of _____ to perfection.

2. The horrific news _____ the team into action.

3. Malcolm apologised for his unfortunate _____ at the party.

4. The husband could hardly get a word in edgeways; his wife was easily the most _____ woman they'd ever met.

5. The Milky Way, consisting of millions of stars, forms part of our _____ .

6. Dorothy Parker wrote that the actress's _____ of emotions ran all the way from A to B.

7. Both Arctic explorers suffered badly from _____ due to frostbite.

8. He used the old joke about Churchill as a _____ to soften the audience.

9. Edouard was decidedly _____ when it came to charming women.

10. The new shopping mall featured a spectacular _____ of four storeys.

Understanding words and their meanings enables you to use them appropriately and expressively. The more extensive your vocabulary, the more choice you have when looking for 'just that right word'. Or, put another way, the greater the choice, the clearer your voice. So if, in this exercise, you placed all the words in their correct contexts, you're well on the way to an eloquent vocabulary. Just the same, check the answers and the meanings of the words on page 217 to make sure you're 100% correct.

What's the Correct Usage?

On the same theme, here are some more useful *'g'* words. In each case one is used correctly, and one is not. Can you identify the sentences, *a* or *b*, that are correct in sense and meaning?

gauche	**a.** The artist presented her with a framed gauche. **b.** The young girl was beautiful but gauche.
gazebo	**a.** They loved sitting in the gazebo for hours and hours. **b.** The orchestra played a tuneful gazebo in Margaret's honour.
gazumped	**a.** The house hunters complained to the agent that this was the second time they'd been gazumped. **b.** The fullback was carried from the rugby field after he'd been gazumped.
generic	**a.** The vicar said that the couple's idea of a wedding was too generic for his church. **b.** He explained that aspirin was a generic drug and could be marketed by any firm.
genre	**a.** Jacob's family had a genre stretching back to the 16th century. **b.** He preferred the realistic fiction of Dickens and works of that genre.
genuflect	**a.** As she entered she genuflected briefly towards the altar. **b.** The three-year sentence gave him ample time to genuflect upon his crime.
geriatric	**a.** Poor old grandad was confined to the geriatric section of the hospital. **b.** The newly developed antiseptic had a beneficial geriatric effect on most patients.
germane	**a.** The ochre shade was attractive, but in the end she preferred the germane. **b.** Mark insisted that consideration of salaries was germane to the factory's inefficiency problem.

gerrymander   **a.** The sitting candidate realised too late that the gerrymander could cost him the election. **b.** The gang boss threatened to gerrymander the FBI by fleeing to a neighboring state.

gestation   **a.** The average gestation time for a heavy meal is five hours. **b.** It was obvious the mare's gestation was in its final weeks.

gesundheit   **a.** "Gesundheit!" he said to his friend, after a whole-hearted sneeze. **b.** Angrily, he sat down. "Gesundheit!" he swore under his breath.

gibe   **a.** Fred had long learned to suffer the gibes from his mates. **b.** One day, thought Wendy, he's going to gibe me in the ribs once too often.

gigolo   **a.** You could tell by his effeminate manner that he was a gigolo. **b.** The widow had plenty of money and a string of eager gigolos.

gilt-edged   **a.** He was one of the partners who'd invented the gilt-edged safety razor. **b.** He regarded the house purchase as a gilt-edged investment.

gimcrack   **a.** The antique armchair lost its value because it was riddled with gimcracks. **b.** Beryl had no taste at all, addicted as she was to gimcrack jewellery.

glasnost   **a.** The new chairman felt that the normally secretive company would benefit from a dose of glasnost. **b.** After the heavy snowfall the windows were glazed with a veil of glasnost.

glitterati   **a.** The famous actress never really cared about being part of the London glitterati. **b.** When in Venice they bought a superb carnival mask, ornamented with glitterati.

gloaming   **a.** As dusk approached, Sir Bernard suggested they follow the old song and do some 'roaming in the gloaming'. **b.** In Scotland the gloaming is a favourite haunt of lovers.

glutinous   **a.** The plant trapped insects in its glutinous nectary. **b.** He came up and spoke to my aunt in his usual glutinous manner.

gobbet   **a.** His body hung for days beneath the evil, creaking gobbet. **b.** The starving prisoners clamoured for the gobbets of rancid flesh.

gobbledegook	**a.** Among Lewis Carroll's creations were the Cheshire Cat, the snark, the boojum and the gobbledegook. **b.** The management's baffling memo was utter gobbledegook.
gossamer	**a.** The dress's fabric was as fine as gossamer. **b.** The leaves of the tree turned as purple as gossamer.
gourmandise	**a.** The factory was built to gourmandise milk into cheese. **b.** Her dream was to gourmandise on fancy Swiss chocolates.
Grand Guignol	**a.** With constant violent arguing, living in the Taylor household must have been pure Grand Guignol. **b.** Having won the lottery, our neighbours thought they were Grand Guignol.
grandiose	**a.** The garden party was a grandiose affair. **b.** Lord Wainscott was always grandiose with his money.
gratuitous	**a.** Not all the diners were gratuitous to the waiters. **b.** The movie was marred by the scenes of gratuitous violence.
gravamen	**a.** The gravamen of the case was the premeditated nature of the attack. **b.** The vicar finally delivered his gravamen to the happy couple.
gregarious	**a.** Jem was a gregarious person and invariably became restive when alone. **b.** When the gregarious mood hit him he would lie in wait for some casual prey.
gremlin	**a.** They hated the painted gremlins in their neighbour's garden. **b.** When the mower kept stalling he blamed the gremlins in the carburettor.
grenadine	**a.** The ex-guardsman had a grenadine manner about him. **b.** The cocktail called for a generous splash of grenadine.
gullible	**a.** Seagulls are so expertly gullible they can swallow a kilo of fish in less than a minute. **b.** Brian was so gullible he was a favourite target of the street traders.
gumption	**a.** The brick pillars were topped with weathered stone gumptions. **b.** The teacher told them that with a bit of gumption they could achieve anything.
gunge	**a.** When all the gunge was finally removed the brasswork looked like new. **b.** The designer favoured the new gunge fashion style so admired by students and ravers.

Slogging through that set might have seemed like a lot of hard work, but if after checking the answers on page 217 you marked 25 or more correct, then surely it was worth it. Reflect a little on the words you missed and explore their full meanings in your dictionary. When you're satisfied that you fully comprehend their meanings, add them to your growing vocabulary.

The '*G*' section might well have concluded with the word *gurney*, a wheeled stretcher used for transporting medical patients from the scene of an accident to an ambulance or hospital. *Gurney* is just one of between 3,000 and 5,000 words created every year, and after a couple of decades or so its usage is now sufficiently widespread as to guarantee a degree of permanence. Words are continually joining and leaving the language. Words like *freet* (a proverb), *frim* (vigorous and healthy), and *frayn* (to ask or inquire) expire from under use to make way for the new words on our lips such as *bimbo* and *yobbo*, *gazumped* and *gazundered*, *fax* and *filofax*. But not all new words make the grade. Remember the *squarial* of the early 1990s? This flat, square satellite aerial had such a short life that it could be termed an *ephemaerial*. But in their anxiety not to be thought of as lexicographically lazy, over-eager dictionary editors fell for it and you'll find it listed in several dictionaries. Not so long ago new words remained in limbo for many years before acquiring lexical respectability, but that never discouraged us from using them. If we used *only* words in dictionaries in our everyday speech and writing our vocabularies would seem rather lifeless indeed. So *vivat!* to *blag, firkinise, Euro, welly, cereologist, grunge, wysiwyg* and their like.

Quickpick: Idioms and Catchphrases

Much of our language is made up of idiomatic expressions and catchphrases – combinations of words that, to a baffled outsider, make no literal sense. So a good grasp of idioms and popular sayings is just as vital a part of our vocabulary as plain words. Can you fill in the missing words from the following idiomatic expressions?

1. I get the feeling that *someone's just walked over my* _____ .
2. Be smart, Kevin, *don't look a* _____ _____ in the mouth.
3. You know that *two can play at that* _____ , don't you?
4. It does rather take the _____ *off the gingerbread*, doesn't it?
5. If it rains tomorrow we'll really *be up a* ____ *tree*.
6. Don't give him any more to drink; he's already a bit _____ *around the* ____ .

7. That officious traffic warden really *gets my* _____ .
8. Don't kill the _____ *that lays the golden egg.*
9. Although he's nearly twelve he's still only *knee-high to a*

   _____.
10. Was it Mae West who said that *a* _____ *man is hard to find*?
11. Aunt Winnie really has the _____ *of the gab.*
12 .The exam will soon *separate the sheep from the* _____ .

The answers are on page 217. These are very popular idioms (and the missing words all start with '*g*') so a score of 10 or even a full score of 12 would not be exceptional. But the real purpose of the exercise is to remind you that much of our everyday speech consists of informal expressions and idioms, all part of a mature English vocabulary.

Word Roots: Guides to Meaning

As with prefixes, suffixes and combining forms (linguistic elements that help form compound words:e.g. *dia* + the combining form *gram* = *diagram*) the ancient roots of many of our words often hint at their meanings. Here are some '*g*' examples.

Word, Element	Origin	Meaning	English words
gamos	Greek	marriage	*monogamous, bigamy, gamete, polygamous, monogyny*
generare	Latin	to beget	*gender, generate, gene*
genus	Latin	kind, type	*genre, genealogy, gentry*
gradus	Latin	a step	*gradual, gradation, graduate*
gravis	Latin	heavy	*gravitas, gravity, grave*
grex, gregis	Latin	flock	*gregarious, congregate*
gune	Greek	woman	*gynaecology, misogynist*

Review, Reappraisal, Reassessment = Revision

Revision by any other name is still revision, but don't dismiss its importance in helping you to enrich your vocabulary. Do you fully understand the meanings of the following words? Can you use them meaningfully in mental sentences?

gauche, gibe, grandiose, gratuitous, gregarious, gullible, garrulous.

Granny Smith and other Eponyms

Many of our words are **eponyms:** names derived from real or mythical persons. The *Granny Smith apple*, for example, derives its name from grandmother Maria Ann Smith who first grew the variety in Australia in the 1860s. Other *eponymous* names are rather better disguised. The one-piece *leotard* was designed at about the same time by Jules Leotard, a French acrobat also remembered as 'the daring young man on the flying trapeze'. Some eponyms are exceedingly ancient. A *Caesarean section* is named after Julius Caesar, who was delivered in this way. Others are quite recent: *Levis* owe their name to a Bavarian immigrant to the US, Levi Strauss, who first came up with the idea of riveting the pockets of trousers; and the *Moog synthesiser*, named after its creator, American engineer Robert Moog, in the 1960s.

Here are some common eponyms (names derived from place-names are called *toponyms*) which are part of our everyday vocabularies.

Biro	Invented by Hungarian Laszlo Biro, who died in 1985.
Buddleia	Named after 17th century English botanist Adam Buddle.
Cardigan	Knitted jacket named after Light Brigade commander, the Earl of Cardigan, and first worn during the Crimean War.
Doberman pinscher	First bred by German dog breeder Ludwig Doberman.
Fuchsia	Named after 16th century German botanist Leonhard Fuchs.
Jack Russell	Breed of English terrier developed by the Rev Jack Russell.
Listeria	Poisonous food bacterium named after British surgeon Sir Joseph Lister.
Mach number	When Concorde flies at a speed of Mach2 we should remember the Austrian physicist Ernst Mach (1838-1916) who devised this system of speed management.

Magnolia	Named after the French naturalist Pierre Magnol.
Maverick	Derives from American frontiersman Augustus Maverick.
Melba toast	A favourite of Australian opera star Dame Nellie Melba.
Platonic	From the Greek philosopher Plato.
Sadism	From the Marquis de Sade (1740-1814) who by all accounts got a buzz from inflicting pain on others.
Salmonella	The American surgeon Dr Daniel Salmon gave his name to this very nasty bacterium.
Saxophone	Blame Belgian musical-instrument maker Adolphe Sax. Place even bigger blame on John Philip Sousa, the American bandmaster who invented the much larger *Sousaphone*.
Shrapnel	Named after British artillery officer Henry Shrapnel.
Teddy bear	The stuffed toy bear derives its name from cuddly US President Theodore (Teddy) Roosevelt (1858-1919).
Watt	Named after Scottish engineer James Watt.
Wellington	The ubiquitous knee-high rubber boot is named after British soldier and statesman the Duke of Wellington.

Choose the Correct Meaning

Which one of the three alternatives, *a*, *b* or *c*, most accurately fits the meaning of the word? Circle or mark your choices (trying not to be tempted into making wild guesses!) and then check the answers on page 217.

habeas corpus	**a.** murder case lacking a body; **b.** demand for a prisoner to appear before a court; **c.** appeal to dismiss a case through lack of evidence.
habitué	**a.** a regular visitor to a place; **b.** a drug addict; **c.** a very stylishly dressed person.
hackneyed	**a.** to be transported by a horse-drawn carriage; **b.** stale and trite; **c.** tired and listless.
hagiography	**a.** a stream of invective; **b.** a catalogue of complaints; **c.** a biography that idolises its subject.
ha-ha	**a.** a sunken fence; **b.** a fountain; **c.** a summer house.
haiku	**a.** a Japanese ceremonial sword; **b.** a 17-syllable Japanese verse form; **c.** the wide sash worn over a kimono.
halation	**a.** the coating of dried salt left by sea-spray; **b.** a greenish deposit on neglected teeth; **c.** a halo effect seen in some photographs caused by pointing the camera at a light.
halcyon	**a.** peaceful and pleasant; **b.** a thick crayon used for stage makeup; **c.** the fringe on an oriental carpet.
halitosis	**a.** body odour; **b.** smelly feet; **c.** bad breath.
hapless	**a.** clumsy; **b.** angry and irritable; **c.** unfortunate and unlucky.

harangue	**a.** the muscle at the back of the tongue; **b.** ornamental brassware on a horse's harness; **c.** to address someone in a loud, abrasive and persuasive way.
harbinger	**a.** someone or something that foretells an event; **b.** a rowboat used for hunting whales; **c.** a species of honey-eating bird.
hauteur	**a.** high fashion; **b.** pride; **c.** causing or deserving hate.
hearsay	**a.** gossip and rumour; **b.** a broken promise; **c.** a method for teaching young children to read and write.
hector	**a.** to tease and bully; **b.** to act strangely in public; **c.** a stage direction in which the actors directly address the audience.
hedonism	**a.** the denial of bodily pleasures; **b.** the pursuit of pleasure as a principle; **c.** the belief that everyone goes to Heaven.
hegemony	**a.** property passing from a mother to her children; **b.** the dominance of one country or power over others; **c.** the state's inherent right to tax its citizens.
heinous	**a.** horse-loving; **b.** evil and atrocious; **c.** rural interests.
helix	**a.** a spiral shape or form; **b.** a four-pronged spear or weapon; **c.** the gold headband of a royal crown.
hellebore	**a.** a rude and tiresome person; **b.** a group of plants; **c.** a type of ship's figurehead.
herbivorous	**a.** plants that are fleshy rather than woody; **b.** plants with medicinal uses; **c.** grass or plant-eating animals.
heresy	**a.** an unorthodox belief; **b.** a wicked lie; **c.** a traitorous act.
hermetic	**a.** self-love; **b.** an aversion for other people; **c.** sealed so as to be airtight.
heterogeneous	**a.** a group made up equally of males and females; **b.** not of the same kind or type; **c.** a preference for the opposite sex.
heuristic	**a.** a process of learning by inquiry and investigation; **b.** an obsession with time; **c.** an admirer of holy artifacts.
hiatus	**a.** a break or gap; **b.** a summer holiday; **c.** acute hiccups.
Hibernian	**a.** pertaining to Scotland; **b.** pertaining to Ireland; **c.** pertaining to the Isle of Man.
hierarchy	**a.** the ruling group of a religion; **b.** persons or things arranged in a graded order; **c.** the chiefs of Scottish clans.

hindsight	**a.** all-round vision; **b.** the part of a gunsight nearest the eye; **c.** to be wise after an event.
histology	**a.** the study of organic tissue; **b.** the study of ancient burial sites; **c.** the study of hay fever.
histrionic	**a.** excessively melodramatic; **b.** referring to the early Victorian period; **c.** the inability to pronounce sibilant letters.
hoary	**a.** covered with cobwebs; **b.** red-faced due to Christmas revelry; **c.** white or whitish-grey in colour.
Hobson's choice	**a.** The best out of three; **b.** a selection so rich that often the worst choice is made; **c.** no choice at all.
hoi polloi	**a.** the toffs and aristocrats; **b.** arrogant public officials; **c.** the common people.
hologram	**a.** a message from the Vatican; **b.** printing by means of gelatin; **c.** a three-dimensional photographic image.
homily	**a.** a religious painting intended for the home; **b.** a moral lesson; **c.** a coarse flour made from barley.
homogeneous	**a.** all of the same kind; **b.** all different; **c.** mixed.
honorarium	**a.** a minor award made to civil servants; **b.** a collection of military medals; **c.** a fee paid for a nominally free service.
hortatory	**a.** pertaining to clocks and time-keeping; **b.** a sleep-walking condition; **c.** giving encouragement.

To score in this round of interesting and useful words, check your choices against the answers on page 217. A score of 35 or more correct would be excellent, but don't feel too put out if yours was around the 30 mark. Just keep revising, that's all.

Supply the Missing Words

Below are ten words and ten sentences. A word is missing from each of the sentences. Can you place the appropriate words in all ten sentences? Each word can be used only once.

hubris	*humane*	*humdrum*	*husbandry*	*hybrid*
hydrofoil	*hyperactivity*	*hypochondriac*	*hyperbole*	*hypothetical*

1. The _____ took only half an hour to travel from Dover to Calais.

2. Many philologists regard English as a _____ language.
3. David's brilliant career was predictably destroyed by his own _____.
4. Despite having a famous father and a socialite mother, Wayne himself led a _____ existence.
5. Since her stroke, grandmother has developed into a veritable _____.
6. Although he had a poor view of humans, the farmer had a _____ side when it came to his animals.
7. Louis was always good fun, even though his claims as a womaniser were generously laced with _____.
8. Although the Ryans were a large low-income family they lived very well, no doubt largely due to Edith's expert_____.
9. Although entirely _____, Sopwith's contention that the firm was cheating them was probably true.
10. Young Robert fell off the wall and broke a tooth, the victim, unfortunately, of uncontainable _____.

It's worth spending a little thought over exercises like this one because if you replace the words correctly the resulting sentences demonstrate their actual *usage*. And if you get the odd one wrong, then you're forced (if you're serious about building your vocabulary) to check the meaning of the word, and to try again. (Answers page 217).

60-Sec Quickpick: Spot the Antonyms

Here are 12 wordgroups in each of which three words have roughly the same meaning (synonyms or near-synonyms) and one (antonym) does not. Inside a minute, can you pick the 'odd men out' – the antonyms? Answers on page 217.

homely, uninhabitable, comfortable, cozy.
haggle, wrangle, quibble, agree.
hillock, knoll, ditch, mound.
hairless, hirsute, hairy, bearded.
handsome, unsightly, ugly, hideous.
harmless, innocuous, harmful, innocent.
humble, proud, arrogant, haughty.

harsh, oppressive, kind, brutal.
Hellenic, Greek, Latin, Athenian.
honour, infamy, glory, esteem.
hypothetical, theoretical, putative, proved.
hinder, hamper, assist, impede.

Heart and Circulation

The heart is an amazingly versatile organ. It can waken, warm, chill, melt, leap, race. swell, bleed and break. It can be engraved upon; it can be worn on the sleeve. But our discussion will confine itself to the heart's organic role, and that's equally versatile. With the heart comes blood, the circulatory system, problems, diseases and hundreds of associated terms, many of which we are expected to understand. Try this heart-to-heart quiz: just answer **True/False** to the statements. Answers on page 217.

	True	False
1. The fluid part of the blood is called *plasma*.	—	—
2. The two pumping chambers of the heart are the *arteries*.	—	—
3. The young man was *anaemic* through the lack of red cells in his blood.	—	—
4. *Thrombosis* is a blood clot that obstructs flow in an artery.	—	—
5. A *coronary bypass* is an operation that substitutes an artificial pump for the heart.	—	—
6. If you have intense chest pain from a blood-deprived heart muscle, it's likely you have *angina*.	—	—
7. The large veins at the front of the neck are the *carotid* veins.	—	—
8. Abnormally fast and violent heartbeats are *palpitations*.	—	—
9. To check his heart, Bert had an *electrocardiogram*.	—	—
10. The little girl had blood poisoning, or *haemophilia*	—	—
11. *Leukaemia* is caused by excessive production of white blood cells.	—	—
12. Someone who lacks the Rhesus factor in the blood is *Rh-negative*.	—	—

More Word Elements: Combining Forms

Combining forms, as we discussed earlier, are elements that can be married to other word roots to form new words: *hydro* + *electric* = *hydroelectric.* Or take another example, *dehydrate,* which is made up of a prefix, a combining form, and a suffix:

Prefix	*Combining form*	*Suffix*
de-	*hydro, hydra*	*-ate*
meaning to remove	meaning water	meaning possessing

If you translate this, the verb **dehydrate** can be understood to mean the removal of water possessed by the substance'. This once again underlines the usefulness of a knowledge of word roots in helping you to figure out the meanings of many words.

Here are some *combining forms* beginning with **'h'** :

Word, Element	Origin	Meaning	English words
haemo-, haema-	Greek	blood	*haemoglobin, haemophilia, haemorrhoids, haemostasis, haemorrhage*
helio-	Greek	sun	*heliograph, heliosphere, heliotrope, heliocentric, helium*
hetero-	Greek	other	*heterodoxy, heterogeneous, heterosexual, heteronym*
homo-, homeo	Latin	the same	*homogeneous, homosexual, homeoeroticism, homogenise*
hydro-	Greek	water	*hydrolysis, hydroelectric, hydrofoil, hydraulic, hydrogen, hydrocephalus, dehydrate*
hypno	Greek	sleep	*hypnotise, hypnosis, hypnogenesis*

Hard Words

So far, in our vocabulary building, we've stuck to words that are in fairly common use – words that anyone might find helpful to know and useful in everyday speech and writing. That takes care of probably 80% of the English lexicon. Most of us can do without the remaining 20% but some writers and speakers persist in sifting through this dark and virtually unknown lexicographical periphery to sneak in words that they know will baffle us and send us searching in our dictionaries. Here are just ten examples of this sneakiness, all lifted from our national broadsheet newspapers. Treat yourself to an Arcanum Award if you know the meaning of *any* of them:

accidie
Spiritual sloth, once one of the seven deadly sins. Its modern meaning is the apathetic attitude of "what's the point".

animadversions
"It is chock-full of brilliant animadversions and unerring disdain" is how a critic described a book by American feminist Camille Paglia. An *animadversion* is a strong criticism.

boskage
This word, along with its alternative spelling *boscage*, crops up occasionally in gardening columns. It means a clump of trees or shrubs; in other words, a *thicket*.

diddicoys
Used wrongly to mean Gypsies; in fact it describes people who are not true Romanies but who just live like Gypsies. 'New Age Travellers' would be a more modern term.

dirigisme
The new Labour government would be "neither old-style dirigisme nor rampant laissez faire", we read. The word means 'control of economic and social matters by the state'.

eleemosynary
Is an adjective meaning 'concerned with or dependent on charity'.

gralloching
A good old Scots word meaning 'to disembowel a deer' but increasingly used to mean removing the guts from any animal.

mumchance
A strange word, meaning 'struck dumb, awed into silence'. Although an adjective, writers tend to use it incorrectly as a verb or noun when they should leave it well alone.

phillipic
"His phillipic was just as dismissive". A *phillipic* is a bitter and impassioned speech of denunciation. Now you know.

sgian-dhu
Perhaps it's unfair to include this Gaelic tongue-twister which merely describes the dirk or knife carried in a Scotsman's sock.

Time for Revising

A few minutes revising your *'h'* words will be time well spent. Do you, right off the cuff, know the meanings of the following?

habitué	*halcyon*	*harbinger*	*hearsay*	*hegemony*
heresy	*hiatus*	*histrionic*	*hoi polloi*	*hubris*

Homophones and Homonyms

A *homophone* is a word that is pronounced the same as another word but which differs in meaning, spelling and origin, such as *boy* and *buoy*, *peace* and *piece*, *him* and *hymn*. "When the crate was opened, out stepped a gnu, and the rest of the zoo wondered what the new gnu knew." The last three words are homophones.

A *homonym* is a word that is spelt the same and sounds the same as another but which differs in meaning, such as *bank* (savings *bank*, river *bank*, and to *bank*, an aircraft turn) and *bow* (the *bow* of a ship; to *bow*, or bend over). The word *bow* is a *homograph*, too, in that it has different pronunciations: to *bow* or incline the head or body, and *bow*, the a stringed weapon that shoots arrows; and also a *homophone*, as in *bow* and *bough*!

There are hundreds of these homo-tricksters lying in wait for the unwary. A women's handicrafts magazine came out with the slogan that "a home of busy sewers is a happy home", which may have inspired a student to paraphrase the witch's scene in *Macbeth*: "Double, double, toilet trouble".

Here are some homophones to watch out for:

air, ere, heir, eyre	*aisle, I'll, isle*	*born, borne, bourne*
braise, brays, braze	*by, buy, bye*	*eau, oh, owe*
ewe, yew, you	*flew, flu, flue*	*heal, heel, he'll*
gnu, knew, new	*holey, holy, wholly*	*knows, noes, nose*
load, lode, lowed	*meat, meet, mete*	*nay, née, neigh*
pair, pare, pear	*peak, peek, pique*	*prays, praise, preys*
rain, reign, rein	*road, rode, rowed*	*seas, sees, seize*
eas, tease, tees	*to, too, two*	*vain, vane, vein*

I

Score 20 with this Score of In-Words

Almost half the words beginning with *'i'* also begin with *'in'*, possibly because the prefix *'in'* is so versatile. It can, for example, impart the meaning of *into* and *within*, as in *incursion* and *intrinsic*, or add the meaning of *not* or *non*, as in *sincere/insincere* and *credible/incredible*. And it can also act as a suffix to form nouns: *aspirin, insulin, penicillin*.

Here are the meanings of a score of *'in'* words, together with bits and pieces of the words the meanings describe. Can you complete the words? Answers on page 218.

1.	Unintentionally careless.	*in _ _ vert _ _ t*
2.	Avoiding recognition by disguise or by assuming another name	*in _ _ gnit _*
3.	Unjust and unfair	*in _ quitab _ _*
4.	Just beginning; undeveloped and immature.	*in _ _ oate*
5.	Something incompatible and discordant, out of place.	*in _ ongr _ _ _ s*
6.	Security against damage or loss.	*in _ _ _ nity*
7.	Native to a particular country or region.	*in _ _ _ enous*
8.	To display scepticism and disbelief.	*in _ _ _ _ ulity*
9.	A naive and ingenuous young girl.	*in _ _ nue*
10.	Something immeasurably small.	*in _ _ _ itesim _ l*
11.	To act unfriendly and hostile	*in _ _ ical*
12.	An oblique hint or suggestion, usually	

derogatory	*in _ _ end _*
13. Cunningly intent on deceiving or betraying.	*in _ _ _ ious*
14. Intemperate and unrestrained, 'over the top'.	*in _ _ dinate*
15. Lacking in interest and taste; quite boring.	*in _ _ _ id*
16. Carefree, careless and unconcerned	*in _ _ _ ciance*
17. Mutually ruinous or destructive.	*in _ _ _ necine*
18. A situation or problem that's very difficult to shape or solve.	*in _ _ _ _ table*
19. Small spaces or cracks between two things.	*in _ _ _ stices*
20. Those interested in their own thoughts, feelings and actions.	*in _ _ _ vert*

Okay, there were some tough ones in that lot, so you should be pleased if you scored 15 or more. But all 20 words are useful to know and use, so they're well worth adding to your expanding vocabulary. Check their meanings again and commit them to memory.

Choose the Correct Meaning

Which of the two alternative meanings most accurately fits the word? Mark or circle your choice, *a* or *b*, and then check the answers on page 000.

iconoclast	**a.** one who attacks established beliefs; **b.** one who believes only in material things.
idiomatic	**a.** expressions common to a particular group or in a particular region; **b.** writing that consists predominantly of slang.
idiosyncrasy	**a.** a slip of the tongue; **b.** a personal mannerism or habit.
idolatry	**a.** worship of idols and images; **b.** desecration of churches.
ignominious	**a.** extreme shyness; **b.** disgraceful and dishonourable.
imbroglio	**a.** a love affair between a husband and sister-in-law; **b.** a complex and confused state of affairs.
imbue	**a.** to instil or inspire with ideas or principles; **b.** to subtly introduce an opposing point of view into an argument.
immolate	**a.** to kill by sacrifice; **b.** to make a generous gesture by

81

	giving away all one's material possessions.
immured	**a.** to be declared an outcast; **b.** to be imprisoned.
immutable	**a.** unchanging and unalterable; **b.** a metal able to combine with other metals to form an alloy.
impartial	**a.** fair and not prejudiced; **b.** relaxed and uncaring.
impasse	**a.** a narrow opening or ledge; **b.** an insurmountable object or situation.
impeach	**a.** to accuse a US president of immoral, although not criminal, conduct; **b.** to accuse a person of a crime, especially treason.
impeccable	**a.** faultless and flawless; **b.** dressed in the latest style.
impenitent	**a.** close to bankruptcy; **b.** unrepentant and not sorry .
imperturbable	**a.** dour and small-minded; **b.** calm and unruffled.
impervious	**a.** unable to be penetrated; **b.** partly water-resistant.
implacable	**a.** unrelenting and not to be appeased; **b.** someone consumed by deep jealousy.
implausible	**a.** most unlikely, prompting disbelief; **b.** a stage variety act that begins well but ends in disaster.
importune	**a.** unfortunate timing; **b.** to demand urgently and persistently.
imprimatur	**a.** sign of good breeding; **b.** a mark of approval.
impromptu	**a.** offhand, without preparation; **b.** amateurish.
impugn	**a.** to challenge the word of someone; **b.** to incite a crowd.
inane	**a.** lazy and slovenly; **b.** senseless and stupid.
incandescent	**a.** to glow white-hot; **b.** to lose one's temper.
incapacitate	**a.** to decrease by a small amount; **b.** to disable or deprive of power or physical capacity.
incipient	**a.** just beginning to happen; **b.** an inherited problem.
inconsequential	**a.** placed in correct numerical order; **b.** insignificant or trivial, not worth worrying about.
incontrovertible	**a.** incapable of being contradicted; **b.** an event that is predicted to end in disaster.
inculcate	**a.** to impress on the mind by repetition and force; **b.** to raise classroom success levels by lowering academic standards.
incumbent	**a.** heavy and bulky; **b.** someone who is currently holding an office or position.

incursion	**a.** a surgical incision involving skin only; **b.** a sudden attack.
indefatigable	**a.** tireless and unflagging; **b.** impossible to defeat.
indigent	**a.** destitute; **b.** the child of an inter-tribal marriage.
ineluctable	**a.** unworthy to be elected; **b.** unable to be avoided.
ineffable	**a.** too overwhelming to be expressed in words; **b.** incapable of being flustered and upset.
inertia	**a.** a disinclination to move or act; **b.** reverse gravity.
inexorable	**a.** unbending and unmoved; **b.** a prediction that turns out to be true.
ingenuous	**a.** inclined to be mean; **b.** open, candid and frank.
ingratiate	**a.** to position oneself so as to invite favours; **b.** to wriggle out of a difficult situation by lying and subterfuge.
inherent	**a.** an inseparable part; **b.** the eldest son in a family.
inimitable	**a.** extremely funny; **b.** unique.
iniquitous	**a.** someone who refuses to take part in a legal inquiry; **b.** an unjust and wicked act.
innate	**a.** an inborn quality; **b.** leaf-shaped.
innocuous	**a.** natural resistance to disease; **b.** harmless.
insalubrious	**a.** unhealthy; **b.** passion for keeping clean.
insular	**a.** imperious; **b.** isolated, narrow-minded, looking inwards.

If you're not too exhausted after that round, check your choices with the answers on page 218 and tot up your score. If you achieved 40 or more correct (with not too many wild guesses) your vocabulary is well above average.

More Merry Pop-Ins

Fifteen words, fifteen sentences with holes in them. Simply pop each of the words in the appropriate hole so that all the sentences make perfect sense. The words are used once only. The answers are on page 218.

inter alia	*interdict*	*intransigent*
intrinsic	*inviolable*	*inured*
inveighed	*inveterate*	*invidious*
iota	*irascible*	*iridescence*
irreparably	*irrevocable*	*itinerant*

83

1. The store told us that the CD player was _____ damaged.
2. Mr Jacob is one of the most mulish and _____ clients I've ever had to deal with.
3. Muriel's decision, she apparently told her boyfriend, was _____.
4. We get our knives sharpened by the _____ handyman who calls here every couple of months or so.
5. By the government's _____ of 1985, fireworks cannot be sold to anyone under the age of fifteen.
6. Grandfather's will went on to say that, _____ , his personal possessions were to be divided between us.
7. As for studying and revision, young John couldn't care one _____.
8. He found himself in the _____ position of trying to placate the family.
9. Difficulty in starting the engine was an _____ part of the charm of the classic sports car, Malcolm insisted.
10. For nearly an hour the MP _____ against the government for its lack of policy on banning fox hunting.
11. Our neighbour, Mr Twine, was an _____ old man and it didn't pay to upset him.
12. They admired the spectacular display of _____ thrown off the male peacock's feathers.
13. Having spent a good part of his life begging and sleeping rough, the man was _____ to hardship.
14. The young couple idealistically regarded their union as _____.
15. Despite all the medical evidence, Beryl was an _____ smoker and would never easily give it up.

There may be instances here where you've popped a word in its right place without *precisely* knowing its meaning. But only *you* will know that, and only you will know that, if your working vocabulary is to benefit, you have to check its meaning in your dictionary. Is your dictionary showing any signs of wear yet?

The ID, the Mind, and the Personality

Do you know your own mind? Do you know the meaning of terms used to describe our mental and emotional processes, conditions and diseases? Here are twenty fairly common terms; you've no doubt heard or read them all, but do you know exactly what they mean?

alter ego	One's other, or second, self.
catharsis	Bringing repressed experiences or ideas into consciousness to relieve tensions.
cognition	(or *cognitive development*). The mental processes by which

knowledge is acquired, including perception, intuition and reasoning.

delusion	Beliefs, ideas and opinions that are firmly held against evidence to the contrary.
ego	One's conscious self, the 'I' of any individual. The *ego* represents the conscious mind concerned with reality, modifying the instinctual *id* and itself modified by the conscience, or *superego*.
Freudian slip	A slip of the tongue believed to indicate repressed thoughts.

id	The instinctive, unconscious and primal element of the human psyche, modified by the *ego* and *superego*.
libido	The psychic energy released from the *id*, including sexual desire.
masochism	An abnormal condition in which pleasure, especially sexual pleasure, is derived from one's own pain.
neurosis	A general mental or emotional disorder (eg anxiety, hysteria, depression, obsessive behaviour) without an identifiable organic cause.
obsessive-compulsive disease (OCD)	A neurosis in which persistent impulses result in compulsive, repetitive actions, such as constant hand-washing.
paranoia	A progressive deterioration of the personality involving delusions, hallucinations and harbouring unreasonable suspicions of others.
precognition	The feeling or belief of knowing something before it occurs.
psychoanalysis	The treatment of mental and emotional disorders by recalling past events to reveal the unconscious.
psychopath	A person with a personality disorder tending towards anti-social behaviour and the carrying out of violent acts.
psychotic	A person suffering a mental disorder involving loss of mental function and withdrawal from reality.
schizophrenia	Psychotic disorders characterised by disorganised, often contradictory thought patterns, delusions, hallucinations, obsessions and withdrawal from reality.
superego	The part of the unconscious mind that is the repository of the conscience and moral standards.
transference	Transferring feelings, attitudes and emotions from one person to another, usually from a patient to his or her psychoanalyst.
trauma	A major emotional shock that may cause neurosis.

30-Sec Quickpick: Add the Final Letters

A quick round to test your speed of response. From the meanings and partial words given, simply add the final two letters to complete the words. Answers on page 218.

1. A set of variable facial characteristics that are built up to create the likeness of someone being sought by the police *identik _ _*

2. Foolishness or pointless stupidity *idio _ _*

3. People who are unable to read or write *illitera _ _*

4   To copy, or to impersonate someone *imita _ _*

5. Something that is about to happen *immine _ _*

6. The chisel-edged teeth at the front of your mouth *incis _ _*

7. Offensive by the usual standards of propriety and morality *indece _ _*

8. A public inquiry into an unexplained death *inque _ _*

9. The state of being unable to meet one's debts and liabilities *insolven _ _*

10. The international criminal police organisation *interp _ _*

You were allowed three seconds in which to complete each word. Did you feel the pressure? A score of seven or more should have been achievable.

Word Roots: Inter- and Itis

You cannot avoid these two common word roots: the prefix *inter-* and the suffix *-itis*. Let's spend a few moments studying their roles in the formation of our words.

Word, Element	Origin	Meaning	English words
inter-	Latin	between, among, together	interact, interbreed, interactive, interchange, international, intercontinental, intercept, interference.
-itis	Greek	inflammation	tonsillitis, appendicitis, meningitis, Mondayitis.

87

Five-Minute Revision

You've just learned or reacquainted yourself with 100 or so *'i'* words – all of them eminently employable in an active working vocabulary. But just to satisfy yourself that you have their meanings nailed down, why not run through the lot again, pausing to check those pernicketty words that continue to confuse you? And, at the very least, try putting the following words into mental sentences of your own:

> *ineluctable   indigenous   internecine   iconoclast   importune*
> *incipient   irrevocable   ingenuous   insular   irascible*

Inept, inert and other Lost Positives

The English lexicon contains its fair share of dysfunctional words – words forever lonely, words that can never have bosom friends or partners no matter how diligently they search. Part of their problem is that they are morosely negative, words without their brighter, positive partners, words without opposites.

If *curable* has its opposite in *incurable*, why is not the antonym of *valuable invaluable*? Inexplicably the words are near-synonyms. But at least *valuable* can claim a range of antonyms: *valueless*, *worthless* and *nugatory* to name just three. No, the words to feel sorry for are words such as *disgruntled*, *dishevelled* and *disgust*.Everyone occasionally feels discontented or *disgruntled* – but conversely you are denied the opportunity to feel *gruntled*. If the *dis-* prefix of such words means *'not'* then what happened to the original word of which it is now the negative? We can feel *disgust* but not *gust*; we can appear *dishevelled*, meaning unkempt and tidy, but even though we might look spiffy we can't describe our appearance as *shevelled*; the word simply doesn't exist. We can *dismantle* a kitchen food processor (take it apart) but we can't *mantle* it (put it together). We can be *intrepid*, but try being *trepid*! And if a *depilatory* removes hair, is there any hope for bald men using a *pilatory*?

The same mystery applies to many *un-* and *non-* words. The lady can be *undone*, but *done*? Well, hardly. We might describe something as *nondescript* and somebody as *nonchalant* or *nonplussed*, but their positives – *descript, chalant* and *plussed* – are missing from the dictionary.

In some cases, however, a former partner, long thought to be dead and buried, can be traced. *Unkempt*, meaning uncombed and slovenly, is in

88

fact happily married to the extremely shy and retiring *kempt,* meaning well-combed and tidy. Another example is *ruthless,* meaning 'merciless and hard-hearted'. If that is what it means then it follows that its positive, *ruth,* should mean 'kind and compassionate'. And, indeed, it does. At least it did in the days of the 17th century English poet John Milton who used it in his poem *Lycidas*:

> *Look homeward Angel now, and melt with ruth,*
> *And O ye dolphins, waft the hapless youth.*

Well, good luck to *ruth.* But shed a tear for *inept, inert, unwieldy, incorrigible, distraught, unruly, disparage* and all those lost and lonely wallflower words forever searching for their partners in the English language.

J

Choose the Correct Meaning

Which of the three alternatives, *a*, *b*, or *c*, most accurately fits the meaning of the word? Tick or circle your choices (if you have to make a guess it's best to be honest and pass) and then check the answers on page 218.

jalousie   **a.** a small commuter bus; **b.** a summer house in the mountains; **c.** a window shutter made from angled slats.

jaundiced   **a.** a distorted, pessimistic point of view; **b.** an optimistic outlook; **c.** a process for making jam from stone fruits.

jejune   **a.** bright and sparkling; **b.** immature, uninteresting and insipid; **c.** young and sexually innocent.

jeopardy   **a.** danger and uncertainty; **b.** the legal status between bail and remand; **c.** the hours between midnight and 6am.

jeremiad   **a.** an extremely unlucky person; **b.** a lament; **c.** a traitor.

jerry-built   **a.** foreign-made; **b.** a manufacture of German origin; **c.** a sloppily built construction of cheap materials.

jettison   **a.** to throw things overboard; **b.** to crash a boat into a dock; **c.** to recover items lost at sea.

Jezebel   **a.** a young girl who loves to dance; **b.** a shameless and wanton woman; **c.** an excessively made-up and ornamented woman.

jihad   **a.** The ruling council of a Muslim state; **b.** a Muslim holy war against infidels; **c.** the confederation of Muslim states.

jingoism	**a.** a compulsion to tell jokes; **b.** chauvinistic, aggressive patriotism; **c.** belief in witch doctor healing.
Job's comforter	**a.** a woollen cardigan of many colours; **b.** the bell or whistle indicating the end of the day's work; **c.** someone who, while claiming to sympathise, only adds to the distress.
jobsworth	**a.** a minor official who sticks to the letter of the law regardless of circumstances; **b.** a particularly ambitious employee; **c.** a job which turns out to be onerous and low-paid.
jocose	**a.** red-faced; **b.** humorous and facetious; **c.** loose-limbed.
joie de vivre	**a.** delight in being aggressive; **b.** addicted to wearing perfume; **c.** joy of being alive.
jubilee	**a.** a 100th anniversary; **b.** a royal anniversary occasion; **c.** any special anniversary occasion.

A short round for which a score of 12 or more correct would be reasonable. Now for the rest of the *'j'* words that should form part of your vocabulary.

Words in Use – Right or Wrong?

If you're truly familiar with the following words you'll have no trouble deciding which of them are being used correctly and which are not. Answers on page 219.

Right Wrong

1. They felt they had been disgracefully deceived and vowed that they would never forgive Tom's *judicial* behaviour. ___ ___

2. Mr Hare decided it might be *judicious* to avoid controversy and to delay the visit for another week. ___ ___

3. At this *juncture* the meeting broke up in wild disorder ___ ___

4. Mrs Siddons, admirably *Junoesque*, swept into the theatre in a swish of skirts and perfume. ___ ___

5. The senior tribal members entered the temple to worship the sacred *junta*.   ____ ____

6. Their eldest daughter had decided to study *jurisprudence*.   ____ ____

7. The prisoner complained to his lawyers that because the trial was *jury-rigged* he was certain to be convicted.   ____ ____

8. Old Mrs Thomson was becoming increasingly *juvenescent*, frail and forgetful.   ____ ____

9. Even though the drawings were obviously *juvenilia* they nevertheless fetched high prices at the studio sale.   ____ ____

10. In flower arranging, the art is skillfully to *juxtapose* contrasting colours, shapes and textures.   ____ ____

In that set, four words were incorrectly used – did you spot them? It's a good idea when you are reading and come across a word unfamiliar to you, to look up its meaning – and also note *how* it was used.

Jargon and Gibberish

Most people recognise jargon when they see it: words and phrases that may have begun life within a particular group, trade or profession, but which are borrowed by those who merely wish to appear cleverer than they are.

The *Concise Oxford Dictionary* defines jargon as 'unintelligible words, gibberish; barbarous or debased language; mode of speech full of unfamiliar terms'.

To be fair, not all jargon is gibberish. For millions, those seemingly baffling and arcane expressions are a form of time-saving professional shorthand, a fast and efficient means of communication between members of a specialist circle. Perfectly intelligible to them but gibberish or 'jargon' to outsiders.

But too often jargon is used by people to trick others into believing they know more than they actually do, and that's how jargon enters the language. At first they're 'vogue' words, then 'buzzwords', and next thing you know we're all using them – words like *parameter, symbiosis, quantum leap, synergy, dichotomy, post-modern.* Yes, we use them, but do we always know precisely what such words mean?

It's hard to believe that Christmas lights can be described as *festive embellishments (illuminary)*; that a supermarket shelf-stacker is called *an ambient replenishment assistant*; a street trader is *an unpremised business person*, and a tourist mountain train is *a visitor uplift facility*. Hard to believe, but true.

Those were extreme examples, perhaps, but nevertheless be on your guard against jargon. Here are a few jargon words you really need to think about before using:

> *accessible, accountability, activist, axiomatic, blueprint, core, down-sizing, dumbing down, geared, hidden agenda, identify with, implement, input, interface, methodology, operational, ongoing, precondition, scenario, state of the art, take on board (in the sense of 'give consideration to'), user-friendly, venue, viable alternative.*

60-Second quickpick: Two Meanings, One Word

Try this 60-seconds of wordplay. From the two meanings, work out what the word is. The number of letters is also given. Answers are on page 219.

No.	Meaning 1	Letters	Meaning 2
1.	Toss one on the fire	_ _ _	A ship's record
2.	Mark of approval	_ _ _ _ _	Nasty biting insect
3.	The deepest voice	_ _ _ _ _	A delicious fish
4.	A line of cottages	_ _ _	To move a dinghy
5.	A dog does it	_ _ _ _ _	A tree has it
6.	A garden tidier	_ _ _ _ _	A dissolute man
7.	Nearly a metre	_ _ _ _ _	At the back of most houses
8.	A useful container	_ _ _	A garden hedge
9.	To conceal yourself	_ _ _ _	The skin of a beast
10.	To grasp	_ _ _ _ _	At the bottom of a ship

Revision: A to J

At this point in your vocabulary enlarging programme it would be an excellent idea to look back over your newly acquired word stock. Of the thousand or so words you've perused so far perhaps a hundred may have been new to you. You may also have been hazy about the *precise* meanings of another hundred. And you may have had a little difficulty using as many again in their appropriate context.

That's the real test of a working vocabulary – whether it consists of words you understand fully and can *use* with ease and familiarity. So how about putting your new words to work? Flip back over the previous sections, A-J, and select a dozen or two words that were new to you but which you think will be useful in your speech and writing. In turn, write them into actual sentences. Let's say the word you select is *abstruse*. It's a word that you could have used a number of times if you had known it existed and what it meant. So have a go now:

> *I found some of the words in this book **abstruse** and hard to understand.*

How's that? Well, we're not quite there; the sentence is tautological. What? Yes, the sentence uses the word *abstruse* correctly, but then it pointlessly repeats the meaning – because *abstruse* itself means 'not easy to understand'. So let's rewrite it:

> *I found some of the words in this book **abstruse**.*

Now try working words into your own sentences. If you're in doubt about how a word should be used, check its meaning or meanings again in the dictionary, which should also provide some grammatical guidance: whether a word is a noun, verb, adjective or some other designation. Take that word *tautological*. Your dictionary will show it as a noun (*tautology*), a verb (*tautologise*), an adjective (*tautologous, tautological*) and as an adverb (*tautologically, tautologously*). All that will help you not only to use the word appropriately in the context of meaning, but grammatically correctly as well.

Janus Words

A **Janus word** is a two-faced word, one that has two directly opposite meanings. The word *peruse* was used a few paragraphs ago. If you check its meaning in your dictionary you will find that it has two meanings: (1) to examine or read with care, and (2) to browse or read through in a leisurely way. This polarisation is also well demonstrated by the word *inflammable*, which can mean 'liable to catch fire' on the one hand, and 'fire-proof' on the other. Because of this confusion *flammable* ('flame-able') is now almost universally used to indicate a substance that is liable to catch fire.

What's the difference between dusting tomato plants to stop mildew and dusting the sideboard? The same word, *dusting*, is describing two completely opposite actions: adding dust, and removing it. When you *draw* the curtains, are you opening them or closing them? A *sanguine* person is optimistic, cheerful and laid back. But the same person can also be *sanguinary* – hot-tempered and murderous. *Sanction* is another lexical hermaphrodite; it can mean 'permission to do something' ("The government sanctioned the flying in of emergency supplies") or 'an order forbidding something' ("The government applied fresh sanctions banning all exports to the country"). Other Janus words – or **contranyms** – include *fast, bolted, handicap, cleave, ravish* and *overlook*, and no doubt there are dozens more lurking in our dictionaries.

Choose the Correct Meaning

Words beginning with *'k'* are somewhat scarce in the dictionary but there are some that you should know. Which of the three choices, *a, b,* or *c,* most accurately fits the meaning of the word? Mark or circle your choices and then check the answers on page 219.

Kafkaesque	**a.** a story with a twist at the end; **b.** middle-European in outlook; **c.** dehumanizing and nightmarish.
kaftan	**a.** a hammock made of woven cane; **b.** a long, loose dress; **c.** the ceremonial headwear of an Indonesian chief.
kamikaze	**a.** an action that is suicidally foolhardy; **b.** a long and persistent artillery blitz; **c.** the cloud that hangs above Fujiyama in Japan.
karaoke	**a.** popular Japanese raw fish and rice dish; **b.** publicly singing songs over a prerecorded backing tape; **c.** fortitude.
kaput	**a.** lost; **b.** irreplaceable; **c.** broken or not functioning.
karma	**a.** the sum of a person's actions that are transferred from one life to the next; **b.** spiritual well-being; **c.** spiritual guidance that cannot be ignored.
kedgeree	**a.** wind-dried whale flesh; **b.** a dish of cooked fish, rice and eggs; **c.** a seabird common in Norway.
Keynesian	**a.** doctrine that recommends government spending to counter economic failure and unemployment; **b.** a

doctrine that favours a free market and with no government intervention; **c.** a doctrine that favours a return to the gold standard.

keystone   **a.** the large carved stone that dedicates a building; **b.** the wedge shaped stone at the top of an arch; **c.** a large masonry block that acts as the base for a pillar.

kibbutz   **a.** Israel's democratic party; **b.** a desert war of attrition, used by Israel to occupy the Left Bank; **c.** an Israeli communal collective settlement.

We're shifting gear here into examples of usage. So keep going! Just select the usage, *a* or *b*, that you think is appropriate and correct. The answers are on page 219.

kinetic   **a.** Brendan thought that kinetic energy was mainly concerned with heat. **b.** Jerry thought that kinetic energy was mainly concerned with motion.

kismet   **a.** The young woman accepted widowhood as her kismet. **b.** To secure her love he promised her his eternal kismet.

kitsch   **a.** It was well known that he published nothing but kitsch. **b.** As a family friend he undertook to act as the children's kitsch.

kleptomaniac   **a.** After a dozen convictions for theft she was finally diagnosed as a kleptomaniac. **b.** His chronic sleepwalking confirmed him as a kleptomaniac.

knell   **a.** The lifeboatmen were pleased to see the knell at last. **b.** The family filed out of the church to the mournful knell of the church bells.

Knesset   **a.** It was a genuine Knesset rug, so obviously very expensive. **b.** The Knesset sat all night to resolve the border problem.

knock-for-knock   **a.** The argument developed into a nasty knock-for-knock confrontation. **b.** Both owners had knock-for-knock insurance agreements so the accident claims were settled quite promptly.

kosher   **a.** The new woollen kosher fitted Elaine perfectly. **b.** Three passengers on the flight had ordered kosher meals.

kowtow   **a.** Lucy had never seen a Chinese with the traditional kow-tow. **b.** Bert hated to kow-tow to his landlord in the big house.

kudos   **a.** Trevor's sales figures brought him plenty of kudos.
                 b. They would spend countless hours playing kudos.

If you find that you tripped up on one or two of these examples of usage, make sure you look up the meanings of the words. Then you can add them to your growing vocabulary.

Karma, Kyrie and Religious Expressions

Few of us confine our lives and thoughts solely to the physical world and most of us hold philosophical or spiritual beliefs of one kind or another. This non-material domain has a considerable lexicon and we're frequently confronted with a word or term, probably familiar to millions, but which leaves us flummoxed. Here are a few:

Apocrypha	The 14 books of the Septuagint not included in Protestant versions of the Bible.
aspersion	Baptism rite involving sprinkling, usually of water.
Brahmans	The highest, priestly caste of the Hindus.
catechism	Question and answer book about the religious doctrine of a Christian church.
Confucian	A follower of Confucius, observing moral order, humanity, respect for ancestors and education.
dharma	In Hinduism, the observance of natural law, religious and moral duty.
Diaspora	The scattering or dispersion of the Jews from ancient Palestine; in modern terms, all Jews outside Israel.
dybbuk	In Jewish folklore, a dead sinner's soul that controls a living person.
ecumenical	Promoting worldwide unity among Christian churches.
Episcopalian	Autonomous American and Scottish branches of the Church of England.
extreme unction	Roman Catholic sacrament of anointing the sick and dying.
Gospel	Any of the first four books of the New Testament.
goy, goyim (pl)	Jewish term for a non-Jew or gentile.

Hare Krishna	Form of Hinduism worshipping the god Krishna.
Hassidim	Sect of ultra-pious Jews founded in Poland.
houri	To Muslims, one of the female guides in Paradise.
Iman	An Islamic prayer leader in a mosque.
Kyrie eleison	Part of the liturgy of the Anglican, Roman Catholic and Greek Orthodox churches. It means 'Lord, have mercy'.
litany	A prayer in which the congregation responds to a series of invocations from the priest or leader.
mantra	In Hinduism and Buddhism, a sacred word repeated as an aid to meditation.
matins	An Anglican service of morning prayer.
muezzin	The mosque official who calls the faithful to prayer five times a day from the minaret.
nirvana	To Buddhists and Hindus, final release from earthly desires and constraints.
original sin	The belief that sin is innate in all mankind.
Paternoster	The Lord's Prayer recited in Latin.
Requiem	A mass celebrated for the dead, or the music for it.
secular	Relating to worldly things, as opposed to sacred things.
Shakers	An Adventist sect stressing celibate communal living.
Shiite	(or *Shia*, *Shiah*) One of the two main branches of Islam mostly centred in Iran.
Sikh	Follower of an Indian religion centred in the Punjab.
Society of Friends	Another name for *Quakers*, who promote informal services and social improvement for mankind.
t'ai chi ch'uan	A Chinese programme for mental and bodily harmony.
Torah	The scroll on which is written the first five books of the Old Testament.
Trappists	Cistercian monks who observe a rule of silence.
Trinity	The threefold godhead of Father, Son and Holy Ghost.
Veda	The ancient sacred writings of Hinduism.
vespers	Church of England evening prayer, or evensong.
yeshiva	Traditional Jewish school devoted to rabbinic texts.
Zen	Buddhism Teaches that contemplation of one's own self to the exclusion of everything else is the only way to pure enlightenment.

30-Sec Quickpick: Odd Man Out

On your mark for a quick round of 'odd man out'. In each group of four words, three are associated in some way while the remaining word is a stranger. Thus of the group *kangaroo, koala, kayak* and *platypus* you will quickly see that *kangaroo, koala* and *platypus* have several things in common: they are living creatures, they are Australian and they are marsupials. A *kayak* on the other hand is inanimate and found in an arctic environment – and is therefore the 'odd man out'. Now try these:

> *racquet, deuce, wicket, court.*
> *carbon copy, software, hard drive, keystroke.*
> *triangle, circle, square, oblong.*
> *kidnap, abduct, deliver, hijack.*
> *mistake, entry, error, flaw.*
> *umbrella, barometer, cirrus, radio.*
> *grapes, vigneron, hops, vintage.*
> *canvas, negative, palette, easel.*
> *desert, deluge, monsoon, cataract.*
> *guffaw, howl, shriek, weep.*

The answers are on page 219. Nothing too profound in that lot, so a score of eight or more correct within the 30 seconds allowed should be expected.

Kitsch, Klutz and Other Yiddishisms

Yiddish, a blend of mostly German and some Hebrew, migrated during the 19th century to America where, even today, it continues to add colour to American-English. Fewer Yiddishisms have entered the British English lexicon but, as much of our reading and entertainment today is American or American-influenced, you're bound to come across the odd *schmuck* and *klutz*. Here are a few you should know.

bupkiss	A nothing; a very boring person.
hutzpah	Barefaced cheek; shameless audacity.
dreck	Rubbish, trash.
fresser	A glutton

kibitzer	Someone who interferes with unwanted advice. *Kibitz* = to interfere.
kitsch	Pretentious, vulgar (but often popular) art, writing or style.
klutz	Someone clumsy and stupid. Often used in self-deprecation: "What a klutz I am!"
kvetch	To constantly complain and whine.
mensch	A kind and humane person.
nebbish	A weak, ineffectual individual.
schemozzle	A thorough mess; a confused argument, a mix-up.
schlemiel	A simple person, usually a man, who has the best intentions but no luck; unlucky but uncomplaining.
schlep	To drag or carry something requiring effort.
schlock	Cheap, inferior, rubbish; in bad taste.
schmaltz	[Lit. chicken fat]Sugary sentimentality.
schmooze	[or *shmooz*]To chat or gossip.
schmuck	A stupid person who always does the wrong thing.
schnorrer	A professional beggar.
shikker	A drunk. To be *shikkered* = to be drunk.
shiksa	Pejorative term for a non-Jewish woman; a Jewish girl by birth but non-practising.
shtik	A routine exclusive to a performer; a special act.
spiel	Glib sales talk. *Spieler* = a very smooth salesman.
tchotchke	[or *tsatske*]Knick-knacks, trinkets. *tchotchkele* = pretty thing; pretty girl.

L

Replace the Missing Words

Below are ten words and ten sentences. A word is missing from each of the sentences. Can you place the appropriate words in all ten sentences? Each word is used only once. Answers on page 219.

labyrinthine	*lachrymose*	*lackadaisical*	*lacklustre*	*laconic*
lacuna	*laissez faire*	*laity*	*lambent*	*lamentable*

1. The coach was unamused by the team's _____ performance, its worst in ten years, losing by four goals to an inferior side.

2. Many economists blamed the market's free-fall on the Government's uncaring, _____ attitude to imports.

3. With his expert knowledge of public life, Sir Gregory was the ideal man to penetrate the _____ workings of the Foreign Office.

4. Although George was an avid churchman he'd always been perfectly satisfied to remain among the _____.

5. Although she didn't lack intelligence, Deborah's _____ efforts when it came to exams almost spelt disaster.

6. The couple chatted for hours in the _____ light of the candles.

7. She loved the strong, silent type of actor, which is probably why Robert Mitchum's _____ style appealed to her.

8. When they read Aunt Hilda's confessional letter it wasn't the contents that intrigued them but the puzzling _____ towards the end.

9. As though she had all the time in the world, Jenny sauntered down the lane in her typically _____ manner.
10. Two days after the funeral Jim had had enough of the _____ household, and headed for the pub.

If you fitted all the pieces of that verbal jigsaw together then you did very well, as several of the words would hardly qualify as common. But all ten would be useful in any person's vocabulary so make sure you're familiar with their meanings and usage.

Chose the Correct Meaning

From the two alternatives, *a* or *b*, mark or circle which one you think represents most accurately the meaning of each word. The answers are on page 219.

lampoon — **a.** a sailing ship's lantern; **b.** a satirical attack in prose or verse.

landau — **a.** A French provincial cottage; **b.** a horse-drawn carriage

langoustine — **a.** a small spiny lobster; **b.** a soup made from pork offal.

languorous — **a.** sleekly beautiful; **b.** to feel sluggish and drowsy.

lapidary — **a.** a doctor specialising in surgery of the abdominal wall; **b.** a worker or dealer in gemstones.

largesse — **a.** a generous gift, usually money; **b.** water that gathers in the hull of a ship.

lascivious — **a.** lustful and lecherous; **b.** given to excessive laughter.

lassitude — **a.** physical and mental weariness; **b.** the relief of escaping from a hurtful emotional situation.

latent — **a.** a temperature just prior to boiling point; **b.** existing but not noticeable or explicit.

lateral — **a.** relating to the top or bottom of something; **b.** relating to the side or sides.

laudable — **a.** praiseworthy; **b.** drugged with opium.

lectern — **a.** a junior university lecturer or assistant; **b.** a raised reading desk or support.

legerdemain — **a.** chain-mail jacket worn by mediaeval knights; **b.** deception or sleight of hand.

leitmotif — **a.** a recurring theme in music, art or literature; **b.** the Berlin subway system.

lese-majesty	**a.** high treason, or an offence committed against the Crown; **b.** the act of bending the knee in the presence of a monarch.
lessee	**a.** a tenant to whom a lease is granted; **b.** an owner who grants a lease of property.
lethargic	**a.** someone suffering from lead poisoning; **b.** drowsy and apathetic.
leviathan	**a.** monstrously huge and powerful; **b.** small, weak and puny.
lexicography	**a.** the study of mathematical puzzles; **b.** the profession of compiling dictionaries.
liaison	**a.** a disastrous relationship; **b.** communication or contact between groups or individuals.
libertarian	**a.** a believer in free thought and expression; **b.** an advocate of 'free love' and polygamous relationships.
libidinous	**a.** excessive sexual desire; **b.** a consummate liar.
libretto	**a.** the soprano section of a choir; **b.** the text of an opera or vocal work.
licentious	**a.** involved in piracy; **b.** sexually unrestrained.
lickspittle	**a.** a person who insists on being uncomfortably close when speaking to others; **b.** a fawning, servile person.
Lilliputian	**a.** very tiny or trivial; **b.** outrageously imaginative.
limbo	**a.** a vague place or condition of uncertainty; **b.** an area used by athletes to warm up before performing.
limpid	**a.** soft and malleable; **b.** clear and transparent.
linchpin	**a.** a person or thing regarded as absolutely essential for a successful outcome; **b.** the lever that operates the trapdoor of a gallows.
lingua franca	**a.** a syrupy cure for hangovers; **b.** a common language used for communication by people with many different mother tongues.
lionise	**a.** to treat someone as a celebrity; **b.** to monopolise a conversation.
lissom	**a.** golden-haired; **b.** lithe and supple.
litany	**a.** the curtains that screen off a crematorium furnace; **b.** a long and tedious recital or speech.

livid	**a.** in red blotches; **b.** greyish discolouration as from a bruise.
lobbyist	**a.** a person who attempts to influence legislators on behalf of a particular interest; **b.** a newspaper reporter specialising in political stories.
locum tenens	**a.** a professional stand-in, usually for a doctor or chemist; **b.** the technique used to locate fractured bones.
logistics	**a.** the management of the supply and flow of materials within an organisation; **b.** forestry science and management.
logorrhoea	**a.** bad breath; **b.** excessive talkativeness.
longevity	**a.** ancestor worship; **b.** long life.
longueur	**a.** the train of a wedding dress; **b.** a period of utter boredom.
loquacious	**a.** excessively talkative; **b.** having red-rimmed eyes.
Lothario	**a.** a seducer of women; **b.** swarthy and crude-mannered.
louche	**a.** calm and laid-back; **b.** shifty and devious.
loupe	**a.** the magnifying eyepiece used by jewellers; **b.** an intrauterine contraceptive device.
lubricious	**a.** obviously effeminate; **b.** lewd and lecherous.
lucid	**a.** brittle and easily breakable; **b.** clear and easily understood.
lugubrious	**a.** excessively mournful; **b.** fulsome and persuasive.
lumpen	**a.** people who are grossly overweight; **b.** deprived and stupid.
luxuriant	**a.** lush, rich and abundant; **b.** devoted to luxury.

That was quite a round, so take a breath and check your choices with the answers on page 219. A score of more than 40 correct would be an excellent achievement, and one of 35 or more very respectable. But shame on you if you missed *lexicography*!

Legalese and the Law

The law may be an ass but it is also a tangle of legal terminology. We come across such terms regularly so they're not unfamiliar to us – but what, exactly, do they mean?

Here are a few well worth knowing about.

accessory	A person involved in a crime but not actually present, whether assisting in the planning (*accessory before the fact*) or being involved afterwards (*accessory after the fact*).
affidavit	A written declaration made under oath.
alibi	Evidence to prove that the accused was elsewhere at the time the crime was committed.
assizes	Formerly principal county court sessions, now replaced by crown courts.
barrister	A lawyer who is qualified to plead in the higher courts.
breach of promise	Failure to carry out a promise to marry.
bylaw, bye-law	Regulations laid down by a local authority which apply only in the area it governs.
circumstantial	[evidence] Indirect evidence that tends to establish a conclusion by inference.
codicil	An addition to a will that revokes or changes it.
complainant	Someone who makes a complaint before a justice.
conjugal rights	Relating to husband and wife and the institution of marriage.
decree nisi	A provisional divorce order which will later be made absolute unless cause is shown why it should not.
deposition	The sworn statement of a witness given to the court.
double indemnity	An insurance clause (in N America) that provides payment of double the policy's face value in the case of accidental death.
double jeopardy	Prosecuting a defendant (in the US) a second time for an offence for which he has already been tried.
ex officio	By virtue of position or office.
ex parte	An application to a court on behalf of only one of the parties concerned in an action.
habeas corpus	A writ requiring a person to be brought before a court or judge to determine whether his or her detention is lawful.
hostile witness	A witness who gives evidence against the side calling him.
indictment	A formal accusation of crime presented to a court on oath.

injunction	An order issued by a court requiring that a party refrain from some specified action.
in loco parentis	A person acting for a child in place of a parent or parents.
kangaroo court	An ad hoc court run on non-legal lines.
larceny	The legal term for theft.
litigious	Excessive readiness to take any dispute to law.
nolle prosequi	An entry into court records that the prosecutor or plaintiff agree to abandon the prosecution or action.
onus probandi	Burden of proof: the obligation to provide evidence sufficient to convince the court or jury that a contention is true.
perjury	Committed by a person who, under oath, wilfully gives false evidence.
petty sessions	Another name for magistrates' courts.
plaintiff	Someone who brings a civil action in a court of law.
probate	The official process of proving the validity of a will.
probation	Placing a convicted offender under the supervision of a court-appointed probation officer.
sine die	Without a day being fixed for the resumption of adjourned business; indefinitely.
stipendiary magistrate	A magistrate who works for a regular salary or stipend.
subpoena	A court writ requiring a person to appear before a court at a specified time.
surety	Responsibility assumed by a person for another person's legal obligation, who then becomes liable if that person defaults.
testator	Any person who makes a will. [female = testatrix].
uttering	In criminal law, putting into circulation counterfeit coin or forged banknotes.
ward of court	A minor or anyone incapable of managing his or her own affairs, placed under the protection of a court or guardian.
warrant	A magistrate's authorisation allowing police to search or seize property or make an arrest.

30-Sec Quickpick: Spot the Dummy

Some words look so weird that you need convincing they're genuine. Conversely, it's not difficult to invent words that, at a quick glance, look to be the real thing. Here's a collection of ten words, half of which are real, with meanings in the dictionary, and half of which are dummy words.

See if you can spot the dummies. The answers are on page 219.

	Real	Dummy

1. The fortune teller told her she could expect *lollapalooza* soon.   ____ ____

2. The decorator quickly decided that the kitchen needed to be *lodoomed* if it was to look welcoming.   ____ ____

3. Jules asked Helena if she'd mind lighting the *lampion*.   ____ ____

4. The old couple sat by the fire and reminisced about **langsyne**. ___ ___

5. The young mother smiled at her sleeping baby, obviously dreaming about the delights of **lushna**. ___ ___

6. Ruth suffered from extreme shyness and desperately wished she possessed the **lackle** to feel confident with strangers. ___ ___

7. When reassembling the clock Brian forgot the **lidget**. ___ ___

8. The ship's cook's meals consisted almost entirely of **loblolly** ___ ___

9. Val thought she spotted a **lentigo** and looked closer in the mirror. ___ ___

10. The bright **lenitude** disappeared when the clouds drifted over. ___ ___

Don't fret too much about your score: the English language, being the *olla podrida* that it is, can make dummies of us all!

Revision: All the Way from K to L

Just when you thought it was safe to assume that revision had been forgotten or abandoned, here we are with a reminder that some *'k'* words might require revisiting, along with the *'l'* words you've just learned. So spare a few minutes to assure yourself that you've really assimilated those vital new words into your vocabulary. How about these, for example:

Keynesian   *kudos*   *kleptomaniac*   *kitsch*   *Kafkaesque*
lachrymose   *laconic*   *lascivious*   *leitmotif*   *louche*

Lust, Sex and Reproduction

You may know all about the subject, but are you familiar with the language of sex and the reproductive system? Here are some terms you may know; or, on the other hand, some you may not. Add the latter to your expanding vocabulary.

androgynous	Having both male and female characteristics.
areola	The brownish area around the nipple.
breech presentation	A baby born with feet or buttocks emerging first.
cervix	The narrow lower part of the uterus that extends into the vagina.
chlamydia	A bacterial form of venereal disease.
D&C	[*dilation and curettage*]Removal of tissue from the lining of the uterus.
ectopic pregnancy	A fertilized egg occurring outside the uterus.
epidural	Anaesthetic injected in the space around the spinal cord, often used during Caesarean sections.
episiotomy	An incision to the vagina to facilitate childbirth.
false labour	Uterine contractions without dilation of the cervix.
in vitro fertilisation	Where egg cells are removed from the ovary, fertilised, incubated and then implanted in the uterus.
labia	Lips or liplike structures, such as the folds of the vulva.
laparoscopy	A tube which, inserted through the abdominal wall, enables the physician to view the uterus, Fallopian tubes and ovaries.
peritoneum	The thin outer layer of the wall of the uterus.
postpartum	The period immediately following birth.
progesterone	The female steroid hormone that prepares the uterus for pregnancy.
prostate	The gland in males that surrounds the bladder and which secretes the fluid in semen.
quickening	When the foetus can first be felt moving in the womb.
scrotum	The protective pouch containing the testicles.
smear test	[or *Pap test*, from Dr Papanicolaou, its inventor] A test for cancer involving screening cells scraped from the cervix.
speculum	An instrument for opening and examining the vagina.
uterus	[also called the *womb*]The muscular organ in females that houses the developing foetus.
vertex presentation	A normal birth with the baby's head emerging first.

It's such a fascinating subject that it's difficult to leave. So here's a terminological test that's not so much about sex and lust, more about procreation and production.Which of the following statements are true, and which false? Enter your choices and then check the state of your birds'n'bees knowledge on page 219.

	True	False
1. The glands in a female that secrete sex hormones and produce egg cells are the *ovaries*.	___	___
2. An *intrauterine device* (IUD) is used by the male to prevent contraception.	___	___
3. *Circumcision* involves the removal of part of the foreskin from the penis, usually at birth.	___	___
4. The tubes in a female that carry egg cells from the ovary to the uterus are called the *mammary tubes*.	___	___
5. The *hymen* is the sensual organ in the female that produces the orgasm or sexual climax.	___	___
6. The tissue in the uterus that nourishes the foetus and is expelled as the afterbirth is the *placenta*.	___	___
7. *Premenstrual syndrome (PMS)* is a pattern of symptoms prior to a menstrual period, often causing tension.	___	___
8. The man required a *double vasectomy*, in which both testicles are removed.	___	___
9. A mother's first milk produced after a birth is the *colostrum*.	___	___
10. *Fertilisation* occurs when a sperm penetrates the ovum.	___	___

Words in Use: Right or Wrong?

There are two good tests to see if a word is well embedded in your vocabulary. One is, "If I hear a word or come across it in my reading, do I know immediately what it means?" And the other is, "Can I use it spontaneously to express my thoughts?" That's what a working vocabulary is all about: instant recognition; easy erudition.

Try the tests on the following words. If you're comfortable with their meaning and usage you'll have no trouble deciding which of them are being used correctly and which are not. Answers on page 220.

		Right	**Wrong**
1.	He placed the thin tissue of *macrocosm* under the microscope.	—	—
2.	With some trepidation they walked into the council chamber and a *maelstrom* of bitter and violent argument.	—	—
3.	She found herself subjected to the *magisterial* gaze of the widely admired but much feared choirmaster.	—	—
4.	True to his *magnanimous* reputation, Sir Richard made sure all the silver was counted before the guests departed.	—	—
5.	After the concert they all agreed that the concerto was undoubtedly his *magnum opus*.	—	—

112

6. Although the professor was brilliant with his students he was distinctly *maladroit* when it came to the simplest household tasks.   — —

7. Bernard could not shake off the *malaise* that had affected him since his return from Nigeria.   — ′ —

8. Mrs Hilton committed the gross *malapropism* of laying out the dinner cutlery in quite the wrong order.   — —

9. Of the two seafood dishes, Claude preferred the *mal de mer*.   — —

10. After hearing the evidence it was clear who the *malefactor* was.   — —

11. It was unfair of Charles to *malign* Mrs Hardcastle, especially as she had been so kind to him.   — . —

12. Robert held the *Malthusian* viewpoint that the Far East would ultimately drain the world's resources to the point of disaster.   — —

When you check the answers on page 220 you'll find that four words were used wrongly. Did you spot them? Did you approve the eight correct examples of usage?

Choose the Correct Meaning

Which of the two alternatives, *a* or *b*, most accurately fits the meaning of the word? Mark or circle your choices (you know now that wild guesses don't count) and then check the answers on page 220.

mandatory **a.** obligatory or compulsory; **b.** officially sanctioned.

manifest **a.** promising; **b.** obvious, easily noticed.

manifold **a.** to accumulate; **b.** multiple or many different kinds.

manna **a.** the remains of a meal; **b.** an unexpected windfall or gift.

manqué **a.** unfulfilled, would-be; **b.** the dust and detritus in an abandoned habitation.

mantra **a.** The sacred cape worn by a Buddhist priest; **b.** a sacred word repeated endlessly as an aid to prayer..

maquette **a.** highly-glazed and ornamented ceramic tile; **b.** sculptor's small preliminary model for a larger piece.

marmoreal **a.** resembling marble; **b.** relating to small monkeys.

materfamilias **a.** family consisting of all daughters; **b.** female head of family.

maudlin **a.** tearfully sentimental; **b.** easily convinced.

maunder **a.** to receive alms on Maundy Thursday; **b.** to talk or act incoherently.

maverick **a.** an independent, unorthodox person; **b.** an injured cow or bull that becomes dangerous.

mawkish **a.** falsely sentimental; **b.** excessively nosey.

maxim **a.** a general truth or rule, briefly expressed; **b.** a rule prescribing a limitation.

mea culpa **a.** the drink is poisoned; **b.** it is my fault.

mealy-mouthed **a.** crudely outspoken; **b.** hesitant, afraid to speak plainly.

median **a.** a hidden mountain plateau; **b.** a middle point or value.

mediate **a.** to intervene in order to bring about agreement in a dispute; **b.** to separate disagreeing parties in the belief that time will heal their differences.

114

megalomania	**a.** fear of spots; **b.** delusions of grandeur or power.
megrim	**a.** a migraine headache; **b.** a horrific, realistic dream.
melange	**a.** a confused mixture; **b.** a milk jelly dessert.
melee	**a.** a lady's long silk dressing gown; **b.** a noisy fight or brawl.
mellifluous	**a.** smooth and honeyed; **b.** soft and billowing.
memorabilia	**a.** manuscripts produced prior to the 15th century; **b.** objects connected to famous people or events.
ménage	**a.** a stable of horses; **b.** members of a household.
mendacious	**a.** prone to lying and deception; **b.** miserly and grasping.
mendicant	**a.** a holistic doctor; **b.** someone dependent on begging.
mephitic	**a.** foul-smelling and poisonous; **b.** a substance that makes the eyes water.
mercenary	**a.** practical: 'act first, think later'; **b.** motivated primarily by greed or gain.
meretricious	**a.** annoyingly repetitive; **b.** vulgarly or superficially attractive.
mesmerise	**a.** to hypnotise; **b.** to cure by immersion in water.
messianic	**a.** having or imitating the appearance of Christ; **b.** an orator promising salvation or an ideal life of peace and prosperity.
metabolism	**a.** the bodily process that converts food to energy; **b.** the theory that base metals like lead can be converted into gold.
metaphorical	**a.** symbolic, illustrative; **b.** relating to philosophical theory.
métier	**a.** one's natural vocation; **b.** a group of art students.
metronymic	**a.** music with a steady beat; **b.** a name or qualities derived from the mother or other female ancestor.
mettle	**a.** decency and honesty; **b.** courage and spirit.
mezzanine	**a.** a basement bar; **b.** an intermediate storey between ground and first floor.
miasma	**a.** a noxious, foreboding atmosphere; **b.** a mass flight of bees, wasps or other insects.
microcosm	**a.** a miniature version of something that is regarded as representing the qualities of the larger original; **b.** extremely thin slices of material prepared for microscopic viewing.
micturate	**a.** preserving crystals in oil; **b.** to urinate.

From that round of 40 a score of 35+ or would be excellent, while one of 30 or more would be above average. Keep in mind, when you check the ones you missed, that many words share two or more meanings, or shades of meaning. The adjective *messianic* is a good example. Even if you were unfamiliar with the word you probably noted that it looks a bit like *Messiah*, and maybe thought there could be a connection. And, indeed, there is. The *OED* records that *messianic* was first used in 1834, relating specifically to the Messiah and therefore capitalised: *the Messianic hopes of the Jews for deliverance and salvation*. Eventually the meaning of the word extended to 'any prophesy or message that similarly promised an ideal world or life'. One could say, for instance, that Martin Luther King's dream of the promised land was delivered in his historic 'messianic speech' to his people in Memphis in 1968.

Fill in the Gaps: Identify the Word

From the meanings given, fill the gaps with the missing letters and identify the words.

Then check the answers on page 220.

1. One's normal surroundings or setting.   *mili _ _*
2. To influence some decision or event.   *milita _ _*
3. The act or art of mimicking or copying.   *mimic _ _*
4. Threatening or menacing.   *minato _ _*
5. A servile, fawning employee or dependant.   *mini _ _*
6. Something, often writing or printing, that is very small.   *minuscu _ _*
7. Small, inconsequential, trifling details.   *minuti _ _*
8. Disliking and distrusting everyone.   *misanthro _ _*
9. The interbreeding of different races.   *miscegenati _ _*
10. To interpret incorrectly, to arrive at a wrong conclusion.   *misconstr _ _*
11. An incorrect or unsuitable name.   *misnom _ _*
12. Hatred of women.   *misogy _ _*
13. To moderate, or make a condition less severe.   *mitiga _ _*

14. An aid to the memory. *mnemon _ _*

15. An attribute that denotes mode, mood or manner. *modali _ _*

16. A small amount or portion. *modic _ _*

17. One of two parts or shares of something. *moie _ _*

18. To soothe and pacify. *molli _ _*

19. Reclusive, like a monk or nun. *monast _ _*

20. The theory that inflation is caused by an excess supply of money in the economy. *monetari _ _*

21. A book, treatise or study concerned with a single subject. *monogra _ _*

22. Mounds and hills of rock debris deposited by former glaciers. *morai _ _*

23. An agreed suspension of an obligation or activity. *moratori _ _*

24. The fundamental values and customs of a society. *mor _ _*

25. A marriage between a man and woman of vastly dissimilar position in which the offspring of the lower ranked partner have no rights to titles and property of the higher ranked partner. *morganat _ _*

26. Without force or vitality; stagnant. *moribu _ _*

27. Ill-tempered and peevish. *moro _ _*

28. The perfect, most appropriate word or expression. *mot jus _ _*

29. Civilian attire, worn instead of a military uniform. *muf _ _*

30. Having many parts of great variety. *multifario _ _*

31. Ordinary, everyday, unexciting and banal. *munda _ _*

32. Extremely generous and liberal. *munifice _ _*

33. The ability to change; adaptability. *mutab _ _*

34. Common to or shared by two or more people or groups. *mutu _ _*

35. Shortsightedness, or inability to see distant objects clearly. *myop _ _*

An easier round, wouldn't you agree? If, after checking the answers on page 220 you find you have completed 30 or more words correctly, congratulate yourself. A lesser score is no disaster, but it tends to indicate that you need to work with determination and enthusiasm to achieve that A1 vocabulary!

Word Roots and Building Blocks

Here are some more word roots which, between them, have provided vital building blocks for dozens, if not hundreds, of our words. Learning their basic meanings will often help you identify the meanings of many words unfamiliar to you.

Word, Element	Origin	Meaning	English Words
macro-	Greek	large, long	*macrobiotics, macrocosm, macro lens, macroscopic*
malus, mal-	Latin	bad	*malevolent, malignant, malady, maladroit, malign*
manus, man-	Latin	hand	*manual, manicure, manuscript*
mater, matri-	Latin	mother	*maternal, matron, matrix, matrimony, matrimonial*
mega-	Greek	great	*megabyte, megalith, megalopolis, megastar*
meta-	Greek	change	*metabolism, metamorphosis*
-meter	Greek	measuring	*metre, barometer, metrication, gasometer*
micro-	Greek	very small	*microcosm, microscope, microfilm, micrometer*
milli-	Latin	thousand	*milligram, millimetre, millibar, millennium*
mis-	Old English	bad, wrong	*misunderstand, misfortune, mistake, misspell, mislead*

monis, mono-	Greek	one, single	*monocle, monody, monograph, monochrome*
-morph	Greek	shape, form	*amorphous, morpheme, morphology*
-most	Old English	superlative	*uppermost, utmost, hindmost, foremost*
multi-	Latin	much, many	*multistorey, multimillion, multiple, multifarious*

60-Sec Quickpick: More Misprints

Here are 10 short passages, each containing a misprint. Being the expert proofreader that you are, first spot the misprint, and then correct it. The answers are on page 221.

119

Your Correction

1. They decided they'd spend the day at the shopping male. _____

2. The Commonwealth Games held in Malasia were a great success. _____

3. She wondered if the week-old mayonaise was still safe. _____

4. Dave laughed when he saw the miniscule fish on the end of his line. _____

5. There aren't many cooks who can whip up a good merangue. _____

6. My father leaned on the mantlepiece, and began the lecture. _____

7. Joyce loved watching the martens and swallows swooping and diving overhead. _____

8. A visit to mecca was included in their middle east tour. _____

9. The Saxons had coarse mating on the floor. _____

10. The nudist colony nearby attracted naturalists from all over the country and even from overseas. _____

It would take sharp eyes and a sharp brain to catch and correct all ten misprints in just sixty seconds, so if you did – well done! *The Grauniad* needs you!

Muscle and Skeleton

Here's a quick tour around the body's skeletal and muscular system, taking in some terms that you may find useful to know.

Achilles tendon The fibrous cord that connects the calf muscles to the heelbone (not an *Achilles heel*, which describes 'a small but fatal weakness').

arthritis Inflammation of a joint.

arthroscopy Observation or surgery of a joint made through small incisions.

bursitis Inflammation of the small fluid-filled sacs (*bursa*) that cushion the joints.

carpal tunnel syndrome	Pressure on the nerve in the passage between the wrist (*carpal*) bones and a ligament.
clavicle	The collar bone.
coccyx	The small triangular bone at the base of the spine.
cranium	The set of bones that enclose the brain.
diaphragm	The dome-shaped muscular partition that separates chest and abdomen, and which moves as you breathe.
dislocation	Any separation of bones from joints and ligaments.
femur	The long, thick bone of the leg from the knee to the pelvis.
fracture	Any break in a bone.
gluteus maximus	The main muscle of the buttocks that moves the thigh.
hamstring	The muscle running from the buttocks to the back of the thigh.
hernia	A rupture or tear in a muscle wall, allowing internal organs to protrude.
humerus	The bone of the upper arm.
ligaments	Tough fibrous bands of tissue connecting and supporting the bones at joints.
lumbago	Pain in the lower part of the back.
mandible	The bone forming the lower jaw.
muscular dystrophy	A genetic disease which causes progressive deterioration and wasting of muscle fibres.
osteoarthritis	Chronic joint disease, especially of weight-bearing joints.
osteomyelitis	Inflammation and infection of the bone marrow.
osteoporosis	Thinning and brittleness of the bones due to loss of calcium.
patella	The kneecap.
radius and ulna	The two bones of the lower arm or forearm.
sphincter	A ring of muscle surrounding the opening of a hollow organ or body and contracting to close it.
spina bifida	A congenital defect in the spinal column.
sternum	The breastbone at the centre of the chest.
tendons	The firm, non-elastic tissue that connects muscle to bone.
tibia and fibula	The two bones of the lower leg.
vertebrae	The bones of the spinal column. The ribs are attached to the *thoracic vertebrae*; the *lumbar vertebrae* form the 'small of the back'.
zygomatic arch	[or *zygoma*] The cheekbone.

A Reminder to Revise

Revision should be instinctive by now. With an urge to move forward, it's understandable that lingering on '*m*' words could be irksome when new '*n*' words beckon from the next page. But before you wrap up this section, double-check your comprehension of the following selection:

macrocosm	*magnanimous*	*mantra*	*mea culpa*	*ménage*
meretricious	*misogyny*	*mollify*	*moratorium*	*mores*

Satisfied? If you are, then by all means move on. But if not . . you know what you have to do . . .

Mallemaroking

For a ship to be icebound these days is something of a rare event; either that, or the newsworthiness of icebound ships is rated about zero. But if, say, a ship *were* icebound, one would think that the sailors on the unfortunate vessel would be a downcast lot, dying from boredom and counting off the weeks and months to the arrival of the thaw. However, a word exists that suggests that such thoughts are way off beam.

That word is ***mallemaroking***, meaning the carousing of seamen aboard icebound ships. Alone among English dictionaries, it seems, *Chambers Twentieth Century Dictionary* has listed the word over many years through several editions, so they must think there's a use for it. Perhaps a clandestine but booming travel business exists, flying tourists to ships purposely icebound in the Arctic Circle for a good old mallemaroking. Perhaps it's listed at the request of Scrabble enthusiasts. Or perhaps *Chambers* is just having us all on.

Are they being used Correctly?

You've probably encountered the following ten words in your reading at some time or other. You may know all their meanings – but are you conversant with their usage? Here are the words integrated into sentences, several of which are completely meaningless. Can you separate the good from the garbage? Simply answer **right** or **wrong**. Answers on page 221.

	Right	**Wrong**
1. She could hardly express the exhilaration and joy she felt at reaching the *nadir* of her ambition.	—	—
2. The interminable silence extended for several *nanoseconds*.	—	—
3. Camilla was very fond of June except for her *narcissistic* streak.	—	—
4. A *nascent* spark of anger ignited in Jack's righteous breast.	—	—
5. Dennis hated the dense, *nebulous* atmosphere of the tropics.	—	—
6. After his release from gaol, Victor returned to his *nefarious* ways.	—	—
7. The two old men liked nothing more than to yarn by the fire, long into the night, fuelled by their mugs of *negus*.	—	—

8. After hours and hours of disastrous betting,
   Sir Randolph prayed that his *Nemesis* would
   arrive soon in the shape of a huge win.   __ __

9. The trendy lecturer confused a good many of
   his audience by his relentless use of *neologisms*.   __ __

10. Hilary admitted that she was a *neophyte* in the
    auction business.   __ __

Your score should read **Right** = 6; **Wrong** = 4. If it doesn't, spend a minute or two more on this exercise before consulting the answers on page 221.

Choose the Correct Meaning

Which one of the three alternatives, *a*, *b*, or *c*, most accurately fits the meaning of the word? Mark or circle your choices and then check the answers on page 221.

ne plus ultra   **a.** that extra effort; **b.** perfection; the highest point attainable; **c.** a place of peace and privacy.

nepotism   **a.** pertaining to the kidneys; **b.** The Muslim principle that the grandmother becomes head of a family; **c.** favouritism shown to relatives and friends by those in positions of power.

nexus   **a.** a link or bond between a group or series; **b.** the central point of a spiral; **c.** a partial vacuum.

nicety   **a.** ridiculous social mannerism; **b.** well-ordered and organised; **c.** a subtle point or distinction.

nihilism   **a.** the rejection of all established authority and institutions; **b.** the doctrine that man is imprisoned by his environment; **c.** the belief that despite superficial circumstances, all men are really equal.

noblesse oblige   **a.** the obligation of the ruled to their rulers; **b.** the supposed obligation of the nobility to be fair and generous; **c.** the obligation of an aristocrat to share his title with his wife.

noisome   **a.** offensive behaviour; **b.** smelly and disgusting; **c.** very loud.

nominal	**a.** theoretical, or token; **b.** a pre-appointment to an office or an official position; **c.** one-tenth of any amount.
nonage	**a.** people enjoying life after 90 years of age; **b.** a woman of 'a certain age'; **c.** the legal state of being a minor.
nonce word	**a.** any term describing homosexuality; **b.** a word coined for a single occasion; **c.** a word invented by Lewis Carroll.
nonchalant	**a.** indifferent, calm and cool; **b.** with a chip on the shoulder; **c.** habitually lazy.
nonentity	**a.** an insignificant person or thing; **b.** a pseudonym; **c.** someone with no known nationality; a stateless person.
nonpareil	**a.** something unmatched or unsurpassed; **b.** something that is out of line with everything else; **c.** any gemstone weighing more than 20 carats.
nonplussed	**a.** to have one's trousers taken away; **b.** to be utterly perplexed; **c.** a person who continually 'misses out'.
non sequitur	**a.** an illogical conclusion; **b.** an unfortunate misunderstanding; **c.** a misunderstanding because of bad timing.
nostrum	**a.** the beginnings of a moustache; **b.** a violent headache or migraine; **c.** a dubious cure-all.
nouveau riche	**a.** a gaudy style of architecture; **b.** a person vulgarly displaying newly acquired wealth; **c.** a ceremonial procession of lawyers.
nuance	**a.** a subtle difference; **b.** a barely discernible breath or breeze; **c.** a lullaby sung to a baby.
nubilea.	a startlingly statuesque woman; **b.** with a shiny, dark skin; **c.** a young woman of marriageable age.
nugatory	**a.** of little or no value; **b.** hardheaded and hard-hearted; **c.** a gold alloy containing very little precious metal.
numinous	**a.** crackling with light; **b.** arousing spiritual or religious emotions; **c.** dismissive, arrogant.
nymphet	**a.** a freshwater mermaid; **b.** a young, sexually precocious girl; **c.** a winged cherub, symbolic of water.

For this quick round, with few challenges, a score of less than 12 would be rather disappointing – but, please, not discouraging! Check your dictionary to make sure you have all the meanings mastered and then add them to the growing number of *'n'* words in your vocabulary.

Neologisms, or New Words

Throughout a millennium or more the English language has borrowed, purloined, adapted and remodelled words from just about every language that ever existed around the globe. It has also invented quite a few: often, seemingly, instantly and out of thin air. It's a continuing, seamless process. The day you read this an estimated twenty to forty new words will be coined to help us describe or explain or express something that never existed before, or to describe, explain or express something familiar in quite a different way. These new words are called **neologisms** and their importance is such that publishers are engaged in a Forth Bridge painting operation to include them in their dictionaries, the irony being that by the time they are listed they are out of date (or worse, out of use) – as is the following selection coined in the 1990s. Are these in *your* dictionary?

acquaintance rape	Rape by a person well-known to the victim.
all gone pear-shaped	Something that has gone wrong.
andropause	Male menopause.
bad hair day	A day when everything goes wrong.
big girl's blouse	A weak, ineffectual or pathetic person.
blag	To dupe or 'con' an advantage from someone.
Blairism	The policies and style of government associated with British Prime Minister Tony Blair.
bobbitt	To sever a man's (usually a husband's) penis.
boracic	[colloq.] To be penniless, broke (from Cockney rhyming slang *boracic lint = skint*).
brollability	The probability of rain.
cereologist	Someone investigating the phenomena of crop circles.
cybersex	Sexual activity or information available through computer networks.
designer stubble	Facial hair on men midway between clean-shaven and bearded.
dumbing down	The policy of excessively appealing to popular taste.
dweeb	A person who is boringly conventional, dull and studious.
firkinised	Off-the-shelf designer pubs, with names such as *Flock & Firkin; Falstaff & Firkin*, etc.

126

gonzo	A crazy, unorthodox person.
jones	Black personification of the male member; penis.
pink pound	Homosexual spending power.
rollover	An unclaimed lottery jackpot that is added to the prize money for the following lottery draw.
saddo	A dull, unsociable person.
scuzz	An unpleasant person.
siblicide	The killing of a young bird by a fellow nestling.
to give it some welly	Extra effort or enthusiasm applied to a task.
wally	An ineffectual, stupid, despised person.
white knuckle	An amusement park ride experience that absolutely terrifies.
wysiwyg	A term indicating that on a computer screen, *what you see is what you get* in a printout.
zilch	Nothing.

30-Sec Quickpick: Same, Opposite or Different ?

Here are ten words, each of which is matched with three other words. In each case the meanings of the three words are the same as the given word, opposite, or have nothing to do with it. In 30 seconds, go down the list, compare the words, and mark your conclusions: the same **(S)**, opposite **(O)**, or different **(D)**

		S	O	D
niggardly	*generous, munificent, benevolent*	__	__	__
nullify	*annul, rescind, void*	__	__	__
normal	*simply, gullible, credible*	__	__	__
neglect	*attention, protection, care*	__	__	__
narrate	*recount, describe, disclose*	__	__	__
neat	*disordered, confused, slovenly*	__	__	__
nearness	*reticular, interwoven, lacelike*	__	__	__
nimble	*maladroit, stolid, clumsy*	__	__	__
noble	*patrician, regal, aristocratic*	__	__	__
nomadic	*vagrant, peripatetic, gypsy*	__	__	__

Now check the answers on page 221. Four of the words were matched with their synonyms, four with their antonyms or opposites, and two were matched with meanings that didn't match in any way. A perfect score?

Numbers, Sizes and Amounts from Word Roots

Although our names for numbers, sizes and quantities are derived from Greek and Latin roots, we chose Arabic numerals rather than Roman. But even though our numerals are Arabic (5, 6, 7) the way in which we express their applications is a glorious mixture of Greek and Latin. For example:

> **7 = hepta** (Greek) and **septem** (Latin). From the former we get *heptagon, heptameter* and *Heptateuch*, while from the latter comes *septuagenerian, septet* and *September* (it was the seventh month of the year in ancient Rome).
> **6 = hex** (Greek) and **sex** (Latin). From the former comes *hexagonal* and *hexagram*, while from the latter derive *sextuple, sextet, sextant* and *sextuplets*.

And so on. This helps to explain why words describing applications of the same numeral often share two different prefixes. The number four has the Greek root **tetra-** (*tetrahedron, tetradactyl, tetralogy, tetragram*) and also the Latin **quad-** (*quadrant, quadrangle, quadrilateral, quadrille, quadroon, quadruped, quadruplet, quadruple*), all expressing some form of the number four. This is a classic case of the English language being unable to make up its mind!

Here's a quick guide to numerical prefixes:

Number	Greek Root	Latin Root
1	*oine*	*unus*
2	*duo*	*duo*
3	*treis, tri*	*tres*
4	*tetra*	*quad*
5	*pente*	*quinque*
6	*hex*	*ex*
7	*hepta*	*septem*
8	*okto*	*octo*

9	ennea	novem, non
10	deca	decem
100	hecto	centum
1000	kilo	milli

Five Minute Revision

Spend a worthwhile five minutes looking back over your '*n*' words. Are you satisfied, for example, that you are fully conversant with the meanings of *nebulous* and *Nemesis*, *neophyte* and *nepotism*? Can you use *nominal*, *non sequitur* and *nugatory* appropriately in sentences? If you're satisfied you can, then let's move on.

Nabokov's Nimieties and Corelli's Conceits

Vladimir Nabokov is noted for many achievements – as a novelist, poet, scholar and lepidopterist – and not least for his controversial fictional nymphet *Lolita*. But, perhaps above all these, Nabokov remains unsurpassed for his linguistic inventiveness in both Russian and English. He was a pyrotechnician with the English language in particular; words and expressions of dismaying felicity and head-spinning expressiveness explode throughout his books in a bravura display of intellectual illumination. But stimulating though it is, there is a downside to reading Nabokov's prose, and that's having to face his cunningly-laid obstacle courses of verbal tripwires: words you've never seen before, words you can barely believe exist, and, frustratingly, words you can't find in any dictionary. Here are some examples, from his novel *Pale Fire* (1962):

> *schmolium, inenubilable, anticomedoists, perlustration, closule, psychomompos, pudibundity, skoramis, lemniscate, lansquenet*

Perhaps each book should display a prominent label:

> **WARNING – This novel contains explicit material**
> **which may be incomprehensible to and upsetting**
> **for readers with normal vocabularies.**

Well, that's Nabokov for you. However, while intellectual challenge of this kind is an acceptable feature of 'literary' novels it comes as a bit of a surprise when it jumps out of the pages of popular fiction. Take the best-selling phenomenon of the late 1990s, *Captain Corelli's Mandolin* by the British author Louis de Bernières. It has sold millions of copies (by word of mouth, rather than hype) around the world and has been rightly praised for its vivid, lyrical narrative. Nevertheless a good many of those millions of readers must have been more than a little perplexed by the unfamiliar and exotic words contained in it. Some – *demotic, immolation, marmoreal* – have been dealt with in our vocabulary exercises, but others you will come across perhaps only once in your lifetime, and you would, in normal circumstances, never have reason to use them. Here's a sampling:

1. *A **gibbous** moon slid filaments of eerie silver light through the slats of the shutters.*
2. *. . . this white death and this snow **incarnadine**, this ungrateful lethal cold . . .*
3. *He was like one of those **saprophytic** orchids . . .*
4. *Misanthropic and **eremitic**, he was scruffy, ill-mannered, unemployable and only went out after dark.*
5. *". . . this tobacco . . . is most unpleasantly **sternutatory**."*
6. *. . . his splendid beard that yet exposed the livid **cicatrice** across his cheek.*
7. *He knew that to leave the island would be to become **deracinated**.*
8. *. . . the many corners of the **malversated** Mediterranean Sea.*

Honestly, how many of those words did you take in your stride, knowing exactly what they meant and what they expressed in the context of the sentence? If you read all eight – or even half of them – without blinking then you wouldn't be reading this book. You shouldn't be the least embarrassed if you were stymied by them all.

Here are their meanings (those in your own dictionary may vary a little):

gibbous	A celestial body that is more than half but not fully illuminated.
incarnadine	A reddish or pink tinge or stain.
saprophytic	A fungus or bacterium that feeds on decayed organic matter.
eremitic	Hermit-like.
sternutatory	Causing or having the effect of sneezing.

cicatrice   A scar caused by a closing or closed wound.

deracinated   To be removed or torn from one's natural environment.

malversated   To be subjected to public misconduct or bad behaviour.

Could not Louis de Bernieres have made it a little easier for us? To make the point, the headline, *Nabokov's Nimieties and Corelli's Conceits*, deliberately didn't. *Nimieties* = excesses. *Conceits* (in this context) = verbal whimsies.

O

Complete the Sentence

Below are twelve words and twelve sentences. A word is missing from each of the sentences. Can you place the appropriate words in all twelve sentences? Each word is used only once. Answers on page 221.

obdurate   obeisance   obfuscate   oblique   obloquy   obsequious
obsolescent   obstreperous   obtuse   obviate   occidental   occlude

1. To the Chinese, confronted by the first Western adventurers, _____ clothing and habits must have seemed totally alien.

2. The professor complained that all his students were equally barbarian, ignorant and _____.

3. They were all of the view that Miss Bertram had gained her various promotions through her grovelling and _____ manner.

4. Despite Emma's pleading, her father remained _____ .

5. The dirt road ran off the highway at an _____ angle.

6. The effect of the nest was to _____ the passage of the smoke up the chimney.

7. Even though he'd served his sentence, Mark found the _____ of his crime too much to bear and withdrew from all public life.

8. As she entered the room Rebecca bowed hesitantly in _____ to the chief on his makeshift throne.

9. The most unruly and _____ boys in the class were moved to the front row of desks.

10. The farmer agreed with the agent that the tractor was _____ and would soon need to be replaced.

11. They felt that installing the new computers would _____ the need for the extra staff the office manager had been requesting.

12. The new handbook only served to _____ the already bewildering maze of unintelligible instructions.

Check the answers on page 221 and feel pleased with yourself if you scored eight or more correct. Now for some more useful 'o' words.

Choose the Correct Meaning

Which of the three alternatives, *a*, *b* or *c*, most appropriately fits the meaning of the word? Mark or circle your choices (remember, blind stabs with a pin shouldn't count!) and then check your answers on page 221.

odium	**a.** bad breath; **b.** intense hatred; **c.** gold amalgam dental filling.
odontologist	**a.** cares for the feet; **b.** cares for the nose; **c.** cares for the teeth.
Odyssey	**a.** any long poem; **b.** a long eventful journey; **c.** a search for the ideal woman.
oeuvre	**a.** a dish of quail's eggs; **b.** a list of soldiers killed in battle; **c.** the whole work of a writer or artist.
officious	**a.** Over-readiness to offer advice or services; **b.** helpful and obliging; **c.** inability to work with others.
olfactory	**a.** a branch of industrial archaeology; **b.** abuse of unionism; **c.** relating to the sense of smell.
oligarchy	**a.** an unbroken line of female descendants; **b.** a government controlled by a privileged few; **c.** a communal olive grove in Mediterranean countries.
omnipotent	**a.** having great or unlimited power; **b.** one whose statements are always true; **c.** one who foresees the future.
omniscient	**a.** knowing everything; **b.** being ruled or overawed by astrology; **c.** fear of the dark.
omnivorous	**a.** eating only herbaceous matter; **b.** eating only animals; **c.** eating anything.

133

onerous	**a.** arduous and oppressive; **b.** selfish; **c.** given to making sarcastic remarks.
opprobrium	**a.** disgrace; **b.** a dark place; **c.** an eye disease.
optimal	**a.** well-balanced eyesight; **b.** the most favourable or advantageous situation; **c.** the unachievable.
opulent	**a.** stout and podgy; **b.** abundant, wealthy; **c.** showing off.
oracular	**a.** roughly elliptical; **b.** prophetic; **c.** squinting.
Orcadian	**a.** the ideal; **b.** sea-loving; **c.** a native of the Orkney islands.
ordure	**a.** excrement; **b.** money distributed to peasants by aristocrats; **c.** the human remains in unmarked graves.
ormolu	**a.** an exquisite black gemstone; **b.** fancy scrollwork in wood; **c.** a gold-coloured alloy used in furniture decoration.
oscillate	**a.** to move up and down; **b.** to swing regularly from side to side; **c.** to vibrate at intervals.
osmosis	**a.** evaporation by use of artificial heating; **b.** diffusion through a porous barrier; **c.** the process of a body turning to dust.
ossified	**a.** transformed into a paste; **b.** turned into rubber; **c.** turned into bone.
ostensibly	**a.** seemingly; **b.** obviously; **c.** incautiously.
ostentatious	**a.** silent and secretive; **b.** pretentious and showy; **c.** using bright, dazzling colours.
osteopathy	**a.** treatment using water and sea products; **b.** using nerve stimulation; **c.** using massage and bone manipulation.
ostracize	**a.** to make a quadruped walk on two legs; **b.** to exclude or banish someone; **c.** to blend various ingredients.
otiose	**a.** useless and futile; **b.** fat and lazy; **c.** slow and lumbering.
ottoman	**a.** a small oriental carpet; **b.** a low padded seat; **c.** a tall brass long-spouted teapot.
overly	**a.** randomly; **b.** excessively; **c.** lately.
overt	**a.** hidden and secret; **b.** open and public; **c.** shy and retiring.
overtone	**a.** an additional meaning or nuance; **b.** the sound from a wrongly tuned stringed instrument; **c.** mild sunburn.

oxymoron **a.** someone consistently using meaningless expressions; **b.** a calf born on Christmas Day; **c.** an expression which combines contradictory terms.

An interesting round and one that should add some fresh words to your vocabulary. A score of around 20 would be average, but if you managed to select 25 or more correct allow yourself an indulgent smile.

The 'Ology Department

There must be by now, since the combining forms *-logy* and *-ology* were introduced in the early 19th century, some thousands of *'ologies*. Many of them you certainly know, but there may be some that remain unfamiliar to you. Here's a selection:

anthropology	Study of man, his origins and physical characteristics.
cardiology	Study of the heart.
cetology	Study of whales.
chronology	Determination of proper sequence of time, dates and past events.
conchology	Study of shells.
cosmology	Study of the origin and nature of the universe.
cytology	Study of plant and animal cells.
dermatology	Study of skin and its diseases.
ecology	Study of the relationships between living creatures and their environment.
gastroenterology	Study of diseases of the stomach and intestines.
haematology	Study of diseases of the blood and blood-forming tissue.
histology	Study of animal and plant tissues.
horology	Art of making clocks and measuring time.
ichthyology	Study of fish.
immunology	Study of biological immunity.
mycology	Study of fungi.
odontology	Study of diseases of the teeth, gums and jaw.
oenology	The study and art of making wine.
oncology	Study and treatment of tumours, especially cancers.

ontology	Theory of the nature of being.
ophthalmology	Study of the eye and its diseases.
ornithology	Study of birds.
palaeontology	Study of fossils and the structure and evolution of extinct animals and plants.
parapsychology	Study of telepathy and mental phenomena.
pathology	Study of the cause, origin and nature of disease.
petrology	Study of the origin and formation of rocks.
pharmacology	Study of drugs, their actions and uses.

philology	Study of the evolution of language.
phrenology	Study of human brain function according to its parts.
pomology	Study of fruit and its cultivation.

primatology	Study of the ape and monkey tribes.
proctology	Study of the anus and rectum.
radiology	Use of radioactivity in diagnosis and treatment of diseases.
seismology	Study of earthquakes.
sociology	Study of the development, functioning and classification of human societies.
speleology	Study of caves.
toxicology	Study of poisons and their antidotes.
volcanology	Study of volcanoes.

30-Sec Quickpick: Spot the Misfits

With a minimum of hesitation, underline or circle the misfits in each word group:

> *obscure, vague, obfuscatory, clear*
> *obligate, bestow, offer, donate*
> *oppress, encumber, assist, hamper*
> *observe, ignore, disregard, overlook*
> *omit, include, exclude, skip*
> *oust, expel, include, eject*
> *owner, landlord, proprietor, tenant*
> *opaque, limpid, transparent, clear*
> *open-minded, receptive, intolerant, amenable*
> *often, repeatedly, rarely, regularly*

The answers are on page 221. In that 30-second dash, two slips could be excused, but if you took longer there should be no excuses for any.

O, Revision! Revision!

Do you think you know your '*o*' words sufficiently to safely stow them in your vocabulary? Just try these again by fitting them into mental sentences:

> *obsequious   obsolescent   oeuvre   orotund   optimal   overt*

137

Make sure you fully understand **obsolescent**; it doesn't mean 'defunct' – that is **obsolete** – but in the *process* of becoming obsolete, defunct or dead. And **orotund**? Oops! Sorry about that. When applied to the voice, it means 'booming and resonant'; with writing, it means 'pompous and bombastic'.

Onomatopoeia

Onomatopoeic words are expressions that imitate the sounds associated with an action or an object, like *buzz, fizz, pop, crackle, whoosh, ping-pong, puff-puff, bubble, sizzle* and so on.

Many of us learn a range of these words at an early age from story books and especially comics such as *Film Fun, Dandy* and *Beano: clang, ping, z-z-z-z, ah-choo! tee-hee, gr-r-r-r, plop, ding-a-ling, thud, boo-hoo* . . . followed inevitably by the shockwave of American comic onomatopoeia (capitalised of course, and with exclamation marks): ***POW! UGH! BOING! BLAM! WHAM! SPLAT! VROOOOM, ARRGGGHHHH! BA-ROOOM! ZAP!***

But onomatopoeia has its serious side, too, being a useful literary tool for conveying emotive mellifluous rhythms and effects. The poet Alfred Tennyson was good at it: *murmuring of innumerable bees . . . myriads of rivulets hurrying thro' the lawn . . . the moan of doves in immemorial elms.* And so were Gilbert and Sullivan. Here's an alliterative sample from their opera *The Mikado:*

> *To sit in solemn silence in a dull, dark dock*
> *In a pestilential prison, with a life-long lock*
> *Awaiting the sensation of a short, sharp shock*
> *From a cheap and chippy chopper on a big, black block!*

P

Choose the Correct Meanings

Which one of the pair of alternatives, *a* or *b*, most accurately fits the meaning of the word? Mark or circle your choices and then check the answers on page 222.

pacifist   **a.** supporter of inter-Pacific Islands economic union; **b.** a person who refuses to undertake military service.

paediatrician   **a.** a specialist in bone diseases; **b.** a specialist in children's diseases.

palaver   **a.** a drawn-out discussion; **b.** a Mexican Indian woven cape.

palimpsest   **a.** a text which has been erased and written over; **b.** a word game in which the player tries to make as many different words as possible from the original.

palliative   **a.** an effective drug but which has severe side-effects; **b.** a treatment that relieves, but without curing.

palpable   **a.** evident and obvious; **b.** barely eatable.

palpitate   **a.** to massage violently; **b.** to flutter or tremble.

panacea   **a.** wishful thinking; **b.** a universal remedy.

panache   **a.** dash and verve; **b.** a vague, irritating ache.

panegyric   **a.** any bitter medicine; **b.** an elaborate, very flattering expression of praise.

panjandrum   **a.** a Punjabi feast; **b.** a self-important official.

pantheism   **a.** the doctrine that the universe is a manifestation of God; **b.** the theory that all souls exist until eternity.

paparazzi	**a.** a long row of marble columns; **b.** tenacious freelance photographers of celebrities.
paradigm	**a.** a model example; **b.** a tongue-twisting phrase.
paragon	**a.** a person held up to ridicule; **b.** a model of excellence.
paramour	**a.** an occasional lover; **b.** the lover of a married man or woman.
paranoia	**a.** fear of criticism or attack; **b.** delusions of persecution.
paraphrase	**a.** a restatement in different words intended to clarify; **b.** a passage rewritten to disguise its real meaning.
pariah	**a.** a West African tribal chief; **b.** a social outcast.
pari mutuel	**a.** a banking system that guarantees depositors a fixed interest rate; **b.** a betting system that divides the total stakes among the winners, less a percentage.
parity	**a.** equality of rank and pay; **b.** an agreed currency exchange rate between two countries.
parlance	**a.** a marble facade of a building; **b.** a particular or idiomatic manner of speaking.
parlous	**a.** poor and embittered; **b.** difficult and perilous.
parodic	**a.** amusingly mimicking the style of another's work; **b.** arriving at an unexpected time or in an unusual way.
paroxysm	**a.** a fatal disease caught from parrots; **b.** a convulsive fit or outburst.
parsimonious	**a.** being frugal; **b.** being unfriendly.
partiality	**a.** biased; **b.** sly greediness.
partisan	**a.** any division into two parts; **b.** a person devoted to one party or cause.
parvenu	**a.** a newly rich social upstart; **b.** a leading patron of the arts.
passé	**a.** up-to-the-minute; **b.** behind the times.
pastiche	**a.** a work that imitates the style of another; **b.** a slow movement for orchestral strings.
paterfamilias	**a.** male head of a household; **b.** the collective uncles of a family.
pathogenic	**a.** pertaining to autopsies; **b.** capable of causing disease.
patina	**a.** circumference of the retina of the eye; **b.** an oxidised layer or the sheen of wear on a surface.
patisserie	**a.** a shop selling pastries; **b.** a shop selling preserved meats.

patois	**a.** a stepped patio; **b.** a regional dialect of a language.
patrial	**a.** pertaining to a person's country of birth; **b.** a person with an unknown father.
patrician	**a.** a fluent speaker of French, Italian or Spanish; **b.** an aristocrat or person of refined tastes.
Pauline	**a.** relating to Pope Paul and his papal bulls; **b.** relating to St Paul or his doctrines.
Pecksniffian	**a.** an admirer of the works of Charles Dickens; **b.** a hypocrite who advocates moral behaviour but behaves otherwise.

That's the first round of five – *'p'* is an extremely productive generator of words – and a lot of interesting and essential ones, too. For this first set of 40 words a score of around 25 would be satisfactory, 30 very good, and one of 35+ excellent.

Words in Use: Right or Wrong?

In some of the following sentences the 'p' word is used correctly; in others incorrectly, resulting in nonsense. Which usages are right and which are wrong? Mark your decisions and then check the answers on page 222.

	Right	**Wrong**

1. He puffed out his chest and the audience admired his *pectorals*. — —

2. The old trader was always on the lookout for a *pecuniary* advantage — —

3. He was a fanatical *pedagogue*, always travelling, never arriving. — —

4. Joanne was always breathlessly *pedantic* and in a hurry. — —

5. Her hair was invariably tied in a crowning *peignoir*. — —

6. The man was thoroughly unpleasant and could never refer to anyone other than in a sneering, *pejorative* manner. — —

7. In the *pellucid* water the divers could see for fifty metres.   ___ ___

8. They were all envious of the beautiful *penchant* she wore that night.   ___ ___

9. Harry jumped all the hurdles but tripped on the *penumbra*.   ___ ___

10. Old Lady Markham was surprisingly alert and *percipient*.   ___ ___

Five are right and five are wrong – did you sort them all out correctly? Check the answers on page 222. Two or three misses would be no great disaster.

Choose the Correct Meanings

Another substantial round in which you are asked again to choose which of the alternative definitions, *a* or *b*, most accurately fits the word. Mark or circle your choices and then check the answers on page 222.

peregrination   **a.** an extensive voyage; **b.** travelling pointlessly in circles.

peremptory   **a.** cautious and hesitant; **b.** decisive and final.

perennial   **a.** annually; **b.** everlastingly.

perfunctory   **a.** careless and half-hearted; **b.** vigorous and positive.

peripatetic   **a.** prone to indigestion; **b.** always travelling.

periphrasis   **a.** a roundabout way of speaking or writing; **b.** an obsession with words.

permeate   **a.** to penetrate or pass through a substance; **b.** to beat two substances together to form a blend.

pernicious   **a.** irritating; **b.** harmful.

peroration   **a.** a memorial address; **b.** the summing up at the end of a speech.

perquisite   **a.** unearned money, favour or benefit; **b.** a service that is required before a payment is made.

persiflage   **a.** frivolous, teasing banter; **b.** embarrassing flattery.

perspicacious   **a.** unduly suspicious; **b.** having the ability to understand things clearly.

pertinacious   **a.** indolent and cheeky; **b.** stubbornly persistent.

pervasive	**a.** to persuasively persist; **b.** to spread subtly and gradually.
philanderer	**a.** a womaniser; **b.** a travelling salesman.
philippic	**a.** a letter expressing deep regret; **b.** a bitter speech of denunciation.
philanthropist	**a.** charitable and benevolent; **b.** a postage stamp collector.
Philistine	**a.** a person indifferent to learning and the arts; **b.** someone who attacks established values.
phlegmatic	**a.** excessively pessimistic; **b.** unemotional and unexcitable.
physiognomy	**a.** the study of cranial bumps and depressions; **b.** a person's facial features.
picaresque	**a.** fictional episodic adventures; **b.** cute and appealing.
picayune	**a.** petty and niggling; **b.** bright and sparkling.
pied-à-terre	**a.** an apartment for secondary or occasional use; **b.** a dish featuring stewed snails.
pinchbeck	**a.** a frugal person; **b.** a cheap alloy imitating gold.
pinnate	**a.** a flagless flagpole; **b.** having the shape or arrangement of a feather.
piquant	**a.** having a stimulating tart taste; **b.** sly joking.
pique	**a.** resentment because of wounded pride; **b.** extreme envy.
pixilated	**a.** slightly dotty; **b.** obsession with garden gnomes.
placate	**a.** to firmly put someone in their place; **b.** to appease.
placebo	**a.** a neutral substance given in place of an effective medicine; **b.** a glass-walled garden summer house.
plagiarism	**a.** falsely attributing genuine documents to fake paintings, manuscripts or antiques; **b.** stealing and using another's work or ideas and passing them off as one's own work.
plangent	**a.** a deep and resonant sound; **b.** a small, square pill.
Platonic	**a.** a blood-bond between two men; **b.** a friendship that's non-sensual and free from physical desire.
plebeian	**a.** a layman who pleads before a court; **b.** common and vulgar.
plenary	**a.** complete and absolute; **b.** intermediate and ongoing.
plethora	**a.** superabundance; **b.** an operation for gallstones.

143

podiatry	**a.** the art of speechmaking; **b.** the treatment of the feet and its disorders.
poetaster	**a.** a degraded person; **b.** a writer of bad verse.
pogrom	**a.** persecution or extermination of an ethnic group; **b.** a coup which leaves a family ruling a government.
poignant	**a.** sad-looking; **b.** distressing and painful to the feelings.

Having consulted the answers on page 222, did you fare any better in this round? It has to be said, however, that there is a fair sprinkling of 'difficult' words in this set, so you should be pleased with any score of 25 or more.

Complete the Sentence

Here are ten words and ten sentences. A word is missing from each of the sentences. Can you place the appropriate words in all 12 sentences? Each word is used only once. Answers on page 222.

polemic	*polyglot*	*polymath*	*poltergeist*	*portentous*
potable	*pragmatic*	*precocious*	*preclude*	*predatory*

1. The campers spent a whole day searching for clean, _____ water.
2. The distant _____ rumbling threatened even further earthquakes.
3. Convinced they'd heard a _____, Margaret and Aunt Edith refused to stay in the old house a moment longer.
4. With an expert knowledge of botany, history, chess and astronomy, and with an amazing talent for writing and painting, William was a true _____.
5. Naturally argumentative, Mark loved to engage in long _____ discussions.
6. Because of the varied ethnic mix, _____ signs were everywhere.
7. Perhaps because most of his family had been convicted for theft at some time or another, the lad could never shake off his _____ instincts.
8. The onset of the rainy season would _____ any further exploration.

9. With makeup, short skirts and high heels, the child looked dangerously _____.

10. The partners feared bankruptcy, but Mr Peters took the _____ view that a rescue package could be arranged without difficulty.

With a little thought, a score of seven or eight should be possible even though you may not have been familiar with half the words. But check them all so that you'll instantly know their meanings in the future. Now for the fifth and final *'p'* round!

Choose the Correct Meanings

Once again, which one of each pair of alternatives, *a* or *b*, most accurately fits the meaning of the word? Mark or circle your choices and then check the answers on page 222.

predicate   **a.** to assert or imply; **b.** to predict firmly, based on fact.

predilection   **a.** a vague dislike for something; **b.** a special liking for something.

prehensile   **a.** in a primitive state; **b.** capable of grasping.

preponderance   **a.** a great amount or number; **b.** a greater amount or number.

prerogative   **a.** a privilege or right; **b.** a person's first public speech.

prescient   **a.** possessing foresight; **b.** easily irritated.

pretentious   **a.** loud and bombastic; **b.** claiming undeserved importance.

prevaricate   **a.** to evade and mislead; **b.** to argue fiercely.

prima facie   **a.** unfounded allegations; **b.** apparently self-evident.

primordial   **a.** pertaining to swamps; **b.** existing from the beginning.

probity   **a.** serious and analytical; **b.** proven integrity.

proclivity   **a.** a tendency or inclination; **b.** a feature of rising ground in a landscape.

procrastinate   **a.** to think things over very carefully; **b.** to defer or postpone until later.

profligate   **a.** Wildly wasteful and debauched; **b.** a financier who takes a profit before everything is accounted for.

prognosis   **a.** the determination of a disease and its treatment; **b.** a prediction of the outcome of a disorder or disease and the chances of recovery.

prolapse	**a.** a recurrence of a disorder; **b.** the downward displacement of an internal organ.
prolix	**a.** tediously long-winded; **b.** the centre of an ellipse.
propensity	**a.** strong and robust; **b.** a natural tendency or disposition.
prophylactic	**a.** germ-free milk; **b.** anything that protects from or prevents disease.
propinquity	**a.** subtle warning signals; **b.** nearness in place or time.
propitious	**a.** prone to lose one's balance; **b.** favourable.
prosaic	**a.** flat and lacking in imagination; **b.** one given to making faintly ridiculous flowery statements.
proscribe	**a.** to condemn or forbid; **b.** to agree under duress.
proselytise	**a.** to translate thoughts into words; **b.** to convert someone from one religious belief to another.
prosthesis	**a.** replacement of a body part with an artificial substitute; **b.** an unwelcome medical opinion.
protean	**a.** versatile and changeable; **b.** of vast size and girth.
protégé	**a.** a legally-appointed guardian; **b.** someone who is helped and protected by another.
provenance	**a.** proof of authenticity; **b.** place of origin.
proviso	**a.** legal advice attached to a document; **b.** a condition or stipulation.
prurient	**a.** highly moral in thought and deed; **b.** inquisitiveness about the smutty and obscene.
psychosomatic	**a.** physical disorder caused by or influenced by the emotions; **b.** a terminal illness.
puerile	**a.** silly and childish; **b.** offensively smelly.
puissant	**a.** self-mocking; **b.** powerful.
pulchritude	**a.** innocence and reverence; **b.** physical beauty.
pullulate	**a.** to vibrate and sway; **b.** to breed abundantly.
punctilious	**a.** paying strict attention to details of conduct; **b.** having an obsession with time and time-wasting.
purlieus	**a.** the fashionable clothes of high society; **b.** a neighbourhood or its boundaries.
pusillanimous	**a.** tending to favour members of one's family; **b.** timid and lacking in courage.
putative	**a.** supposed or reputed to exist; **b.** emerging and growing.
Pyrrhic victory	**a.** a victory in which the victor's losses are as great as those of the defeated; **b.** a victory that has emerged from the ashes of defeat.

If you've stayed the *'p'* course for all five rounds you'll have mulled over the meanings of no less than 150 words – a lexicographical marathon! And, surely, in the process, added considerably to your vocabulary. As with similar rounds, a score for this one of 25 or more would be commendable. If it's any consolation, the low-quota *'q'* section is next.

Politics and Public Life

It is a part of life we can't escape. If you can't beat 'em, join 'em (or confuse 'em, as US President Teddy Roosevelt once said). Here are some useful terms.

autarky	An economically self-sufficient country.
autocracy	Government by an individual with unrestricted authority.
by-election	A local or regional election to fill a vacant legislative seat.
canvass	To solicit votes.
coalition	An alliance between two groups or factions.
colonialism	A country's rule over usually weaker foreign territories.
coup d'état	A sudden violent and illegal seizure of government.
fascism	A right-wing, nationalist authoritarian ideology that is fundamentally opposed to democratic principles.
federalism	A union of states giving some or all power to a central government.
filibuster	Obstructing legislation, usually by over-long speeches.
gerrymander	To divide constituency boundaries to gain an unfair advantage.
green paper	Policy proposals to be discussed by Parliament.
hereditary peers	[also known as the Lords Temporal] Peers formerly entitled by birth to a seat in the House of Lords.
home rule	Domestic self-government of a member state or dependency.
impeachment	The commitment for trial of a public officer, including a president.
imperialism	Extending one state's rule over other territories.
junta	Rule by a group of military officers.
life peers	Peers created by a government entitled to sit in the House of Lords but whose titles lapse on death.
Lords Spiritual	Archbishops and senior Church of England bishops entitled to sit in the House of Lords.

mandate	Support given to a newly elected government for its policies.
ombudsman	An official with powers to protect citizens from government abuse.
plebiscite	A vote by a state or region on a question of national importance.
prorogue	To discontinue discussion and business in Parliament without actually dissolving it.
socialism	A system in which the key economic features are controlled by the state, democratically or not.
stalking horse	A supposed candidate put up to mask the intended candidate and divide the opposition, and who then withdraws.
theocracy	Government by a priesthood or deity.
veto	The power exercised to prevent legislation.
whip	Party members in a legislature appointed to organise and discipline members, especially on voting behaviour.
white paper	An official report setting out a government's policy on a matter that will come before Parliament.

30-Sec Quickpick: Add the Final Letters

From the following definitions, can you supply the final two letters to correctly complete the words? Answers on page 223.

1. A writing material used by the ancient Egyptians. — *papyr _ _*

2. To become aware of something. — *percei _ _*

3. To penetrate or make holes in something. — *perfora _ _*

4. The inhabitants of a country or area. — *popula _ _*

5. The treatment of mental disorders. — *psychiat _ _*

6. The sport of fighting with the fists, or boxing — *pugili _ _*

7. The first public performance of a film or play — *premie _ _*

8. An overabundance or excess. — *pletho _ _*

9. To induce or urge someone do something.   *persua _ _*
10. A public walk along a seaside resort   *promena _ _*

One or two pauses perhaps, but otherwise these should have given you no trouble.

Words from Ancient Beginnings

If you look at the pair of words *suspend* and *pendulum* for a few moments, you'll see that they are connected by a common syllable, **pend** – as a suffix in *suspend* and as a prefix in *pendulum*. The source for **pend** is the Latin *pendere*, meaning 'to hang', and if you think for a minute you'll probably come up with some more words containing the same element, such as *pendant, pendulous* and *pending*. You might also wonder about *depend* – and, yes, that too derives from the old Latin word. If you were, for example, to ask a favour of a friend, he might reply, "Well, . . . that **depends** . . " In other words, he's letting your request hang for a while before making up his mind or inventing some conditions. You can thus see that even a flimsy knowledge of word elements can often help you suss out the approximate meaning of words not in your vocabulary. Here are a few more worth thinking about.

Word, Element	Origin	Meaning	English Words
pan-	Greek	all, everything	*panacea, pan-American, pantheism, panchromatic*
para-	Latin	protection	*paramedic, parachute*
ped-	Latin	foot	*pedestrian, pedal, pedestal, quadruped, centipede*
per-	Latin	through	*pervade, percolate, persist*
phon-	Greek	voice, sound	*phonetics, phonograph, telephone*
poly-	Greek	many, much	*polygon, polygamy, polyglot*
port-	Latin	to carry	*portable, porter, support*
post-	Latin	after, behind	*postpone, posterior, postwar, p.m. (post meridian)*

pre-	Latin	before	*preface, predate, preschool, premeditation, pre-eminent*
pro-	Latin	forward in place of in favour of	*proceed, progress, prologue, pronoun, proactive, project, pro-European*

Revision Suggestion

For a change, try DIY revision – browse through the *'p'* section and spend a minute or two with any words whose meanings don't *instantly* spin out of your memory.

Prose and Poetry

Writers, being writers, are naturally prone to make references to their raw materials (words, literature), their craft (writing, publishing), and to other writers. Specialised terms aside (*dactyl, apophasis, paroxytone*), it's handy to know a few 'literary' words that crop up from time to time in books, reviews, magazine articles and newspaper reports.

alliteration	The repetition of consonants in stressed words, as in Coleridge's line from *Kubla Khan: Five miles meandering with a mazy motion . . .*
anthology	A collection of short pieces or excerpts of works by one or more authors.
aphorism	A succinct statement of a truth, principle or opinion.
apothegm	[or *apophthegm*] A pithy cryptic remark, expressed wittily.
bon mot	A clever, well-phrased witticism.
couplet	A pair of rhymed lines in poetry.
Delphic	An obscure or ambiguous statement.
denouement	The final resolution of a mystery or problem in a fictional plot.
dialectic	The investigation of truth through reasoning and intellectual discussion.
ephemera	Printed matter of short-lived interest.
epistolary	A narrative told solely through personal correspondence.

genre	A subject classification, e.g. science fiction, romance, historical.
holograph	A document written in the handwriting of its author.
hyperbole	Exaggeration for emphasis or rhetorical effect.
incunabula	Any book printed in moveable type before the 16th century.
irony	Using words to imply the opposite of what they normally mean: e.g. one person saying to another on a miserable, rainy day, *"Lovely weather, isn't it?"*
litotes	Understatement by using negatives: i.e., *not bad,* meaning good.
longueur	A long and tedious section of a book or play.
metaphor	A figure of speech in which an image replaces the given word to imply a certain quality: *Mrs Kershaw's an absolute dream.*
metre	The rhythmic arrangement of syllables in a line of verse.
paean	A joyous hymn of thanksgiving or victory.
pleonasm	The use of redundant words.
precis	A precise, clear summary of the essentials of a text.
rhetoric	The art of using the language to please and persuade.
roman a clef	A novel whose characters and narrative represent actual people and real events, although usually disguised.
semantic	The concern with verbal meaning.
simile	A figure of speech that compares two essentially unlike things, usually after the words *as* or *like*: *He was as thick as a plank.*
sonnet	A lyric poem of 14 lines with a fixed rhyme of three quatrains and a closing couplet.
sophistry	Cleverly persuasive but fallacious reasoning.
split infinitive	When a word is inserted in an infinitive: *to [boldly] go.*
Sturm und Drang	Literally 'storm and stress' it usually denotes a literary style that employs turbulent emotions to excess.
syntax	The grammatical pattern of word arrangement in a language.

The terms *Shakespearean, Dickensian, Kafkaesque* and *Orwellian* are in fairly common use and most us know roughly the meanings intended: the allusions are to the style, subject matter, period or characters of those authors. Unfortunately such terms can be vague or ambiguous, especially when the work of the author referred to is extensive and varied. The word *Dickensian*, for example, can conjure up a host of images ranging from stark pictures of Victorian working-class misery to merry scenes of feasting around a roaring fireside; from rotund, comical eccentrics to coarse and brutal characters such as Bill Sykes. The allusion could be to Dickens's sometimes turgid plots, or merely to mid-19th century England. How are we to know?

Here are some more that are far from uncommon in general reading:

Brechtian, Byronic, Carrollian, Chaucerian, Chekhovian, Churchillian, Dantesque, Flaubertian, Homeric, Jamesean, Joycean, Proustian, Rabelaisian, Runyonesque, Shavian, Swiftian, Thurberesque, Trollopian, Wildean, Zolaesque.

And, of course, *Johnsonian* : Typical of or resembling the thought, writing, or generally lofty, authoritative opinionising of Samuel Johnson; showing good common sense and elevated diction; or derogatorily pontifical and given to pompous, Latinate phraseology. (David Grambs: *Literary Companion Dictionary,* 1985)

Select the Correct Usage

For each word there are two examples of usage: one in which the word is used in its correct sense, and one in which it is not. Obviously the example of incorrect usage will make no sense at all. Try to select, in each case, the example of correct usage. Circle or mark your choice, *a* or *b*, and then check the answers on page 223.

qualm	**a.** Miranda sailed in and, without a *qualm*, commanded the dogs to be quiet. **b.** John grew more restless as evening approached, and the eerie *qualm*, which usually presaged a violent storm, was almost palpable.
quandary	**a.** With the majority unexpectedly voting against him, Councillor Evans found himself in a *quandary*. **b.** Guy was always confused between the one-humped *quandary* and the two-humped Bactrian camel.
quango	**a.** Sir Edward seemed always to be running from one *quango* meeting to another. **b.** Although it has to air-freighted from the Pacific, the *quango* has become a popular delicacy in Britain.
quantum	**a.** She decided that perhaps half a *quantum* would be better than none. **b.** There wasn't a *quantum* of evidence to support the case against him.
quasar	**a.** It wasn't until 1963 that the rare *quasar* jelly was extracted from the queen bee's honey. **b.** One *quasar* has been detected up to 10 billion light years away from earth.

querulous	**a.** The matron was fed up with her patient's *querulous* attitude. **b.** The teacher was delighted with Anne's *querulous* approach to difficult problems.
quiddity	**a.** They were both amused and appalled by the poor man's *quiddity*. **b.** The *quiddity* of a pun is its wit.
quidnunc	**a.** His snobbishness, vanity and *quidnunc* passion for uniforms was well known. **b.** Being a hairdresser and thus the confidante of several dozen women, Mrs Mount was in the ideal situation to hone her talents as the village *quidnunc*.
quiescent	**a.** The volcano last erupted in 1878 and was now *quiescent*. **b.** The doctor said that Bill would recover; his heartbeat was now steady and *quiescent*.
quietus	**a.** The bell tolled its long and lonely *quietus*. **b.** The coup d'état celebrations were short-lived, silenced by the inevitable, even bloodier, *quietus*.
quintessence	**a.** Jason thought himself to be the *quintessence* of the modern male. **b.** Lingering in the air was that faint *quintessence* typical of early apple blossom.
quisling	**a.** The man was completely unaware that his grovelling, *quisling* manner made him an object of derision. **b.** The suspicion never died that Mr Bender was some sort of *quisling* during the war.
quixotic	**a.** Albert's face reddened with *quixotic* anger. **b.** He lived rough in the country most of the time, trying to stop bypasses and motorway extensions in his usual *quixotic* style.
quoin	**a.** He pointed to the huge *quoin* and claimed to have laid it when he was working on the building fifty years ago. **b.** The machine counted the sheets and stacked them in *quoins* of twenty-five.
quondam	**a.** In exchange for the pawned rings he received a *quondam* note as a receipt. **b.** The horse cantered up to us and nuzzled its *quondam* owner.
quorum	**a.** The conductor surveyed the orchestra and the enormous *quorum* of singers. **b.** Satisfied that a *quorum* was present, the chairman announced the start of the meeting.
quotidian	**a.** The neighbours were maddened by the *quotidian* uproar from the boarding house. **b.** Jules was a polished *quotidian* from Milton to Wordsworth.

Of the seventeen '*q*' words offered here, how many were strange to you? Or, more to the point, how many – from your knowledge and experience – were you able to immediately confirm were being used correctly? Check the answers on page 223 and also your dictionary to . make sure you have this tiny '*q*' section well buttoned-up in your vocabulary.

Quickpick: Questions! Questions!

What's that, Mummy? Dad – what's that thing called? Most children's requests for the names of things are easily satisfied, but occasionally they catch us out. What, for example, do you say to a child who asks:

1. What's that fringed bit of paper wrapped around the end of the cutlets?

2. When you went and had your gold ring valued, what was that magnifying thing the jeweller wore on his eye?

3. What's the place called where they keep and breed cats?

4. When they cut hedges into all those funny shapes, what's it called?

5. What are those little holes called that separate postage stamps?

6. When you go upstairs you step on the treads, but what are the upright bits called that keep the treads apart?

7. In that Western film the cowboy kept spitting tobacco into a sort of bowl on the floor. What's it called?

8. What's that great big marble basin in the church they use for baptising babies?

9. What's that little bit of plastic called that they use to strum a guitar or a banjo?

10. What do you call that long thing with a handle that you rub your knives up and down on to sharpen them?

Well, how many times would you have been able to answer these classic ankle-biter questions? Answers on page 223.

Qantas, Qintar and other U-less Q-words

Lurking outside the selection of words listed under Q in most dictionaries is an exclusive and exotic tribe of words beginning with *'q'* – but without the customary following *'u'*. **Qantas** (it's not so much a word as an acronym formed from the original company (Queensland And Northern Territory Air Services), **qintar** (Albanian currency unit, 100 to a lek) and **qwerty** (the standard typewriter keyboard layout) aside, it's debatable whether these are acceptable as English words or simply just foreign words. Addicts of the game *Scrabble* welcome them; dictionary makers generally refuse admission. Here are a few for the record:

qabbala	Secret and mystical versions of the scriptures.
qawwali	An Islamic religious song.
qadi	A Muslim judge of religious law.
qaf	A letter in the Arabic alphabet.
qaid	A Muslim official.
qantar	A unit of weight.
qat	A narcotic Arabian shrub.
qazaq	A brightly-coloured Caucasian woollen rug.
qiblah	The direction Muslims turn to during ritual prayer.
qinah	A traditional Hebrew elegy.
qiviut	Wool from the undercoat of the Arctic musk ox.
qobar	A dry fog affecting the upper Nile.
qoph	The nineteenth letter of the Hebrew alphabet.
qvint	A Danish measurement of weight.

R

Pop the Word in Place

Below are ten words and ten sentences with holes in them. Simply pop each of the words in the appropriate hole so that all the sentences make sense. Each word is used once only. The answers are on page 223.

> *Rabelaisian   raconteur   raffish   raillery   raison d'étre*
> *rapprochement rancour   rapport   rara avis   ratiocination*

1. Never able to forgive, the resentful old colonel was still full of _____ towards his former superiors.

2. Lucas was that _____, a farmer who genuinely loved all animals, both his own and all the wild creatures too.

3. Their boisterous and ribald sessions at the pub took on an even more _____ flavour as closing time approached.

4. After a decade of hostility, Britain and Iran were keen to seek a _____ .

5. Most of his listeners would agree that forty years of mixing with the rich and famous had a lot to do with Philip's urbane skills as a _____ .

6. The _____ for the impromptu party was Fiona's engagement.

7. Although Mr Bennett took his time, his partners appreciated that his unflappable _____ invariably resulted in the right solution.

8. Along with his knowledge of antiques, Basil had the kind of
_____ manner and appearance that seems to make a successful
dealer.

9. Dressed in that outrageously sexy gear it was little wonder that June
attracted a good deal of _____ from the backstage staff.

10. A lot of their success as a comedy act was due to the long-established
_____ between the two men.

Despite a couple of head-scratchers in that batch, a little thought
should have resulted in a score of at least seven correct. Eight would be
good and the perfect score of ten, of course, excellent!

Complete the Words

From the meanings given, supply the missing letters to complete
the words. The answers are on page 223.

1. It sounded harsh and hoarse and loud.   *r _ _ cous*

2. He was hostile to change and progress.   *react _ _ nary*

3. The whole atmosphere of the place was repellent
   and forbidding.   *re _ arbative*

4. The old horse proved to be stubborn and
   uncontrollable.   *recalci _ rant*

5. She decided to publicly retract her former
   opinions.   *rec _ _ t*

6. To make sure they all understood, he decided
   to restate the main points of his argument.   *re _ _ _ itulate*

7. She was always searching for the rare, strange
   and exquisite.   *re _ herché*

8. His habitual relapse into criminal behaviour
   was not unexpected.   *recidiv _ sm*

9. Having won, she was the delighted owner of a
   new fridge.   *re _ ipient*

10. In return for their help they decided to give
    their neighbours a party.   *recip _ _ cate*

11. The two families were always at war, with a constant barrage of charge and counter-charge and mutual accusations. *recrim _ _ ation*

12.1Professor Home's speciality was obscure and profound philosophies. *rec _ _ dite*

13. After nearly a year the dreadful disease broke out afresh. *recru _ escent*

14. Mr and Mrs Jones were models of moral integrity. *rectit _ _ e*

15. The vandalism occurred repeatedly, on an almost regular basis. *recu _ _ ent*

16. The house smelled of something that stirred her memory. *red _ lent*

17. He was still a formidable figure, commanding respect. *redou _ table*

18. They decided to invite the electorate to vote on the issue. *ref _ _ endum*

19. As a child he was always obstinate and unmanageable. *refra _ tory*

20. In the clear sky the stars were radiant and shining brightly. *reful _ ent*

21. With the fresh evidence he was able to prove that all the charges against him were false. *ref _ _ e*

22. The doctor decided to put him on a new course of treatment. *reg _ men*

23. The man was repeating it over and over again. *re _ _ erate*

24. It was obvious he was negligent and lacked attention to duty. *remi _ s*

25. She went outside to object strongly about their noisy behaviour. *remon _ trate*

26. Although he liked the job, the pay was poor. *remun _ _ ation*

27. The lovers agreed to meet at a certain place. *rende _ vous*

28. Should he go back on his promise? *ren _ ge*

29. After the bombing he sought compensation for the damage. *re _ _ ration*

159

AFTER A FEW DRINKS . . .

30. After a few drinks he was a master of the
sharp and witty response. *repart _ _*

There was surely nothing too *recondite* or *recherché* in that round,
so a score of 25 correct would be a reasonable effort. But in any case
consult your dictionary for the meanings of any of the words that tripped
you up.

Choose the Correct Usage

Which one of the two alternatives, *a* or *b*, most accurately
expresses the usage of the word? Circle or mark your choices (a reminder:
don't count 'correct' wild guesses!) and then check the answers on page
223.

repertoire   **a.** Bill's *repertoire* of jokes was getting a bit thin. **b.** Lucy
enjoyed an enviable *repertoire* with her two sisters.

replicate   **a.** The judge decided to *replicate* the publican and
withdraw his licence. **b.** The professor decided to
replicate the experiment to make sure the initial findings
were correct.

reprehensible **a.** Mandy found it difficult to overcome her *reprehensible* feelings towards George. **b.** Larry's awful behaviour towards his parents was utterly *reprehensible*.

reprobate **a.** Uncle's will was the subject of a *reprobate* for the third time. **b.** Archie was a confirmed *reprobate* for whom there was little sympathy among his few exasperated friends.

repudiate **a.** The breakaway group threatened to *repudiate* the latest agreement with the council. **b.** The court agreed to *repudiate* the prisoner on compassionate grounds.

repugnant **a.** The patient's breathing was becoming *repugnant* to a dangerous degree. **b.** Although driven by her Christian principles, Marcia found her work at the old men's home undeniably *repugnant*.

rescind **a.** The board agreed to *rescind* the total ban on smoking. **b.** After the fire they sifted through the *rescind* for anything of value.

resonant **a.** When he tapped the gourd the *resonant* sound indicated it was empty. **b.** The hive was *resonant* with honey, and in minutes he was up to his elbows in it.

respite **a.** The old lady was full of bitter *respite* and accusations. **b.** They fully deserved the unexpected but welcome *respite* from the searing heat.

resplendent **a.** The governor at last appeared, *resplendent* in his white uniform and plumed helmet. **b.** Harold was fearful that he would be cited as a *resplendent* in Lady Hatfield's divorce case.

resurgent **a.** Her father had signed up as a *resurgent* in the Spanish Civil War. **b.** After the war everyone looked forward to a *resurgent* nation with a fair deal and prosperity for all.

reticent **a.** Harvey was always *reticent*, so on the few occasions he did speak, everyone listened in surprise. **b.** Josephine was not *reticent* when it came to knowing the sleazy bars in the city.

retrench **a.** With an empty order book and a poor economic outlook ahead, the firm decided to *retrench*. **b.** The man was asked to *retrench* his allegations or face legal action.

retrograde **a.** We sped through the chicane and then down the steep *retrograde*, with the other car in pursuit. **b.** Motorists agreed that changing to the one-way system was a *retrograde* step.

retroussé   **a.** His smart suits and immaculate grooming were marks of his *retroussé* charm. **b.** With her wide blue eyes and pert, *retroussé* nose, Dawn had all the attributes of a natural model.

reverberate   **a.** The sound of the explosion continued to *reverberate* through the town. **b.** Although the attack was moderating, the man's limbs continued to *reverberate*.

reverie   **a.** Martha was accustomed to falling on her knees and reciting her *reverie* twelve times every day. **b.** Leonard was a dreamer and we would often find him lost in a *reverie*.

rhetorical   **a.** Trevor was fascinated by the *rhetorical* past and loved poking around in ruins. **b.** As a speechmaker, he was rather too *rhetorical*, and facts were few and far between.

rictus   **a.** The *rictus* that affected his legs was painful to see. **b.** After the shocking apparition he glanced around and saw the *rictus* on Ellen's horror-stricken face.

riparian   **a.** The country house came with nearly a mile of *riparian* rights and privileges. **b.** Joyce hated *riparian* creatures such as snakes and lizards.

riposte   **a.** The jockey sensed that he was in a *riposte* position and certain to win. **b.** The stand-up comedian responded to the jeering with a withering *riposte* that silenced the audience.

risible   **a.** His dramatic performances on stage were unintentionally *risible*, often causing an undercurrent of giggling. **b.** The skin of the porpoise has a smooth, slithery *risible* quality.

rococo   **a.** The disease that hit *rococo* plantations in the 1960s threatened chocolate production for nearly a decade. **b.** The interior was decorated in the elegant *rococo* style.

roué   **a.** For the sauce the chef first prepared a *roué* to which he added the stock and herbs. **b.** Although handsome in his youth Brendan today was a decrepit old *roué*.

rubicund   **a.** The gardener's *rubicund* face creased with amusement. **b.** Hilda's thoughts turned to *rubicund* musings, of former lovers and love's regrets.

rumbustious   **a.** The rugby team were undoubtedly a *rumbustious* lot. **b.** Larry closely searched the old musician's *rumbustious* features for some sign of appreciation.

ruminate   **a.** Jack went away to *ruminate* upon his defeat. **b.** The recipe called for the beef to *ruminate* in the wine sauce for several hours.

rusticate   **a.** The surface of the desk was subtly *rusticated*, a sure sign of many years of use. **b.** His parents decided to *rusticate* and began looking for a suitable property in Hampshire.

The point about usage exercises such as the above is that they make you think about the word, its meaning, and its application in the context of the sentence. But there is a problem with words whose meanings you simply don't know. In such cases, consult the answers on page 223 or, better still, look up the more complete meaning (or meanings) in your dictionary. Then refer back to the example of usage to see how the word is actually employed.

Respiratory Matters

As human activities go, drawing breath is a not unimportant function. Here are some terms relating to the body's respiratory system that you may find useful.

asbestosis	Inflammation of the lungs caused by breathing asbestos dust.
asphyxiation	Suffocation through lack of oxygen.
bronchitis	Inflammation of the bronchial tubes.
bronchoscopy	Examination of the bronchial tree using a flexible instrument.
catarrh	Increased production of mucus due to inflammation of the mucous membrane in the nose and throat.
cot death	As yet unexplained sudden infant death syndrome (SIDS).
cystic fibrosis	A genetic disease characterised by chronic infection of the respiratory tract, especially in young children.
emphysema	Enlargement and loss of elasticity of the lungs, resulting in breathlessness and wheezing.
epiglottis	The flap that covers the larynx during swallowing.
halitosis	Bad breath.
laryngitis	Inflammation of the larynx (vocal cords).

163

mumps	An acute viral disease of the parotid or salivary glands.
palate	The roof of the mouth, separating the oral and nasal cavities.
pharynx	The throat, from the mouth to the oesophagus.
pleurisy	Inflammation of the pleura (the lining of the outer lungs and inner chest cavity).
pneumoconiosis	Disease of the lungs caused by inhalation of mineral particles such as coal dust.
quinsy	Abscesses of the tonsils and surrounding tissues.
rhinoplasty	Plastic surgery of the nose.
scrofula	Tuberculosis of the lymphatic glands.
septum	The fleshy division between the two nostrils.
silicosis	Disease of the lungs caused by inhaling silica, slate, quartz dust.
sinuses	The cavities in bones near the nose.
trachea	The tube or windpipe that carries air from the larynx to the bronchi.

Quickpick: Spot the Misprints

Here's a quick DIY editing task: spot the misprint or mistake in each of these ten sentences, and enter your correction. The answers are on page 223.

Correction

1. The book included a racey account of Cyril's love affair. _____

2. The pupils were asked to resite the examination. _____

3. The workers were looking forward to the rum steak and chips. _____

4. The old boy lived alone and was a bit of a Ripe Van Winkle. _____

5. Unfortunately the carpet had to be relayed twice. _____

6. He was being prosecuted for refusing to pay his council rats. _____

7. He'd reached the rank of rare admiral before he retired. _____

8. She'd studied the fertility rights of many New Guinea tribes. _____

9. The pilot decided to use the alternative runaway. _____
10. The roll of Shylock in the play was taken by
    Mr Patten. _____

You probably twigged early on that the misprints began with an *'r'* – so
there's little excuse for scores of less than eight correct.

Three Word Elements: Re, Retro and Rupt

Word, Element	Origin	Meaning	English Words
re-	Latin	back, again	*return, renew, recall, re-do, reuse, refresh, remarry*
retro-	Latin	backwards	*retroactive, retrograde, retrospective, retrorocket*
rupt	Latin	break	*disrupt, interrupt, rupture, eruption, corrupt*

Revision: Q to R

Take a breather and spend a few minutes reviewing any of the *'q'*
and *'r'* words that were unfamiliar to you – and also words the meanings
of which you were a little hazy about. For example, can you, without too
much hesitation, mentally place the following words appropriately in
sentences?

querulous	*quiescent*	*rapprochement*	*rebarbative*	*redolent*
refute	*repudiate*	*retroussé*	*rhetorical*	*riposte*

The five minutes required to tuck these ten words securely away in
your expanding vocabulary is surely worth it.

Rare and Unusual Words

Here's a heartfelt letter from a reader to *The Sunday Times*:

*If you ask Martin Cropper to write another review for you, please
insist that he cleans up his act. On August 9 I had to delve into the*

dictionary three times, for **cyclothymic**, **melanophobe** *and* **lacustrine**. *Using the Shorter Oxford English Dictionary I found lacustrine and managed to construct melanophobe, but still seek cyclothymic. May I please have the definition? I, too, wish to show off.*

You have to sympathise. What protection does the average reader have from smarty-pants columnists and reviewers? Even a good dictionary can sometimes fail to protect readers from lexicographical humbug. In the case above, instead of *cyclothymic*, the reviewer might have used the standard medical term, *manic depression*, and we would have understood. *Lacustrine* relates to lakes, but *melanophobe*, meaning someone fearful of dark skin, is not to be found in most dictionaries.

Apart from showing off, is there any point in using words that the vast majority of people don't understand and, perhaps lacking a comprehensive and up-to-date dictionary, will never figure out? There is, of course, the occasional need for a rare or unusual word where no other exists to define aptly and accurately a particular meaning. But if the reader doesn't know the word and has difficulty discovering the meaning, then the usage is self-defeating.

Here is a selection of '*r*' words – rare but real words – you're unlikely ever to meet or use in your lifetime. Want to show off? Go right ahead.

rabiator	A violent person.
rantallion	A man whose scrotum is longer than his penis.
ratamacue	A drum roll of a certain pattern.
rebullition	Renewed bubbling or boiling on a liquid surface.
rectopathic	One who is easily hurt emotionally.
refocillation	Revitalisation, revival.
remontado	One who has fled or retired to the mountains.
rhadamanthine	Inflexibly, unbendingly just.
rhigosis	The sensation of cold.
rhonchisonant	Snoring.
rixatrix	A disagreeable old woman.
roral	Dewy, or pertaining to dew.
rounceval	Huge and strong.
rurigenous	Born in the country.

S

What's the Correct Meaning?

Which of the two choices, *a* or *b*, most accurately fits the definition of the word? Mark or circle your choices before checking the answers on page 224.

sacrilegious	**a.** taking something regarded as sacred for secular or inappropriate use. **b.** excessive deference to the church hierarchy.
sacrosanct	**a.** shaped like the head of an arrow. **b.** sacred and inviolable.
sagacious	**a.** circumspect and proper. **b.** wise and perceptive.
salacious	**a.** obscene and bawdy. **b.** obsessively jealous.
salient	**a.** highly conspicuous. **b.** favoured with a following wind.
salubrious	**a.** prone to catch infections easily. **b.** wholesome and favourable.
salutary	**a.** intending to have a beneficial effect. **b.** a well-earned rest.
sanctimonious	**a.** pretending to be generous but in actuality very mean. **b.** making a display of piety and purity.
sang-froid	**a.** composed and self-possessed. **b.** a haughty manner.
sanguine	**a.** gloomy and despondent. **b.** cheerful and optimistic.
sardonic	**a.** sneering and scornful. **b.** shy and retiring.

sartorial	**a.** relating to shooting stars and comets. **b.** relating to tailoring.
Sassenach	**a.** a primitive Scotsman, from an English point of view. **b.** an Englishman, from a Scots point of view.
saturnine	**a.** having a mane of black hair. **b.** having a gloomy temperament.
savoir-faire	**a.** extremely witty. **b.** having a fine sense of what's right and wrong socially.
scatology	**a.** having a great knowledge of trivia. **b.** an unhealthy interest in excrement.
sceptic	**a.** a cut or bruise that becomes infected. **b.** a person who habitually questions accepted beliefs.
schadenfreude	**a.** delight in another's misfortune. **b.** to remain calm in a heated argument.
schism	**a.** the division of a group into opposing factions. **b.** a fissure that threatens to deepen and become wider.
scintilla	**a.** a group of bright stars. **b.** a tiny, minute amount.
scion	**a.** a descendent, heir or young member of a family. **b.** a small, shallow-gabled porch.
scrupulous	**a.** obsessively clean. **b.** careful and precise.
scurrilous	**a.** obscenely abusive and defamatory. **b.** in a hurried manner.
sebaceous	**a.** prone to skin complaints. **b.** fatty and greasy.
secular	**a.** pertaining to sacred things. **b.** pertaining to worldly things.
sedentary	**a.** involving little or no exercise, such as sitting about. **b.** involving work that requires extreme concentration.
sedulous	**a.** assiduous and diligent. **b.** casual and uncaring.
semantics	**a.** concerned with the sounds of words. **b.** concerned with the meanings of words.
semiotics	**a.** the study of signs and symbols in communications; **b.** the study of American Indian languages.
senescent	**a.** becoming young again. **b.** growing old.

If after checking the answers on page 224 you find that you failed to identify the correct meanings of some of the words, you'll find it worthwhile to revisit those that caused you to stumble and to commit their meanings to memory. If you scored 25 or more correct you did very well.

Words into Spaces

Below, twelve words and twelve incomplete sentences.Each of the sentences has a space for a missing word. Which word goes into which space? Take your time and with a little thought a perfect score should be possible. Each word is used only once. The answers are on page 000.

sententious	*sequestered*	*serendipitous*	*serpentine*
serrated	*servile*	*shibboleth*	*sibilant*
sidereal	*simian*	*similitude*	*simulacrum*

1. With his long arms and grossly hairy chest the man looked positively
    _____.

2. Archie looked the man over and decided there was a certain
    _____ that reminded him of an old school friend – and who
    turned out to be his twin.

3. Judith had always been fascinated by astrology and the stars and her
    _____ interests eventually led to a lucrative newspaper column.

4. He thought the philosopher's lectures, loaded with aphorisms, sound
    bites and moralising, were just a lot of _____ nonsense.

5. The road wound its _____ way around the sides of the
    canyon.

6. Colin declined to join the society, saying that the members could keep
    its ridiculous and secret _____ to themselves.

7. The old couple were quite content with their quiet and
    _____ life.

8. After nearly half a century as a butler to the household it was
    understandable that Mr Nobbs' demeanour was _____ and
    unassertive.

9. The _____ edge of the knife cut deeply into the assailant's bare
    arm.

10. Linda's _____ discovery of the kind and helpful Bailey
    family undoubtedly changed her life.

11. The ghostly image that began to emerge from the gloom was a
    _____ of his grandmother.

12. The gap between Bernard's two front teeth gave his speech a
    pronounced _____ sound that put paid to his disc jockey
    ambitions.

Some tough ones in that lot, admittedly, so a score of nine or more correct would be quite an achievement. Words beginning with 's' are prolific in the English language, so prepare yourself for another extended round of 'Choose the Meaning'.

Choose the Correct Meaning

As before, choose one of the alternatives, *a* or *b*, that most accurately fits the meaning of the word. Wild stabs that turn out to be correct shouldn't score, so try not to guess. Mark or circle your choices before checking the answers on page 224.

sinecure   **a.** a cushy, well-paid and secure job. **b.** the inability to bend an arm at the elbow.

sinistral   **a.** a hot wind that blows off the Mediterranean. **b.** left-handed.

Sisyphean   **a.** someone who will attempt anything regardless of the consequences. **b.** an activity or task that is endless and futile.

skulk   **a.** to lurk unseen with wrongdoing in mind. **b.** to run away from trouble.

slander   **a.** false or defamatory words spoken about somebody. **b.** false or defamatory words written about somebody.

sobriety   **a.** the state of drunkenness. **b.** the state of being sober.

sobriquet   **a.** flowers presented to a singer after a performance. **b.** a humorous epithet or nickname.

sodality   **a.** malicious scheming. **b.** fellowship and fraternity.

soi-disant   **a.** a devil-may-care attitude. **b.** so-called or self-styled.

soignée   **a.** an elegantly groomed woman. **b.** a jewelled clasp for the hair.

soirée   **a.** an evening of conversation and music. **b.** a gathering of female friends.

solecism   **a.** a recorded sun-spot. **b.** a grammatical or social mistake.

solicitous   **a.** excessive use of legal means to achieve one's ends. **b.** showing concern and consideration.

soliloquy   **a.** a speech made to oneself. **b.** a poem full of musings.

solipsism   **a.** the denial of the possibility of all knowledge except that of one's own existence. **b.** an unforgivable social gaffe.

sommelier	**a.** a brandy warehouse. **b.** a wine waiter.
somnambulism	**a.** communicating with the spirit world. **b.** sleep-walking.
somnolent	**a.** in a depressive mood. **b.** feeling drowsy and sleepy.
sonorous	**a.** giving out a full, rich sound. **b.** a person with a knowledge of the Spanish and Portuguese languages.
sophistry	**a.** the use of fallacious and deceptive argument to win a point. **b.** having a preference for one's own sex.
soporific	**a.** unpleasantly oily. **b.** sleep-inducing.
sotto voce	**a.** slightly inebriated. **b.** in an undertone.
soupçon	**a.** the lowliest, poorest-paid employee in a restaurant kitchen. **b.** a tiny amount.
spasmodic	**a.** happening at sudden and brief intervals. **b.** any drug or preparation that induces vomiting.
spatial	**a.** existing or happening in space. **b.** exhausted.
spavined	**a.** worn out and broken down. **b.** split in two.
specious	**a.** undersized. **b.** seemingly true and correct but actually false and wrong.
splenetic	**a.** a tendency to be constantly ill. **b.** spiteful and bad-tempered.
spoonerism	**a.** the wrong placement of cutlery on a formal dining table. **b.** the inadvertent transposition of consonants or words often resulting in confusion and ambiguity, sometimes with comical results.
sporadic	**a.** at regular intervals. **b.** occurring intermittently or irregularly.
spurious	**a.** not genuine or real. **b.** a freshly broken or trained horse.
staccato	**a.** abrupt and clipped. **b.** a long kettle-drum roll or solo.
stasis	**a.** in a static or stagnant state. **b.** an irregular heartbeat.
statutory	**a.** held down by force. **b.** authorised by legislation.
stentorian	**a.** an excessively strict teacher. **b.** uncommonly loud.
stigmatise	**a.** to identify as bad or to be avoided. **b.** to cross-fertilise plants.
stoical	**a.** resigned to bearing problems and pain. **b.** rejecting pleasures of the flesh.

stolid	**a.** massively built. **b.** showing little emotion or interest.
stringent	**a.** highly aromatic and stinging. **b.** requiring strict attention to rules and detail.
stultify	**a.** to make useless or ineffectual. **b.** to check growth.
Stygian	**a.** bottomless depths. **b.** dark and gloomy.
subjugate	**a.** to make subservient or submissive. **b.** to divide equally.
sublimate	**a.** to drift into very deep sleep. **b.** to refine and make pure.
subliminal	**a.** a brief or subtle stimulus of which the individual is unaware. **b.** so deeply buried in the unconscious as to be irretrievable.
subservient	**a.** deferential and submissive. **b.** in any series, the second number, place or position.
substantiate	**a.** to be bold. **b.** to establish as valid or genuine.
subsume	**a.** to incorporate or absorb into. **b.** to reduce or diminish.
subterfuge	**a.** a major underground tunnel for conveying water supplies. **b.** a stratagem designed to conceal or evade.
succinct	**a.** easily dissolved. **b.** sharp and concise.
supercilious	**a.** extremely superficial. **b.** arrogant and indifferent.
superfluity	**a.** an oversupply or excess of what is needed. **b.** an officious and superior manner.
supernumerary	**a.** any number greater than a billion. **b.** a person or something that exceeds normal requirements.
supplant	**a.** to take the place of. **b.** an alternative or emergency supply.
suppurate	**a.** to vibrate. **b.** to fester.
surrogate	**a.** a person appointed as a substitute for another. **b.** a person wholly dependent upon charity or public funds.

Sisyphean? Spoonerism? Stygian? Surely these shouldn't be expected to be in an average vocabulary? But the record shows that these unlikely words occur in print with surprising regularity, no doubt intriguing or irritating a few million 'average' readers. So perhaps, after all, there's a good case for knowing what they mean.

Sisyphean is an old word now in vogue: an example from *The Times*: "The painters who undertook the sisyphean work on the mile-long Forth rail bridge will down brushes for a year because of spending cuts by ScotRail." It derives from Greek mythology and the story of King Sisyphus who was punished in Hades by having to roll an enormous boulder eternally up a hill. As it neared the top the boulder was always fated to roll down again. Is there another word in the language that combines the definitions of an endless task and utter futility? Search and ye may find. Or not.

Spoonerism derives from a real person, the Rev William Archibald Spooner, one-time warden of New College, Oxford. Dr Spooner suffered from the rare condition of *metathesis,* or the inadvertent transposition of sounds. Thus, intending to say "Is the Dean busy?" he would say, "Is the bean dizzy?"; or "Three cheers for the queer old Dean" instead of the intended "Three cheers for the dear old Queen". Anyone can utter these mirthful slips of the tongue, or spoonerisms, and there doesn't seem to be another word that so engagingly describes them.

Stygian, like *Sisyphean*, also derives from Greek mythology – in this case the infamous Underworld River Styx whose water killed everybody who drank it and corroded any vessel that tried to contain it. **Stygian**, therefore, means dark and hateful and hellish – and words don't come with meanings much more frightening than that!

But notwithstanding this curious trio, a score of 30 correct would be commendable.

Words in Use: Right or Wrong?

Here are ten sentences, each containing a highlighted word. In some sentences the words are used correctly and appropriately, but in others they are not and the resulting sentences make no sense at all. Can you identify correct and incorrect usage? In each case make your choice by marking **Right** or **Wrong**. The answers are on page 224.

	Right	Wrong
1. By **surreptitious** means the landlord had managed to prove that the family had broken their lease agreement.	____	____
2. Ravishingly **svelte**, Priscilla showed off the designer ball gown to perfection.	____	____
3. Mr Marlar was a reputed worshipper of Satan and other dark **sybaritic** cults.	____	____
4. The lawyer was so **sycophantic**, constantly niggling over relatively unimportant details.	____	____

5. From the argument that mice are just small rats, and that all rats are pests, David produced the *syllogism* that all mice are pests.   ____ ____

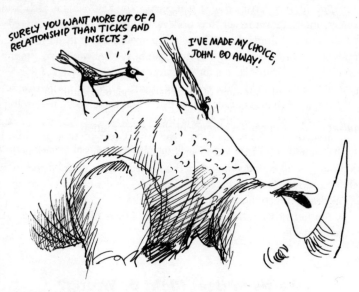

6. They concluded that the small bird, by cleansing the rhino of ticks and other insects, had a *symbiotic* relationship with its host.   ____ ____

7. The *synchronous* material allowed the fluid to permeate through it and to be completely absorbed.   ____ ____

8. The directors felt that the merger would result in productive *synergies* and enhanced profitability.   ____ ____

9. Hugh might have been a competent writer had he had a better understanding of *syntax* and the importance of correct spelling.   ____ ____

10. Thinking it might be poisonous the doctor decided to ask the laboratory to *synthesise* the substance in the bottle.   ____ ____

A rather tricky lot, so if after checking the answers on page 224 you managed a score of seven or more correct choices, you can feel reasonably pleased with your effort.

Skinny Dipping

Skin: our outer covering, our hide, our epidermis, and the source of a lot of associated words. Skin also figures largely in our idiomatic speech: *thin-skinned; thick-skinned; skin deep; skinflint; by the skin of my teeth; he gets under my skin; skinned alive; it's no skin off my nose; I nearly jumped out of my skin* . . and so on.

But idioms apart, here are some useful words relating to our skin.

acne	Inflammation of the sebaceous glands, common in adolescence.
albinism	Congenital absence of skin pigmentation.
carbuncle	Staphylococcal infection causing deep and extensive skin eruption.
carcinoma	A malignant tumour of the skin tissues.
cellulite	Subcutaneous fat supposed to resist dieting.
chilblains	Inflammation of the extremities caused by damp and cold.
cuticle	Dead skin around the base of fingernails and toenails.
dermatitis	General reddening or inflammation of the skin.
eczema	Scaly or crusty skin inflammation, often causing itching.
follicles	Small sacs in or below the skin which have excretory, secretory or protective functions.
haemangioma	Non-malignant tumour of blood vessels in the skin, often known as 'strawberry mark' and 'port wine stain'.
hangnail	Partly detached skin at the side of a nail.
impetigo	Contagious bacterial skin disease developing into pustules.
keritosis	Any skin condition marked by a horny growth, such as a wart.
liver spots	Brown spots on the skin due to age and sun.
lunula	The white crescent-shaped area at the base of the fingernails.
melanoma	A malignant tumour occurring in the skin, usually as a result of excessive exposure to sunlight.

175

mole	[naevus] A congenital growth or pigmented blemish on the skin.
pruritis	Intense itching of the skin.
psoriasis	A skin disease characterised by reddish spots and patches covered with silvery scales.
scabies	A contagious and itchy skin infection caused by a mite.
sebaceous glands	Small oil glands that lubricate the skin and hair follicles.
subcutaneous	Situated under the skin.
tinea	[ringworm] A fungal skin infection that shows up as itchy circular patches.
urticaria	[hives; nettle rash] An allergic skin condition characterised by raised red or white patches.
verruca	[wart] An abnormal elevation of the skin caused by a virus.

30-Sec Quickpick: Complete the Simile

A simile is, as you know (page 224), a figure of speech that compares two dissimilar entities, usually linked by *as* or *like*: *He was as tough as nails*. Here are ten potential similes, the missing elements of which you should be able to instantly supply. Have a go, anyway. Answers on page 000.

1. As cool as a _____.
2. As bright as a _____.
3. As dry as a _____.
4. As sick as a _____.
5. As white as a _____.
6. As quiet as a _____.
7. As sober as a _____.
8. s proud as a _____.
9. As red as a _____.
10. As dull as _____.

Word Elements: Script to Syn

Once again, a glance at some ancient word elements that can often help to identify the meanings of words.

Word, Element	Origin	Meaning	English Words
script, scrib	Latin	to write	inscription, scripture, postscript, description
se-, separare	Latin	apart	separate, segregate, secede, select
sect	Latin	cut	intersect, section, sector, sectile, vasectomy
sed	Latin	seat,	situated sediment, sedate resident, sedentary, sedan chair
sequ, secut	Latin	to follow	sequence, consecutive, sequel, consequence
soph	Greek	wise	sophistry, sophisticated, sophomore, philosophy
spec	Latin	look	spectacle, spectrum, spectre, spectator, conspicuous
-some	Old English	tendency	awesome, wholesome
sub-	Latin	under, beneath	subterranean, subordinate, submarine, sub-editor
super-	Latin	above, over	supervisor, superior, superman, supermarket
syn-	Greek	with, together	synchronise, synagogue, syndicate, synchromesh

A Little Light Revision

Yes, it may be tiresome, but periodical revision does help you to remember. What's the point of filing useful and interesting words in your vocabulary if you can't, or only vaguely, remember the meanings? So cast your eyes – and memory – over this selection of 's' words.

sanctimonious	*sanguine*	*savoir-faire*	*sequestered*
sinecure	*soi-disant*	*solecism*	*stoical*
stultify	*subsume*	*surrogate*	*sacrosanct*

Sloshed, Shickered and Squiffy

After what must have been a marinated marathon, the American wordsmith Paul Dickson came up with 2,231 words, phrases and expressions for intoxication. Here are just a few of them.

aced	*aglow*	*banjaxed*	*besotted*	*bibulous*
blasted	*blimped*	*blitzed*	*blotto*	*bombed*
bunnied	*cockeyed*	*corked*	*crapulous*	*crocked*
ebriose	*elephant's*	*embalmed*	*floored*	*flummoxed*
fogmatic	*frazzled*	*ga-ga*	*gone*	*half-sprung*
high	*juiced*	*lathered*	*it-up*	*lushed*
motherless	*petrified*	*non compos*	*obfuscated*	*ossified*
out to lunch	*overloaded*	*owl-eyed*	*pie-eyed*	*plastered*
roostered	*sauced*	*soused*	*chnoggered*	*shellacked*
shickered	*shit-faced*	*smashed*	*tight*	*tipsy*
tired and emotional		*totalled*	*varnished*	*zippered*

T

Complete the Word

Here's a round of 30 words. Each word is incomplete, with one or more letters missing. Your task is to fill in the missing letters to complete the words. To help you, the meaning of each word is given. Answers on page 225.

1. An instrument, often seen in cars, that measures
   speed of rotation   *ta _ _ ometer*

2. Something indirectly expressed: implied or
   inferred   *tac _ t*

3. Habitually silent and uncommunicative   *tacitu _ n*

4. Relating to the sense of touch   *t _ ctile*

5. A small object believed to protect the wearer
   from evil   *ta _ isman*

6. Something real, capable of being seen and
   touched   *tan _ ibl _*

7. As good as, or equivalent in effect   *tantam _ _ nt*

8. A brownish-grey colour   *ta _ pe*

9. Using words that unnecessarily repeat a
   meaning already conveyed   *tautolog _ _ al*

10. Moving things without touching them, as
    though through willpower   *te _ ekinesis*

11. Rashness or boldness   *temer _ ty*

12. Relating to earthly rather than spiritual or religious affairs · *tempora _*

13. To delay in order to gain time or arrive at a compromise · *temp _ rise*

14. Showing an intentional bias · *tendent _ ous*

15. A belief, dogma or opinion · *te _ et*

16. Something insignificant, flimsy or delicate · *ten _ ous*

17. A 300th anniversary · *te _ centenary*

18. Relating to the earth, as opposed to the sea and air · *te _ _ estrial*

19. There's primary, then secondary, and then . . . · *tert _ ary*

20. Paved or inlaid with a mosaic of small tiles · *te _ sellated*

21. Any person who makes a will · *testa _ or*

22. A steroid hormone secreted in the male · *testestestost _ _ one*

23. A private conversation between two people · *téte-à-t_ _ e*

24. The belief in one God as creator of the universe · *the _ sm*

25. Relating to maintaining health and the treatment of disease · *the _ apeutic*

26. Relating to drama, the theatre, and to actors · *thesp _ _ n*

27. Being subjected to the power and control of another person · *thra _ l*

28. Fearful and timid · *timor _ _ s*

29. A ringing, hissing or booming sensation in the ears · *ti _ _ itus*

30. An alarm or warning signal, especially the ringing of a bell · *to _ sin*

Not too difficult, was it? Therefore a score of 25 or more correct should be expected. Make sure you double-check the meanings of the words that tripped you.

Choose the Correct Meaning?

Another round of '*t*' words. This time each word has three definitions, only one of which is correct. Choose the one optional from **a**, **b**, or **c**, which you think is the correct meaning.

torpid	**a.** apathetic and sluggish. **b.** uncomfortably warm. **c.** slithery.
tort	**a.** a junior judge. **b.** a civil wrong or injury, liable for a claim for damages. **c.** the laws regarding criminal offences.
tortuous	**a.** causing physical and mental agony. **b.** twisted and winding. **c.** writhing and wriggling.
touché	**a.** the acknowledgement of a witty response. **b.** a challenge. **c.** a gentle warning of a problem ahead.
tractable	**a.** something easily traced. **b.** something easily swallowed. **c.** docile and easily controlled.
traduce	**a.** to defame someone. **b.** to pursue the favours of an older woman. **c.** to subtly persuade.
tranche	**a.** a French government bond. **b.** a portion or instalment of something, usually money. **c.** divided into three parts.
transcend	**a.** to gradually disappear. **b.** to rise above or go beyond a limit. **c.** to travel across difficult territory.
transient	**a.** speedy. **b.** fleeting or temporary. **c.** a lover of travelling.
translucent	**a.** semi-transparent. **b.** having the appearance of opal. **c.** dull.
traumatic	**a.** the effects of a shock or injury. **b.** lapsing into unconsciousness. **c.** loss of memory or absentmindedness.
travail	**a.** uncomfortable travelling. **b.** painful toil or exertion. **c.** the sound of wailing at a funeral.
travesty	**a.** a ceiling-to-floor wall hanging. **b.** a farcical imitation or parody. **c.** a deep disappointment.
tremulous	**a.** lisping. **b.** singing in a low register. **c.** trembling, wavering.
trenchant	**a.** forceful and incisive. **b.** eating with greedy gusto. **c.** living underground.
trepidation	**a.** the magical art of suspending a person without support. **b.** rapidly vibrating. **c.** a state of fear or anxiety.
trichology	**a.** the study of shells. **b.** the study of combustible matter. **c.** the study of hair.
tridactyl	**a.** having a long tail. **b.** having three fingers or toes. **c.** having armoured scales.
triptych	**a.** a painting on three panels. **b.** a religious sculpture, especially of the Madonna. **c.** a three-handled vase or urn.

triumvirate	**a.** a gathering of cardinals. **b.** joint rule or the sharing of power by three individuals. **c.** an 18th century three-cornered hat.
troglodyte	**a.** a dwarfish gargoyle. **b.** a large toad. **c.** a cave dweller.
trompe l'oeil	**a.** lavender bath oil. **b.** a painting that portrays a convincing illusion of reality. **c.** a resounding victory.
trope	**a.** a figure of speech. **b.** a malarial infection. **c.** a woman's pith helmet worn in Africa.
truculent	**a.** someone who prefers to be last rather than first. **b.** defiantly sullen and aggressive. **c.** rowdy and attention-seeking.
truism	**a.** a falsehood masquerading as truth. **b.** an obvious truth. **c.** a proverb the truth of which is in doubt.
truncate	**a.** to cut off or shorten. **b.** to divide into many parts. **c.** to reduce by more than half.
tsunami	**a.** an assortment of Japanese raw fish delicacies. **b.** the sash worn by geishas in Japan. **c.** huge, destructive sea waves produced by earthquakes or volcanic eruptions.
tumescent	**a.** decaying. **b.** gently dozing. **c.** becoming swollen.
turbid	**a.** muddy or clouded. **b.** distended. **c.** sexually aroused.
turgid	**a.** red-faced. **b.** swollen and congested. **c.** over-active.
turpitude	**a.** inherent depravity. **b.** moral uprightness. **c.** admirable strength of character.
tyrannise	**a.** a process to protect timber from rotting. **b.** to rule in a cruel or oppressive way. **c.** to habitually steal.
tyro	**a.** a notorious seducer. **b.** a lazy good-for-nothing. **c.** a novice or beginner.

A score of 25 or less for this round (answers on page 225) would indicate the need for some serious revision. If you scored 30 or more you can relax a little – but don't relapse into complacency!

Treatments, Tests and Therapies

We can all be thankful that treatments such as bleeding went out of fashion a couple of centuries ago, but beware – cupping and leeches are making a comeback! Here are some medical treatments, tests, tools and therapies that are very much part of our lives today – terms that you may find useful to know.

acupressure	See *shiatsu*.
acupuncture	Insertion of needles into the skin at specific points, stimulating nerve impulses to treat various disorders.
Alexander technique	Relaxation via improved posture and movement.
anaesthesia	Inducing a local or general loss of body sensation.
anthroposophy	Rudolph Steiner's spiritual philosophy of the therapeutic and educational value of certain creative activities.
antibiotics	Drugs capable of destroying or inhibiting growth of bacteria.
aromatherapy	Massaging the skin with aromatic oils to relieve tension.
ayurveda	Ancient Hindu healing techniques involving diet, herbs, yoga, breathing exercises and massage.
biofeedback	Control of certain body functions including breathing and heartbeat.
biopsy	Microscopic examination of tissue to determine nature and extent of a disease.
CATscan	[Computerised Axial Tomography] X-ray technique that produces cross-sectional images of body organs.
cauterisation	Treating wound tissue with heat or caustic agents.
chavutti massage	Indian technique of massage and body movements to maximise the strength and power.
chemotherapy	The treatment of disease, especially cancer, with combinations of toxic drugs.
chiropody	Medical treatment of the feet.
chiropractic	Treatment of bodily disorders by manipulation of the spine and other areas of the body.
endoscopy	Examination of internal organs through a hollow flexible tube.
forensic medicine	Medical evidence for legal proceedings.
holistic medicine	The consideration of the complete person, physically and psychologically, rather than treatment of specific organs or symptoms.
homeopathy	Treatment with minute amounts of a substance that in healthy people would produce symptoms similar to those of the disease.
hydrotherapy	Exercising in water to treat joint and muscular complaints.
hypnotherapy	The use of hypnotism to treat emotional and stress problems.

macrobiotics	Dietary system in which foods are classified according to the principles of Yin and Yang.
naturopathy	Treating disorders with herbs, organic foods, sunlight and fresh air.
NMR	[nuclear magnetic resonance] The use of a magnetic field and high frequency radiation to produce images of body organs.
osteopathy	Treatment of disorders with massage and bone manipulation.
paediatrics	Treatment of children and childhood diseases.
periodontics	Treatment of gums and tissues that surround the teeth.
physiotherapy	Therapeutic use of heat, massage and manipulation to treat disease or injury.
prosthetics	The branch of surgery concerned with replacement of body parts with artificial substitutes.
radiotherapy	Treatment of disease, especially cancer, with high-energy radiation.
reflexology	Massage and stimulation of pressure points in the feet to relieve pain and tension.
shiatsu	[also called acupressure] Massage in which pressure is applied to specific points of the body, as in acupuncture.
suture	In surgery, the means by which bodily surfaces are joined.
transcendental	meditationHindu technique for relaxing and rejuvenating the mind through the silent repetition of a mantra.
triage	The principle of allocating limited medical resources to those who will benefit most from treatment.
ultrasound	The use of ultrasonic waves to detect and diagnose internal bodily structure and disorders.

30-Sec Quickpick: Complete the Simile

Let's have some more fun with similes, which allow us to make quick and vivid comparisons: *as dead as a dodo; as soft as putty*. Many similes are now so familiar that they are part of the language. Can you complete these?

1. As drunk as a _____
2. As slippery as an _____
6. As deaf as a _____ .
7. As mad as a _____ .

3. As flat as a _____

4. As blind as a _____

5. As tough as _____

8. As warm as _____ .

9. As keen as _____ .

10. As fresh as a _____ .

In the unlikely event that you are unable to cap them all, the answers are on page 225.

Word Elements: Tact to Tude

Some of these word elements – *trans* meaning 'across' for example, giving us words such as *trans-Siberian* and *transcend* – may seem too familiar to bother about, but they are worth parking away in your memory as useful pointers to the meaning of words that are not so familiar. Here are some word elements beginning with '*t*' .

Word, Element	Origin	Meaning	English Words
tactus, tact	Latin	touching	*tact, tactile, contact, tangible*
tele-	Greek	far, distance	*telepathy, telephone, telegram, telescope, telecommunication*
temp, tempore	Latin	time	*temporary, contemporary, temporise, extempore*
terr, terra	Latin	land	*terra firma, territory, terrestrial*
theo	Greek	god	*theology, theocracy, theomancy, apotheosis, pantheon*
topo, topos	Greek	place	*topography, toponym, topology*
tract, tractus	Latin	to drag, pull	*attract, traction, tractor, protract, distract, extract*
trans-	Latin	across, beyond	*transgress, transact, transcribe, transform, translate*
-tude	Latin	state	*solitude, magnitude, plenitude, , exactitude*

Time to Revise

Yes, revision time again. Just to make sure your vocabulary has assimilated its full intake of '*t*' words, take a little time to refresh your memory with this sampling. In each case, preferably without hesitation, try to frame the word in a sentence.

tacit	*tendentious*	*traduce*	*truism*	*turpitude*
turbid	*trenchant*	*transient*	*temporise*	*tantamount*

Transatlantic Differences

Travellers and tourists and freight form only part of the traffic that flows across the Atlantic between Britain and America. One of the most restless voyagers is the English language, incessantly making the transatlantic crossing not only in the form of human communication but also in magazines, books, songs and movies. This traffic is, however, somewhat one-way; the remorseless international spread of American popular culture and products over the last century or so has demanded that users of British English possess at least a working knowledge of the variant words, spellings and idioms of American English. For most Americans, however, English as she is spoke and wrote across the Atlantic is largely regarded as merely quaint.

Here is a selection of the more pronounced Anglo-American differences.

British	**American**
aerial	antenna
aeroplane,	aircraftairplane
air hostess	flight attendant
aluminium	aluminum
anti-clockwise	counter-clockwise
aubergine	eggplant
autumn	fall
banknote	bill
barrister, solicitor	trial lawyer, attorney
behind	in back of

biscuit	cookie
bonnet	(car)hood
boot (car)	trunk
braces	suspenders
bumper (car)	fender
car (estate)	station wagon
car (saloon)	sedan
cheque	check
chips French	fries
courgette	zucchini
crisps	chips
crystallised (fruits, etc)	candied
cupboard, wardrobe	closet
dinner jacket	tuxedo
district	neighborhood
draught	draft
dressing gown	bathrobe, housecoat
dummy (baby's)	pacifier
dustbin	trashcan, garbage can
engaged (phone)	busy
estate agent	realtor, real estate agent
ex-serviceman	veteran
flat	apartment
fortnight	two weeks (no equivalent term)
frying pan	skillet
full stop (punctuation)	period
gents, gentlemen (lavatory)	men's room
grey	gray
grill	broil
ground floor	first floor
handbag	pocketbook, purse
high street	main street
jewellery, jeweller	jewelry, jeweler
jug	pitcher
jumper	sweater
kerb	curb

ladder (stockings, tights)	run
ladies (lavatory)	women's room
lavatory, WC	bathroom, washroom, restroom
lawyer	attorney
lift	elevator
lorry	truck
maths	math
minced meat	ground meat
motorway	expressway, freeway
mum, mummy	mom, mommy
muslin	cheesecloth
nappy	diaper
noughts and crosses	tick-tack-toe
paraffin	kerosene
pavement, footpath	sidewalk
petrol, petrol station	gasoline, gas/service station
postcode	zip code
plait	braid
post, postbox, pillar	boxmail, mailbox
pram	baby carriage

pyjamas	pajamas
queue	line
railway	railroad
ring road	beltway
serviette	napkin
shop assistant	sales clerk
silencer (car)	muffler
soda water	seltzer
spanner	wrench
spring onions	callion
swede (vegetable)	rutabaga
talk to; meet	talk with; meet with
tap	faucet
tie	necktie
tights (hosiery)	panty-hose
timber	lumber
tin (food, drink container)	can
tram	streetcar, trolley car
treacle	black molasses
treacle (golden syrup)	corn syrup
trousers	pants, slacks
trunk call	long-distance call
underground, tube	subway
undertaker	mortician
upmarket	upscale
vest	undershirt
zed (the letter z)	zee

There are, of course, countless other examples of Br/Am English differences, besides thousands of spelling variants (calibre/caliber, dialled/dialed, furore/furor, homely/ homey, tyre/tire). But as far as your own vocabulary is concerned, when in Rome (or Britain, or the US) do as the Romans (or the Brits, or the Americans) do.

U

Select the Correct Usage

Opposite each of the following words are two sentences. In one sentence the word is used correctly and appropriately; in the other it is used wrongly, with the result that the statement makes no sense at all. Your task is to select the sentence, **a** or **b**, in which the usage is correct. The answers are on page 225.

ubiquitous	**a.** In summer the *ubiquitous* dandelions and daisies dazzle the eye. **b.** The *ubiquitous* landlord extracted ferocious rents from his tenants.
ullage	**a.** The shipowner was fined for discharging *ullage* in the docks. **b.** The wine merchant complained about the excessive *ullage* in the barrels.
ululation	**a.** The crowd gasped at the dancer's incredible *ululations*. **b.** The *ululation* of the mourners was almost too much to bear.
umbrage	**a.** Lucy took *umbrage* at the slightest criticism. **b.** The cellar was dark and damp and reeked with *umbrage*.
unanimity	**a.** The choir sang with a *unanimity* that was sometimes even off key. **b.** There was, for once, *unanimity* among all members.
unconscionable	**a.** John took an *unconscionable* time to walk to the rostrum. **b.** On occasions Roberta would lapse into *unconscionable* dreams.
unctuous	**a.** After the sermon a good many felt decidedly *unctuous*.

b. He addressed them in his usual *unctuous* tone.

unequivocal   **a.** The bank's message was *unequivocal:* pay up or face legal action. **b.** Unable to get his views across, the man felt he was the victim of an *unequivocal* action.

unguent   **a.** The victim's room was in a terrible state, filthy and *unguent*. **b.** The herbalist prepared an *unguent* incorporating comfrey and chamomile.

unilateral   **a.** The convoy steered on a *unilateral* course. **b.** the governor made a *unilateral* decision to suspend the constitution.

uninhibited   **a.** Always *uninhibited*, Sabrina was, predictably, the life of the party. **b.** In his *uninhibited* way, Silas made sure all his valuables were securely hidden away.

unison   **a.** The chairman felt that at last there was *unison* between all the parties. **b.** The family was affected by the hereditary *unison* of only ever having male children.

unmitigated   **a.** After the storm and flooding, the landslip was an *unmitigated* disaster for the village. **b.** The agreement was *unmitigated* at the lawyer's request.

unprecedented   **a.** The document was *unprecedented* and had no legal standing. **b.** The celebrations were *unprecedented* in the history of the city.

unreconstructed   **a.** The minister felt that the hill farmers were an *unreconstructed* lot and would never accept the EC ruling. **b.** Most critics felt that the book was a collection of *unreconstructed* nonsense.

unseemly   **a.** The committee concluded that the machinery was *unseemly* and should be replaced. **b.** Gordon was suspended because of his *unseemly* behaviour at the Christmas party.

untenable   **a.** The consensus was that the professor's theory was *untenable*. **b.** The patient's condition was *untenable* and probably terminal.

untoward   **a.** Harry was fundamentally *untoward*, with no sense of direction. **b.** The boy had been missing for nearly two days and everyone hoped that nothing *untoward* had happened to him.

unwonted   **a.** The Queen's visit to the village was a most *unwonted* event. **b.** As a child he spent many *unwonted* hours in sad isolation.

urbane	**a.** Georgina arrived with her new, rich, *urbane* escort. **b.** The man looked utterly *urbane* in his string vest and seedy jacket.
usurious	**a.** The upheaval left them all anxious and *usurious*. **b.** He had no alternative but to borrow the money at *usurious* rates.
usurp	**a.** The old tyrant was afraid to leave the country as he knew his son would *usurp* the presidency. **b.** Lord Southwell knew that by leaving the property to Robert it would *usurp* his wife and other children.
utilitarian	**a.** The chairs were plain and strictly *utilitarian*. **b.** The former colonel still retained his *utilitarian* views on discipline.
Utopian	**a.** Jacob lived in fear of having to return to his old *Utopian* existence of begging and homelessness. **b.** As they left for the island the family wondered if life on Desmonia would be the *Utopian* paradise everyone said it would be.

Usage vs Abusage

Roughly speaking, there is **Correct English** and there is **Common Usage**. Common usage is what the majority of people *do* with the language, and it is often at odds with what is considered to be 'correct'. It sometimes happens that people will begin to use a word wrongly, and soon everyone is doing the same. When this happens, many linguists believe that the wrong usage then becomes the right usage. If most people say and believe that *hoi polloi* are the toffs and upper class (it actually means the opposite – the ordinary people) then that becomes an accepted alternative meaning. If people believe that *lemmings* are animals that blindly follow each other in large numbers and hurl themselves off cliffs into the sea (which only the Scandinavian species does and then in only extremely rare circumstances) then that becomes an acceptable definition. The word *aggravate* is another case. It means to worsen, but many people think it means to annoy or irritate (confirmed by usage databases) and this belief is growing. All dictionaries now allow the meaning, albeit as 'informal' – a necessary recognition but one which many people would regard as a cop out. If you are careful about your vocabulary you would be wise to observe a simple rule: always use the definition which will leave no doubt about your intended meaning.

Quickpick: Defusing Confusables

Here are ten confusables – words that look alike but which have quite different meanings – in ten sentences. One makes sense, the other nonsense. Mark or circle the correct word in each case before checking the answers on page 225.

1. The couple had always wanted to (*adapt* / *adopt*) a child.
2. When they returned the barn was (*raised* / *razed*) to the ground.
3. Jennifer always had a (*flair* / *flare*) for smart clothes.
4. The children watched the Punch and Judy show with (*baited* / *bated*) breath.
5. The baked beans in the shop had (*past* / *passed*) their sell-by date.
6. An avowed (*septic* / *sceptic*), he never believed I had climbed the mountain.
7. The young midshipman agreed to fight a (*duel* / *dual*) with the lieutenant.
8. The (*geyser* / *geezer*) was amazing when it shot a hundred feet into the air.
9. The Sherlock Holmes story he read (*wetted* / *whetted*) his appetite for more.
10. Old Mrs Craddock looked (*hale* / *hail*) and hearty on her 90th birthday.

Revision: In a Word

A quick revision exercise. From the single-word meanings, can you recognise the words listed in the *'u'* section?

1. wailing	2. ointment	3. unusual	4. insupportable
5. offence	6. unconstrained	7. oily	8. everywhere

Unlovely and Lovely Words

Quite apart from their meanings, many people have pronounced emotional feelings about some words. Unlovely words, words they can really do without, they say.

In recent polls in *The Times* and the *Daily Telegraph*, thousands of readers responded to invitations to nominate the words they loved to hate, and here is a selection:

actually	*structured*	*core*	*meaningful*	*gobsmacked*
on-going	*scenario*	*pro-active*	*iffy*	*parameters*
totally	*hardline*	*chomp*	*fayre*	*concept*
seriously	*basically*	*whatever*	*famously*	*prioritise*
fax	*marginalise*	*stuff*	*burglarise*	*workshop*

In isolation these words don't look or sound too hateful, but it is the usage of them that sends them to Coventry: *The **core** problems will be addressed soon, the spokesman promised. We are determined to **prioritise** the complaints and to have a **meaningful** discussion about them. The **workshop** will be **structured** to be **basically pro-active** to serve the **disadvantaged**, the organisers promised.* Clichés all.

But there are also many words in the English language that are undeniably beautiful, either pleasing to the eye or mellifluous to the ear. Again, let newspaper readers have their say. Here are the top ten choices of readers of *The Sunday Times*:

melody	*velvet*	*gossamer*	*crystal*	*autumn*
peace	*tranquil*	*twilight*	*murmur*	*caress*

If they seem a little flat, here are some rather more whimsical and romantic choices. A poll conducted by the *US Literary Digest* came up with *illusion, mirage* and *azure* as their top three, followed by *celestial, quintessence, ravish, whisper, twilight, meander, lovely, evanescent, taffeta* and, yes, *mellifluous*. In Britain, the learned journal *Logophile* published the words most loved by celebrities. These included *shimmering, moonlight, rapture, pure, innocent, divine* and *God* (the romantic novelist Barbara Cartland, who else?); *pellucid, aquiline, lily, silken, alembic* (Bernard Levin); *spume, vanilla, dingle, hellebore, dusk, heirloom, treacle, chocolate, flummery* (cartoonist Posy Simmons); *mandragora, valerian, polysyllable, adamantine* and *cellar door* (writer Jilly Cooper).

The poet John Kitching, in his *Sunday Words*, plumped for, among many others, *syllabub, myrrh, eiderdown, antimacassar, celandine, harlequin, chrysalis, enigma, gazebo* and *didgeridoo*.

But for the American columnist and wit Dorothy Parker the two most beautiful words in the language were *check enclosed*.

Choose the Correct Meaning

Which of the two alternatives, a or b, most accurately fits the meaning of the word? Mark or circle your choices and then check the answers on page 225.

vacillate	**a.** to be indecisive and inclined to waver. **b.** to become increasingly angry.
vacuous	**a.** talking interminably. **b.** empty and mindless.
vagary	**a.** an inveterate wanderer. **b.** a whim, an erratic idea or notion.
vainglorious	**a.** vanity and boastfulness. **b.** excessive patriotism.
valedictory	**a.** a collection of biographies of only dead people. **b.** a farewell occasion or speech.
valetudinarian	**a.** a chronically sick invalid. **b.** a person aged between 90 and 100.
vanguard	**a.** the leading position. **b.** a position at the back or rear.
vapid	**a.** insipid, dull and lifeless. **b.** a faint musky smell.
variegated	**a.** too many to count. **b.** displaying a variety of colours.
vegetate	**a.** to believe in the healing power of vegetables and fruit. **b.** to lead a life of mental inactivity.
vehement	**a.** vigorously emphatic. **b.** narrowness of viewpoint.
venal	**a.** easily bribed and corrupted. **b.** slyly envious.
vendetta	**a.** a small boat, used on the Italian lakes. **b.** a prolonged personal feud or quarrel.

veracity	**a.** habitual lying. **b.** consistently honest and truthful.
verbatim	**a.** using exactly the same words. **b.** an exact translation from one language to another.
verbose	**a.** speaking nasally, sneering. **b.** boring and long-winded speech.
verisimilitude	**a.** the appearance or quality of seeming to be true. **b.** a ghostly apparition that resembles a recognisable person.
vernacular	**a.** a long flight of steps. **b.** the common language or dialect of a particular people or place.
vernal	**a.** pertaining to or occurring in spring. **b.** a temperate climate.
vertiginous	**a.** extremely steep. **b.** the sensation of imbalance and dizziness.

Nothing too demanding in that lot, so a score of 15 or more would be respectable and one of 18+ exceptional. But watch out for *venal* (listed above) and its rather rarely seen lookalike *venial*, which means 'easily excused or forgiven': *In the vicar's view it was merely a venial error.*

Complete the Sentence

Here are ten words and ten sentences. A word is missing from each of the sentences. Can you place the appropriate words in all 10 sentences? Each word is used only once. Answers on page 226.

viable	*vicarious*	*vicissitudes*	*vilify*	*vindicate*
vindictive	*virago*	*virulent*	*virtu*	*vis-à-vis*

1. Mr Hornby said that, _____ the matter discussed yesterday, it would be dealt with as soon as possible.

2. When he married Edna, Bill never had a clue she'd turn out to be an embarrassing and embittered _____.

3. Over the years the couple had accumulated a fine display of objects of _____ .

4. The farmer wondered if raising turkeys would be a _____ business.

5. Looking at the old fisherman's craggy face I could see he'd had his share of life's _____ .

6. Marcia disliked her sister's resentful and _____ nature.

7. Why do you ridicule and _____ your boss just because you didn't get your expected promotion?

8. The infection was so _____ that it laid him low for three weeks.

9. We suspected that Brian's colourful accounts of his Sahara adventures were mostly _____ experiences culled from library books.

10. The barrister produced a file of documents that would _____ his client's claim to the property.

If after checking the answers on page 226 you find you scored eight or more correct, well done.

Identify the Word

From the meanings given, fill in the gaps to identify the words. Answers page 226.

1. Intuitive or instinctive, rather than intellectual.   *visce _ al*
2. Thick and sticky.   *vis _ ous*
3. To debase, spoil or make faulty.   *v _ tiate*
4. Relating to or made of glass.   *vitre _ _ s*
5. Caustic and acrimonious.   *vitr _ olic*
6. Abusive and defamatory language.   *vit _ peration*
7. Lively and full of high spirits.   *vi _ acious*
8. Performing experiments on animals involving surgery.   *vivi _ ection*
9. Clamorous, loud and noisy.   *vocif _ _ ous*
10. The faculty of exercising one's own choice or decision.   *vo _ ition*
11. A reversal of attitude or opinion.   *volte-fa _ e*
12. A person addicted to luxury and sensual pleasures.   *volu _ tuary*
13. A whirling, spiralling mass or motion.   *vor _ ex*
14. A person who dedicates himself or herself to religion.   *vota _ y*

15. To agree or condescend to give or grant
    something.   *vouch _ afe*
16. The voice of the people.   *vox po _ uli*
17. A Peeping Tom.   *vo _ eur*
18. Crafty and clever: relating to or resembling
    a fox.   *vulp _ ne*
19. Predatory and rapacious: relating to or
    resembling a vulture   *vult _ rine*

For that round a score of 15 or more would be a reasonable attainment. But don't be despondent if your score was lower: after all, you don't come across words such as *vit _ peration, vouch _ afe* and *visce _ al every day.*

The Visual Arts

Apart from existing as a visual medium, art overflows with a fountain of words – many of them strange and puzzling. Here are some you may find useful.

aquatint	An etching process that produces prints with varying tones.
Art Deco	Stylised geometrical decorative art style of the 1920s and 1930s.
Art Nouveau	Art style of the 1890s based on natural forms, flowers and leaves.
Bauhaus	Influential German school of art and architecture founded in 1919 by Walter Gropius.
Byzantine	Highly coloured and stylised religious art style of the Eastern Roman Empire.
catalogue raisonné	A descriptive catalogue of an artist's work.
chiaroscuro	Monochrome contrast between light and dark.
collage	A work of art formed of pasted-together materials.
cubism	The original abstract art form which aimed to present the three dimensional structure and different viewpoints of the subject on a flat surface.

Dada	[or Dadaism] Early 19th century artform that set out to shock, to be incoherent, anti-sense and anti-art. The precursor of surrealism.
drypoint	Engraving using a steel needle on a soft metal printing plate.
etching	Engraving by drawing the design on a wax-coated plate which is then etched, using acids, to varying depths and printed.
expressionism	Early 20th century German art form that aimed to express emotion, involving distortion and crudeness of line and colour.
Fauve	[*Les Fauves* = wild beasts] Early 20th century anti-academic artists who revelled in distortion and violent colours.
fresco	Wall painting using water-based paint on fresh plaster.
Gothic	Style of architecture from the 12th to 15th centuries.
gouache	Painting using opaque watercolours.
impasto	Painting with thick raised layers of paint .
Impressionism	French painting movement of the 1870s that aimed to capture fleeting impressions and natural light effects.
intaglio	A design cut or engraved into metal or stone.
lithograph	A print made from metal or smooth stone on which the design attracts ink and the blank area repels it.
mezzotint	A print made from a metal plate on which a fine engraved background is burnished off to produce a soft-toned image.
neoclassical	19th century style of decorative art and architecture based on the classical art of Greece and Rome.
pentimento	The re-emergence of a previous image or images through a surface that has been painted over.
pieta	A painting, drawing or sculpture of the dead Christ supported by the Virgin Mary.
pointillism	A post-impressionist style of art, employing dots of colour.
pre-Raphaelite	A mid-19th century revival of the style of Italian painting before Raphael, aiming at realistic colour and fidelity to nature.

scrimshaw	Fine and elaborate carving on bone or ivory.
serigraphy	[silk screen printing] Printing from a stretched sheet of fine material on which all areas except the image are coated to block off the ink forced through the fabric during the printing process.
surrealism	Art movement of the 1920s based on elements of dreams and the juxtaposition of incongruous or unexpected images or objects.
ukiyoe	Traditional Japanese colour woodblock prints.

Quickpick: Odd Man Out

With a minimum of hesitation, underline or circle the 'odd man out' in each of these word groups. The answers are on page 226.

1. *vacant, abandoned, void, occupied*
2. *velocity, idling, dawdling, passive*
3. *verdant, greenish, barren, grassy*
4. *vexed, satisfied, irritated, peeved*
5. *vicious, pleasant, inviting, sympathetic*
6. *voracious, ravenous, insatiable, satisfied*
7. *vivid, dreary, resplendent, refulgent*
8. *veto, interdict, authorise, proscribe*
9. *vigilant, watchful, careless, attentive*
10. *vulgar, seemly, fastidious, refined*

For this snap test of your grasp of word meanings you should have been aiming for a score of eight or more. Did you achieve it?

The Penultimate Revision

Yes, the end is near! But all the more reason to make sure your *'v'* words are neatly and securely stored away in your vocabulary. Very quickly, *right* or *wrong*?

Right Wrong

To *vacillate* is to become increasingly angry ____ ____

A *vainglorious* person is excessively chauvinistic
   or patriotic. ____ ____

A *vernal* climate is a pleasant, temperate climate.   ___ ___

Have you ever climbed up a *vertiginous* mountain
    slope?   ___ ___

The *vortex* is the highest point of any structure.   ___ ___

A *votary* is the church helper who lights the candles.   ___ ___

To *vitiate* something or someone, you bring it to life.   ___ ___

To be *virulent* is to act foolishly and irresponsibly.   ___ ___

If you marked any of those definitions or usages as being right,
then you need even further revision. Every one is, in fact, wrong.

Voodoo, Hoodoo and other Borrowings

The English language, as already noted, is a prolific borrower of
other languages – originally from Greek and Latin, then from German,
Scandinavian and French, not to mention Celtic and Gaelic. Then, as
England and other European nations began to explore the wider world, a
fresh supply of words poured into our lexicon. Here are some of them.

Africa	hoodoo, voodoo, safari, banana, banjo
Arabia	algebra, alcohol, alkali, elixir, zero, cotton, lemon, harem
Australia	corroborree, boomerang, koala, kookaburra, wombat
Brazil	jaguar, piranha, bossa nova
Canada	pecan, toboggan, cache, portage, rapids
Caribbean	canoe, barbecue, cannibal, potato, rotisserie, picayune
China	ketchup, sampan, kowtow, tycoon, chop suey, lichee
Czechoslovakia	howitzer, pistol, robot
Egypt	paper, ivory, oasis, ebony
France	aide, crêche, coupe, malaise, gourmet, petite, salon, vogue
Germany	droll, plunder, lager, waltz, kindergarten, gimmick
Greece	angel, anonymous, bishop, lexicon, moussaka, tonic
Greenland	anorak, igloo, kayak
Holland	brandy, drum, knapsack, wagon, yacht, yawl
Hungary	hussar, goulash
Iceland	geyser, mumps, saga

India	bandana, chintz, cot, bungalow, chutney, pyjamas, shampoo
Israel	babel, behemoth, leviathan, kosher, kibbutz, shibboleth
Italy	altar, brigand, bark, million, onus, nervous, ulcer, vertigo,
Japan	kimono, sake, bonsai, karate, geisha, haiku, hara-kiri
Malaysia	bamboo, bantam, gong, caddy, kapok, gingham, launch
Mexico	coyote, mescal, taco, tortilla
North America	moccasin, moose, skunk, pow-wow, totem, wigwam
Norway	fjord, lemming, ski, slalom
Peru	condor, inca, quinine, puma
Poland	horde, mazurka
Polynesia	aloha, lei, hula, taboo, tattoo, muu-muu
Portugal	albatross, dodo, marmalade, molasses, sargasso
Russia	czar, steppe, borscht, samovar, vodka, glasnost, sputnik
South Africa	apartheid, kraal, spoor, trek, veldt
Spain	armada, comrade, matador, sierra, embargo, junta, bonanza
Sweden	ombudsman, verve
Turkey	coffee, jackal, kiosk, shish kebab

WXYZ

Choose the Correct Meaning

Yes, the final round at last! Which of the three choices, *a*, *b* or *c*, most accurately matches the true definition of the word? Mark or circle your answers (last warning: blind guesses shouldn't count!) and then check them on page 226.

wagon-lit   **a.** a coach lamp. **b.** a sleeping car on a continental train. **c.** the driver's seat at the front of a coach.

waive   **a.** to set aside or relinquish a privilege. **b.** a circumambulatory walk in the country. **c.** a choice between two similar options.

wanton   **a.** a Chinese dumpling served with soup. **b.** an orphan. **c.** dissolute, capricious, unnecessarily destructive.

whet   **a.** a short canal barge. **b.** to sharpen or stimulate. **c.** a cause of worry or anxiety.

winsome   **a.** sweet singing voice. **b.** charming and engaging. **c.** attractively chubby.

wizened   **a.** enlightened after years of experience. **b.** shrivelled and wrinkled. **b.** relating to wizards and wizardry.

wraith   **a.** a thin, swirling mist. **b.** a long, thin silken women's scarf. **c.** a deathly apparition of someone still living.

wunderkind   **a.** a child prodigy. **b.** the doctrines of the Lutheran church. **c.** a former pupil of Winchester College.

xanthic **a.** yellowish in colour. **b.** ability to thrive with little water or moisture. **c.** easily bleached by sunlight.

Xanthippe **a.** an army general of commanding stature. **b.** a nagging, peevish, irritable woman. **c.** a person who can speak in a language with which they are totally unfamiliar.

xenophobic **a.** hatred or fear of foreigners. **b.** hatred or fear of aliens and UFOs. **c.** Hatred and fear of bodily tissues, even one's own.

yahoo **a.** a brutish, half-human creature. **b.** a type of lemur found in Madagascar. **c.** a tin whistle with a vibrating reed.

yashmak **a.** cheese made from yak's milk. **b.** the veil worn by Muslim women in public. **c.** a colourful blanket woven from yak's wool.

yclept **a.** called, or having the name of. **b.** stone stairs leading down to a crypt. **c.** any yew tree over 500 years old.

zealot **a.** a fanatic. **b.** an ornamental brass tray. **c.** an arab horseman.

zeitgeist **a.** the spirit of an age or period. **b.** the collective spirits of the dead. **c.** a spirit that keeps returning to haunt.

zenith **a.** the furthest point. **b.** the lowest point. **c.** the highest point.

zwieback **a.** a wild boar. **b.** a type of twice-baked bread. **c.** a spinal defect in cattle.

zygote **a.** the cell resulting from the union of an ovum and sperm. **b.** an instrument used for measuring the intensity of mirrors. **c.** the small skullcap worn by dignitaries of the Catholic church.

zymotic **a.** frozen with fear. **b.** relating to or causing fermentation. **c.** fervent, fanatical religious zeal.

A tough final round. But *yclept*! What sort of a word is that, many of you may complain. But as with *xanthic*, *Xanthippe* and *zymotic*, such words did turn up on several occasions in the national press in a 12-month period, so who's to say they're not coming back into vogue? As this last test was undeniably tough, why don't we settle on a score of 12 correct out of 20 as a better than passable attempt, and any score greater than that, a real lexicographical achievement.

Word Roots: Final Dig

Here's a final selection of word elements which, as has been noted many times, can help in identifying the meanings of words that are unfamiliar to you.

Word, Element	Origin	Meaning	English Words
un-	Old English	not, contrary to	*unable, unaware, unbend, unclean, undated, unbuilt*
ver, verax	Latin	truth	*veracity, veracious, verify, verily, veritable, verity*
vert, versum	Latin	change, turn	*reverse, invert, convert, versus, version, diversion*
vict, vinc	Latin	win, defeat	*victory, victim, convict, convince*
vid, visus	Latin	to see	*vision, visage, visit, vista, evident, video, television*
viv, vit	Latin	live, life	*vital, vivacious, vitamin, vivid, vivify, vivacity*
voc, vocare	Latin	call, voice	*vocal, vocalist, vociferous, evoke, provoke, vocation*
volvare, volt	Latin	to turn	*revolve, evolve, volte-face, revolt, convolvulus*
-wise	Old English	way, manner	*businesswise, clockwise, otherwise, likewise*
-y, -ey, -ie	Old English	smallness	*daddy, granny, bunny, mummy, doggie*
zoo	Greek	animal	*zoology, zoological*

Quickpick: X-Quiz

Not a crossword, but a x-quiz. Check your x-rating:

1. What in *Xanadu* did Kubla Khan decree in Coleridge's poem?
2. Who was the unfortunate husband of *Xanthippe*?
3. The process of *xerography* was responsible for the creation of a

famous trade name. What is it?

4. When were *X-rays* discovered? *a.* 1875 *b.* 1895 *c.*1905?
5. Is *xenon* a *a.* petroleum byproduct; *b.* a rare gas; *c.* a luminous liquid?
6. Does the *Xhosa* tribe hail from *a.* West Africa; *b.* East Africa; *c.* Southern Africa?
7. What does the *'xylo'* in the percussion instrument *xylophone* stand for?
8. In *Xmas* – the abbreviation for *Christmas*, what or who does the letter *'x'* represent?

The answers are on page 226. Any score of five or more: excellent!

A Final Revision

The mere 20 words in the **WXYZ** section hardly need revision: they should still be iceberg fresh in your memory. Just the same, are you sure about the precise meanings of *zeitgeist*, *xenophobic* and *Xanthippe*? If not, your dictionary beckons.

Words of the Century: 1900-2000

To salute the advent of the millennium Collins Dictionaries decided to define the last century by the words that came into the English language in each of its years. As thousands of words and names are coined every year, the choice of a single one would be expected to meet with dispute and controversy – and so it was. But the publishers, HarperCollins, determined boldly to go ahead anyway, and here is their list of words that they believe defines the 20th century and the modern age.

1900 Labour Party	1950 Nato
1901 Fingerprint	1951 Discotheque
1902 Teddy bear	1952 Stoned
1903 Tarmac	1953 Rock'n'roll
1904 Fifa	1954 Teddy boy
1905 Sinn Fein	1955 Lego
1906 Suffragette	1956 Angry young man
1907 Allergy	1957 Psychedelic

1908 Borstal	1958 Silicon chip
1909 Jazz	1959 Hovercraft
1910 Girl Guide	1960 Laser
1911 Air raid	1961 Catch-22
1912 Schizophrenia	1962 Montezuma's revenge
1913 Isotope	1963 Rachmanism
1914 Vorticism	1964 Moog synthesiser
1915 Tank	1965 Miniskirt
1916 Dada	1966 Cultural Revolution
1917 Cheka	1967 Pulsar
1918 Bolshie / Bolshy	1968 Fosbury flop
1919 Fascism	1969 Moon buggy
1920 Robot	1970 Butterfly effect
1921 Chaplinesque	1971 Workaholic
1922 Gigolo	1972 Watergate
1923 Spoonerism	1973 VAT
1924 Surrealism	1974 Ceefax
1925 British Summer Time	1975 Fractal
1926 Television	1976 Punk rock
1927 Talkie	1977 ERM
1928 Penicillin	1978 Test-tube baby
1929 Maginot Line	1979 Rubik's cube
1930 Pluto (the planet, not the pup)	1980 Solidarity
1931 Oscar	1981 SDP
1932 Neutron	1982 CD
1933 Gestapo	1983 Aids
1934 Belisha (beacon)	1984 Yuppie
1935 Alcoholics Anonymous	1985 Glasnost
1936 Mickey Mouse	1986 Mexican wave
1937 Surreal	1987 PEP
1938 Nylon	1988 Acid house
1939 Walter Mitty	1989 Velvet Revolution
1940 Jeep	1990 Crop circle
1941 Radar	1991 Ethnic cleansing
1942 Robotics	1992 Clone
1943 Dam Busters	1993 Information superhighway
1944 Doodlebug	1994 National Lottery

1945 Tupperware	1995 Road rage
1946 Bikini	1996 Alcopop
1947 Flying saucer	1997 Blairite
1948 Scrabble	1998—-
1949 Big Brother	1999—-

You are invited to nominate your own century-defining words for 1998-2000, and doubtless you could assign a good number of alternatives for many of the other years. The editors of the *Oxford English Dictionary* chose to do just that, but confined their alternative choices to the years 1978-1997. Here is their late-finishing selection:

1978 BMX, Teletext	1988 Lager lout
1979 Space Invaders	1989 Poll tax

1980 Reaganomics	1990 Global warming
1981 Walkman	1991 Citizen's charter
1982 Exocet	1992 Grunge; annus horribilis
1983 Star Wars	1993 Whitewater; Bobbitt

1984 Aids	1994 World Wide Web
1985 Yuppie	1995 Britpop
1986 Perestroika	1996 Ecowarrior; scratchcard
1987 Freemarket; Black Monday	1997 New Labour

The century, as you see – lexicographically at any rate – began much as it ends, with *Labour Party* coined in 1900 and *New Labour* and *Blairite* in 1997.

Answers, Definitions and Meanings

Keep in mind that many, if not most, words have more than a single definition, and that they can also convey various subtleties of meaning according to the context of their use.

In this book only one definition is given for each word, but this will reflect the usual, most commonly accepted meaning.

So it is important that if you are in doubt about what a word means, check its precise meaning or meanings and, if possible, its usage, in your dictionary.

A

CHOOSE THE CORRECT MEANING. aberration, **b**; abeyance, **a**; abnegation, **c**; abrogate, **b**; abstruse, **b**; accede, **a**; accolade, **a**; accrue, **c**; accretion, **a**; Achilles heel, **c**; acolyte, **a**; acquiesce, **b**; acrid, **c**; acrimonious, **a**; actuary, **c**; acuity, **a**; acumen, **b**; adamant, **b**; ad hoc, **a**; adjunct, **b**; adroit, **b**; adventitious, **a**; aegis, **a**; affidavit, **b**; aficionado, **c**; aggrandize, **b**; agnostic, **c**; agronomy, **c**; akimbo, **b**; alacrity, **a**; alfresco, **c**; allude, **b**; alter ego, **b**; altruism, **a**; amalgam, **a**; amanuensis, **b**; ambidextrous, **c**; ambience, **c**; ambivalent, **b**; ameliorate, **b**; amenable, **a**; amoral, **b**; amortise, **a**; anachronism, **c**; analgesic, **b**; analogous, **b**; anathema, **a**; ancillary, **c**; angst, **b**; annuity, **c**.

IDENTIFY THE WORD. annul; anomalous; anorexia; anthology; antipasto; antipathy; antithesis; antonym; aperient; aphorism; apiarian; aplomb; apocalypse; apocryphal;apogee; apostasy; apothegm (*sometimes apophthegm); apotheosis; apposite; approbation; appurtenance; apropos; apse; aquiline; arable; arachnid; arbitrary; arcane; argot; Armageddon; armoire; arraign; arriviste; ascetic; asinine; aspersion; asperity; assiduous; assuage; atrophy; attenuate; attrition; atypical; au fait; auspicious; autonymous; avocation; avuncular; awry; axiomatic.

QUICKPICK: SPOT THE MISFITS. coarsen; eager; abrogate; contend; antedate; anneal; antithesis; whim; ascetic; audition.

ASTRONOMY, SPACE AND THE UNIVERSE. 1. true; 2. false - diurnal means happening daily or during the day; 3. true; 4. false - a light year is an astronomical unit of distance, equal to the distance travelled by light in a year; 5. true; 6. true; 7. true; 8. false - an aurora features bright coloured flashes that light up the polar night sky; 9, false - a supernova is a star that explodes; 10. true.

B

RIGHT OR WRONG? 1. right; 2. wrong - badinage is teasing banter or repartee; 3. right; 4. right; 5. right; 6. wrong – banal means trite or commonplace; 7. wrong – a barmitzvah (or Bar Mitzvah) is the celebration when a Jewish boy assumes his religious obligations; 8. right; 9. right; 10. wrong - a bayou is a marsh, and certainly not parched; 11. right; 12.

wrong – a behemoth is a gigantic beast, something huge; 13. wrong – bel canto is a style of singing; 14. right; 15. right; 16. wrong – a bellwether is a leader (usually a sheep) others follow blindly; 17. wrong – bemused means bewildered and confused; 18. right; 19. right; 20. wrong – something bespoke is individually made, so cannot be mass-produced.

CHOOSE THE CORRECT MEANING. béte noire, **b**; bibelot, **a**; biennial, **b**; bifurcate, **a**; bijou, **a**; bilateral, **b**; billabong, **b**; billet-doux, **a**; binary, **a**; biodegradable, **b**; biopsy, **b**; bisque, **b**; Black Maria, **a**; blag, **a**; blandishments, **b**; blasé, **b**; blench, **a**; blithe, **b**; bombastic, **a**; Bombay duck, **b**; bona fide, **a**; bonhomie, **b**; bon vivant, **b**; boondocks, **a**; boreal, **b**; bourgeois, **a**; bowdlerise, **a**; boycott, **b**; braggadocio, **a**; braise, **a**; brasserie, **a**; bravura, **b**; breccia, **b**; breviary, **b**; bric-a-brac, **a**; brioche, **b**; Brobdingnagian, **a**; brouhaha, **a**; brusque, **a**; bucolic, **b**; bulimia, **b**; bum steer, **a**; bumptious, **b**; burgeoning, **a**; burgher, **a**; burlap, **b**; burnish, **a**; buttress, **b**; Byronic, **a**; Byzantine, **b**.

BONES AND MUSCLES.1. **a**; 2. **b**; 3. **b**; 4. **b**; 5. **b**; 6. **a**; 7. **b**; 8. **a**; 9. **b**; 10. **a**.

QUICKPICK: NAME THE SYNONYM. bribe/backhander; ballpark/approximate; beau/sweetheart; bemuse/bamboozle; bedraggled/untidy; bland/uninteresting; boisterous/noisy; bosh/nonsense; brazen/shameless; broach/initiate.

CAN YOU GIVE IT A NAME? 1. Braille; 2. baguette; 3. betel; 4. bodegas; 5. Bactrian; 6. Bloody Mary; 7. breech; 8. bovine spongiform encephalopathy; 9. borscht; 10. bollards.

C

WHAT'S THE APPROPRIATE WORD? 1. cabriole; 2. cache; 3. cajole; 4. calisthenics; 5. calumny; 6. camaraderie; 7. campanile; 8. campanology; 9. canard; 10. candour; 11. cantankerous; 12. carcinogenic; 13. cardinal; 14. carte blanche; 15. cartel; 16. castellated; 17. castigated; 18. catalyst; 19. catharsis; 20. catheter.

COMPLETE THE WORD.1. catholic; 2. caucus; 3. cavil; 4. cerebral; 5. cessation; 6. chancel; 7. charismatic; 8. charlatan; 9. chauvinism; 10. chicanery; 11. chiffonier; 12. chimera; 13. choleric; 14. chutzpah; 15. cineaste; 16. circumspect; 17. circumvent; 18. clandestine; 19. claque; 20.

clement; 21. climactic; 22. coalesce; 23. codicil; 24. coerce; 25. cogent; 26. cognoscenti; 27. collateral; 28. colloquial; 29. comatose; 30. commensurate; 31. compatible; 32. complacent; 33. complaisant; 34. complicity; 35. concomitant; 36. concision; 37. concupiscence; 38. concurrent; 39. condign; 40. conflation.

CHOOSE THE CORRECT MEANING. congenital, **a**; congeries, **a**; congruence, **b**; connotation, **a**; consanguinity, **b**; construe, **b**; consummate, **a**; contiguous, **a**; contrapuntal, **b**; contretemps, **a**; contrite, **b**; contumacious, **b**; contusion, **a**; convoluted, **b**; corollary, **a**; corroborate, **b**; corrugated, **a**; coruscate, **b**; costive, **b**; coterie, **a**; crapulous, **b**; credo, **a**; credulity, **a**; crepuscular, **a**; criterion, **b**; cruciform, **b**; culpable, **a**; cupidity, **b**; curmudgeon, **a**; cursory, **a**; cynosure, **b**.

QUICKPICK: IDENTIFY THE ANTONYM. 1. calm - agitated; 2. captious - easygoing; 3. curb - encourage; 4. circumscribe - distend; 5. compromise - dispute; 6. circumlocution - brevity; 7. cheerful - forlorn; 8. condemn - absolve; 9. confess - dissemble; 10. conquer - capitulate.

CHEMICAL COMPETENCE. 1. false – water boils at 100 degrees Celsius or 212 degrees Fahrenheit; 2. true; 3. false; alcohol is produced by fermentation; 4. false - a kilogram is 1,000 grams;5. true; 6. false – 'dry ice' is solidified carbon dioxide; 7. true; 8. true; 9. false – neon is an elemental gas that is often used in glass tubes to make illuminated signs; 10. true.

COLLECTIVE NOUNS: TWO OR MORE OF A KIND. 1. murder; 2. pride or troop; 3. business; 4. exaltation; 5. dray; 6. covey; 7. herd or pod; 8. flight.

D

CORRECT THE CONFUSABLES. 1. debarred; 2. descent; 3. defused; 4. dependants; 5. deserts; 6. detracted; 7. discrete; 8. uninterested; 9. dual; 10. decried.

CHOOSE THE CORRECT MEANING. dado, **b**; dalliance, **a**; dearth, **b**; debacle, **c**; debilitate, **c**; decant, **a**; déclassé, **a**; declivity, **b**; décolletage, **c**; decrepitude, **b**; de facto, **a**; deferential, **a**; déjà vu, **c**; deleterious, **a**; deliquescent, **a**; Delphic, **c**; demagogue, **c**; demeanour, **a**; demimonde, **b**; demotic, **a**; demurrer, **a**; denigrate, **b**; denouement, **c**; depilatory, **b**;

deprecate, **b**; depreciate, **a**; derogatory, **c**; deshabille, **a**; desiccated, **b**; desuetude, **a**; desultory, **b**; determinism, **c**; devolution, **a**; dextral, **b**; dharma, **b**; dialectic, **a**; Diaspora, **b**; diatribe, **b**; dichotomy, **c**; didactic, **a**.

WHAT'S THE WORD? 1. diffident; 2. dilatory; 3. dilettante; 4. Dionysian; 5. dipsomaniac; 6. disabuse; 7. discommode; 8. disconcert; 9. disconsolate; 10. discrepancy; 11. discrete; 12. discursive; 13. disingenuous; 14. disinterested; 15. disparate; 16. dissemble; 17. dissonance; 18. diurnal; 19. diva; 20. divertissement; 21. doctrinaire; 22. doggerel; 23. dolorous; 24. domicile; 25. double entendre; 26. doughty; 27. doyen; 28. Draconian; 29. drugget; 30. dubious; 31. ductile; 32. dudgeon; 33. dulcet; 34. duodenum; 35. duopoly; 36. duplicity; 37. duress; 38. dynasty; 39. dyslexia; 40. dyspeptic.

QUICKPICK: SAME, OPPOSITE OR DIFFERENT? 1. opposite; 2. same; 3. same; 4. same; 5. different; 6. opposite; 7. same; 8. different; 9. opposite; 10. same; 11. different; 12. same; 13. opposite; 14. same; 15. different.

DIGESTION AND THE DIGESTIVE SYSTEM. 1. true; 2. true; 3. true; 4. true; 5. true; 6. false - it is a suppository; 7. true; 8. true; 9. true; 10. true.

RIGHT OR WRONG? 1. right; 2. wrong – eclectic means broad-based and comprehensive; 3. right; 4. right; 5. right; 6. wrong – effete means weak and enfeebled; 7. wrong - efficacious means effective; 8. right; 9. wrong – effulgent   means radiant and shining; 10. right; 11. wrong – to be egocentric is to be selfish and self-centred; 12. right; 13. right; 14. right; 15. wrong – elephantine means huge; 16. right; 17. right; 18. wrong – elliptical is having the curved shape of an ellipse; 19. wrong – to elucidate is to make clear and intelligible; 20. right.

TOP AND TAIL THE WORDS. 1. emanate; 2. emancipate; 3. emasculate; 4. embargo; 5. embolism; 6. embryonic; 7. emendate; 8. emeritus; 9. emetic; 10. emollient; 11. empathy; 12. empirical; 13. empyrean; 14. emulate; 15. encomium; 16. endemic; 17. energise; 18. enervate; 19. enfant terrible; 20. engender; 21. enigma; 22. enjoin; 23. enmity; 24. ennui; 25. enormity; 26. entreat; 27. enunciate; 28. ephemera; 29. epicure; 30. epigram.

WHICH IS THE CORRECT MEANING? epitome, **a**; eponymous, **a**; equable, **b**; equanimity, **b**; equinox, **b**; equitable, **a**; equivocal, **a**; ergonomics, **b**; erogenous, **a**; ersatz, **b**; eructation, **b**; erudite, **a**; eschatology, **b**; eschew, **b**; esoteric, **a**; esprit de corps, **a**; ethos, **a**; etymology, **b**; eugenics, **a**; eulogise, **b**; euphemism, **b**; euphonious, **a**; euphoria, **a**; Eurasian, **b**; euthanasia, **b**; evanescent, **a**; eviscerate, **a**; exacerbate, **b**; excoriate, **b**; exculpate, **a**; execrable, **a**; exegesis, **b**; exemplary, **a**; exigency, **a**; exonerate, **b**; exorcise, **b**; expatiate, **a**; expiate, **a**; exponentially, **a**; expropriate, **b**; expunge, **a**; expurgate, **b**; extempore, **b**; extenuating, **a**; extraneous, **a**; exuberant, **b**.

QUICKPICK: ODD MAN OUT. 1. discomfort; 2. entry; 3. attract; 4. comprehensible; 5. unstable; 6. reject; 7. disguise; 8. pleasant; 9. beginning; 10. give.

INCREASE YOUR WORD POWER! 1. facetious, **c**; 2. facile, **a**; 3. facilitate, **d**; 4. factotum, **b**; 5. fait accompli, **c**; 6. fallacy, **a**; 7. Falstaffian, **d**; 8. farcical, **d**; 9. farinaceous, **a**; 10. farrago, **c**; 11. fascism, **b**; 12. fastidious, **b**; 13. fatuous, **a**; 14. fatwa, **d**; 15. faux pas, **b**; 16. fealty, **d**; 17. febrile, **c**; 18. feckless, **a**; 19. fertile; **c**; 20. feign, **b**.

FILL IN THE MISSING LETTERS. feisty; felicitous; felonious; feral; fifth columnist; filial; filibuster; finial; flaccid; flagrant; flamboyant; flippant; florid; fluent; foetid; foible; foment; footling; foray; forbearance; forensic; forestall; forte; fortuitous; fracas; fractious; Francophile; fratricide; frenetic; friable; fruition; fulminate; fulsome; fundamentalism; funereal; furbelow; furore; fustian.

FOOD AND DRINK.1. true; 2. true; 3. false – the drink is the Margarita; 4. false – prosciutto is cured ham; 5. true; 6. true; 7. true; 8. true; 9. false – taramasalata is a pâté made from fish roe; 10. true; 11. false – lasagna is a pasta dish with meat and cheese; 12. true; 13. false – the salad described is a Caesar salad; 14. true; 15. false – the sausages are chorizos; 16. true; 17. false – the only Swiss cheese of the three is Gruyere; Havarti is Danish and Gouda is Dutch; 18. false – a menu with each dish priced separately is à la carte; 19. true; 20. true.

QUICKPICK: SPOT THE MISPRINT. 1. faraway; 2. forty-four; 3. fazed; 4. Millennium; 5. beck and call; 6. custody; 7. Call me Ishmael; 8. amock; 9. Whooping cough; 10. transsexual.

G

REPLACE THE MISSING WORDS. 1. gamine; 2. galvanised; 3. gaffe; 4. garrulous; 5. galaxy; 6. gamut; 7. gangrene; 8. gambit; 9. Gallic; 10. galleria.

WHAT'S THE CORRECT USAGE? gauche, **b**; gazebo, **a**; gazumped, **a**; generic, **b**; genre, **b**; genuflect, **a**; geriatric, **a**; germane, **b**; gerrymander, **a**; gestation, **b**; gesundheit, **a**; gibe, **a**; gigolo, **b**; gilt-edged, **b**; gimcrack, **b**; glasnost, **a**; glitterati, **a**; gloaming, **a**; glutinous, **a**; gobbet, **b**; gobbledegook, **b**; gossamer, **a**; gourmandise, **b**; Grand Guignol, **a**; grandiose, **a**; gratuitous, **b**; gravamen, **a**; gregarious, **a**; gremlin, **b**; grenadine, **b**; gullible, **b**; gumption, **b**; gunge, **a**.

QUICKPICK: IDIOMS AND CATCHPHRASES. 1. grave; 2. gift horse; 3. game; 4. gilt; 5. gum; 6. green around the gills; 7. goat; 8. goose; 9. grasshopper; 10. good; 11. gift; 12. goats.

H

CHOOSE THE RIGHT MEANING. habeas corpus, **b**; habitué, **a**; hackneyed, **b**; hagiography, **c**; ha-ha, **a**; haiku, **b**; halation, **c**; halcyon, **a**; halitosis, **c**; hapless, **c**; harangue, **c**; harbinger, **a**; hauteur, **b**; hearsay, **a**; hector, **a**; hedonism, **b**; hegemony, **b**; heinous, **b**; helix, **b**; hellebore, **b**; herbivorous, **c**; heresy, **a**; hermetic, **c**; heterogeneous, **b**; heuristic, **a**; hiatus, **a**; Hibernian, **b**; hierarchy, **b**; hindsight, **c**; histology, **a**; histrionic, **a**; hoary, **c**; Hobson's choice, **c**; hoi polloi, **c**; hologram, **c**; homily, **b**; homogeneous, **a**; honorarium, **c**; hortatory, **c**.

SUPPLY THE MISSING WORDS. 1. hydrofoil; 2. hybrid; 3. hubris; 4. humdrum; 5. hypochondriac; 6. humane; 7. hyperbole; 8. husbandry; 9. hypothetical; 10. hyperactivity.

QUICKPICK: SPOT THE ANTONYMS. 1. uninhabitable; 2. agree; 3. ditch; 4. hairless; 5. handsome; 6. harmful; 7. humble; 8. kind; 9. Latin; 10. infamy; 11. proved; 12. assist.

HEART AND CIRCULATION. 1. true; 2. false – the pumping chambers of the heart are ventricles; 3. true; 4. true; 5. false – in a coronary bypass a narrow or blocked coronary artery is bypassed by grafting a replacement section of healthy blood vessel taken from another part of the body; 6.

true; 7. false – the carotid artery is the main blood vessel to the brain; 8. true; 9. true; 10. false – haemophilia is an inherited disease which impairs the clotting ability of the blood; 11. true; 12. true.

I

SCORE 20 WITH THIS SCORE OF IN-WORDS. 1. inadvertent; 2. incognito; 3. inequitable; 4. inchoate; 5. incongruous; 6. indemnity; 7. indigenous; 8. incredulity; 9. ingénue; 10. infinitesimal; 11. inimical; 12. innuendo; 13. insidious; 14. inordinate; 15. insipid; 16. insouciance; 17. internecine; 18. ineluctable; 19. interstices; 20. introvert.

CHOOSE THE RIGHT MEANING. iconoclast, **a**; idiomatic, **a**; idiosyncrasy, **b**; idolatry, **a**; ignominious, **b**; imbroglio, **b**; imbue, **a**; immolate, **a**; immured, **b**; immutable, **a**; impartial, **a**; impasse, **b**; impeach, **b**; impeccable, **a**; impenitent, **b**; imperturbable, **b**; impervious, **a**; implacable, **a**; implausible, **a**; importune, **b**; imprimatur, **b**; impromptu, **a**; impugn, **a**; inane, **b**; incandescent, **a**; incapacitate, **b**; incipient, **a**; inconsequential, **b**; incontrovertible, **a**; inculcate, **a**; incumbent, **b**; incursion, **b**; indefatigable, **a**; indigent, **a**; ineluctable, **b**; ineffable, **a**; inertia, **a**; inexorable, **a**; ingenuous, **b**; ingratiate, **a**; inherent, **a**; inimitable, **b**; iniquitous, **b**; innate, **a**; innocuous, **b**; insalubrious, **a**; insular, **b**.

MORE MERRY POP-INS. 1. irreparably; 2. intransigent; 3. irrevocable; 4. itinerant; 5. interdict; 6. inter alia; 7. iota; 8. invidious; 9. intrinsic; 10. inveighed; 11. irascible; 12. iridescence; 13. inured; 14. inviolable; 15. inveterate.

QUICKPICK: ADD THE FINAL LETTERS. 1. identikit; 2. idiocy; 3. illiterate; 4. imitate; 5. imminent; 6. incisor; 7. indecent; 8. inquest; 9. insolvency; 10. Interpol.

J

CHOOSE THE CORRECT MEANING. jalousie, **c**; jaundiced, **a**; jejune, **b**; jeopardy, **a**; jeremiad, **b**; jerry-built, **c**; jettison, **a**; Jezebel, **b**; jihad, **b**; jingoism, **b**; Job's comforter, **c**; jobsworth, **a**; jocose, **b**; joie de vivre, **c**; jubilee, **c**.

WORDS IN USE - RIGHT OR WRONG? 1. wrong – judicial relates to the law courts and justice; 2. right; 3. right; 4. right; 5. wrong – a junta is a ruling group of military officers; 6. right; 7. wrong – nautically, a jury-rig is a makeshift mast or sail; 8. wrong – juvenescent means regaining youth and vitality; 9. right; 10. right.

QUICKPICK: TWO MEANINGS, ONE WORD. 1. log; 2. tick; 3. bass; 4. row; 5. bark; 6. rake; 7. yard; 8. box; 9. hide; 10. hold.

K

CHOOSE THE CORRECT MEANING. Kafkaesque, **c**; kaftan, **b**; kamikaze, **a**; karaoke, **b**; kaput, **c**; karma, **a**; kedgeree, **b**; Keynesian, **a**; keystone, **b**; kibbutz, **c**; kinetic, **b**; kismet, **a**; kitsch, **a**; kleptomaniac, **a**; knell, **b**; Knesset, **b**; knock-for-knock, **b**; kosher, **b**; kowtow, **b**; kudos, **a**.

QUICKPICK: ODD MAN OUT. 1. wicket; 2. carbon copy; 3. circle; 4. deliver; 5. entry; 6. radio; 7. hops; 8. negative; 9. desert; 10. weep.

L

REPLACE THE MISSING WORDS. 1. lamentable; 2. laissez faire; 3. labyrinthine; 4. laity; 5. lacklustre; 6. lambent; 7. laconic; 8. lacuna; 9. lackadaisical; 10. lachrymose.

WHAT'S THE RIGHT MEANING? lampoon, **b**; landau, **b**; langoustine, **a**; languorous, **b**; lapidary, **b**; largesse, **a**; lascivious, **a**; lassitude, **a**; latent, **b**; lateral, **b**; laudable, **a**; lectern, **b**; legerdemain, **b**; leitmotif, **a**; lese-majesty, **a**; lessee, **a**; lethargic, **b**; leviathan, **a**; lexicography, **b**; liaison, **b**; libertarian, **a**; libidinous, **a**; libretto, **b**; licentious, **b**; lickspittle, **b**; Lilliputian, **a**; limbo, **a**; limpid, **b**; linchpin, **a**; lingua franca, **b**; lionise, **a**; lissom, **b**; litany, **b**; livid, **b**; lobbyist, **a**; locum tenens, **a**; logistics, **a**; logorrhoea, **b**; longevity, **b**; longueur, **b**; loquacious, **a**; Lothario, **a**; louche, **b**; loupe, **a**; lubricious, **b**; lucid, **b**; lugubrious, **a**; lumpen, **b**; luxuriant, **a**.

QUICKPICK: SPOT THE DUMMY. 1. real word; 2. dummy; 3. real word; 4. real word; 5. dummy; 6. dummy; 7. dummy; 8. real word; 9. real word; 10. dummy.

LUST, SEX AND REPRODUCTION. 1. true. 2. false – an intrauterine

device is used by the woman to prevent contraception; 3. true; 4. false –
the tubes that carry egg cells from the ovary to the uterus are the
Fallopian tubes or oviducts; 5. false – the hymen is the membrane over a
female virgin's vagina; 6. true; 7. true; 8. false – there is no such operation
as a 'double vasectomy'; nor are the testicles removed. A vasectomy is the
cutting and tying off of the duct that conveys sperm from the testicles to
the urethra; 9. true; 10. true.

M

WORDS IN USE: RIGHT OR WRONG? 1. wrong – a macrocosm is a
large and complex structure, such as the universe, or human society, as
opposed to a microcosm; 2. right; 3. right; 4. wrong – a magnanimous or
generous person wouldn't bother to count the silver; 5. right, although
more usually applied to literary works; 6. right; 7. right; 8. wrong – a
malapropism is a verbal gaffe, such as "He's at his wick's end" or "You
could have knocked me down with a fender";9. wrong – mal de mer is
French for seasickness; 10. right; 11. right; 12. right, if Robert's view was
that the increasing population in the Far East would eventually exceed its
means of subsistence.

CHOOSE THE CORRECT MEANING. mandatory, **a**; manifest, **b**;
manifold, **b**; manna, **b**; manqué, **a**; mantra, **b**; maquette, **b**; marmoreal, **a**;
materfamilias, **b**; maudlin, **a**; maunder, **b**; maverick, **a**; mawkish, **a**;
maxim, **a**; mea culpa, **b**; mealy-mouthed, **b**; median, **b**; mediate, **a**;
megalomania, **b**; megrim, **a**; melange, **a**; melee, **b**; mellifluous, **a**;
memorabilia, **b**; ménage, **b**; mendacious, **a**; mendicant, **b**; mephitic, **a**;
mercenary, **b**; meretricious, **b**; mesmerise, **a**; messianic, **b**; metabolism, **a**;
metaphorical, **a**; métier, **a**; metronymic, **b**; mettle, **b**; mezzanine, **b**;
miasma, **a**; microcosm, **a**; micturate, **b**.

FILL IN THE GAPS: IDENTIFY THE WORD. 1. milieu; 2. militate; 3.
mimicry; 4. minatory; 5. minion; 6. minuscule; 7. minutiae; 8.
misanthrope; 9. miscegenation; 10. misconstrue; 11. misnomer; 12.
misogyny; 13. mitigate; 14. mnemonic; 15. modality; 16. modicum; 17.
moiety; 18. mollify; 19. monastic; 20. monetarist; 21. monograph; 22.
moraine; 23. moratorium; 24. mores; 25. morganatic; 26. moribund; 27.
morose; 28. mot juste; 29. mufti; 30. multifarious; 31. mundane; 32.
munificent; 33. mutable; 34. mutual; 35. myopic.

QUICKPICK: MORE MISPRINTS 1. mall; 2. Malaysia; 3. mayonnaise; 4. minuscule; 5. meringue; 6. mantelpiece; 7. martins; 8. Mecca; 9. matting; 10. naturists.

N

ARE THEY BEING USED CORRECTLY? 1. wrong – the nadir is the deepest or lowest point; 2. wrong – it must have been an extremely short silence; a nanosecond is one thousand-millionth of a second; 3. right; 4. right; 5. wrong – nebulous means lacking in form, shape and content; 6. right; 7. right; 8. wrong – Nemesis is an agent not of good fortune but of vengeance and retribution; 9. right; 10. right.

CHOOSE THE CORRECT MEANING. ne plus ultra, **b**; nepotism, **c**; nexus, **a**; nicety, **c**; nihilism, **a**; noblesse oblige, **b**; noisome, **b**; nominal, **a**; nonage, **c**; nonce word, **b**; nonchalant, **a**; nonentity, **a**; nonpareil, **a**; nonplussed, **b**; non sequitur, **a**; nostrum, **c**; nouveau riche, **b**; nuance, **a**; nubile, **c**; nugatory, **a**; numinous, **b**; nymphet, **b**.

QUICKPICK: SAME, OPPOSITE OR DIFFERENT? niggardly - opposite; nullify - same; normal - different; neglect - opposite; narrate - same; neat - opposite; nearness - different; nimble - opposite; noble - same; nomadic - same.

O

COMPLETE THE SENTENCE. 1. occidental; 2. obtuse; 3. obsequious; 4. obdurate; 5. oblique; 6. occlude; 7. obloquy; 8. obeisance; 9. obstreperous; 10. obsolescent; 11. obviate; 12. obfuscate.

CHOOSE THE CORRECT MEANING. odium, **b**; odontologist, **c**; Odyssey, **b**; oeuvre, **c**; officious, **a**; olfactory, **c**; oligarchy, **b**; omnipotent, **a**; omniscient, **a**; omnivorous, **c**; onerous, **a**; opprobrium, **a**; optimal, **b**; opulent, **b**; oracular, **b**; Orcadian, **c**; ordure, **a**; ormolu, **c**; oscillate, **b**; osmosis, **b**; ossified, **c**; ostensibly, **a**; ostentatious, **c**; osteopathy, **c**; ostracize, **b**; otiose, **a**; ottoman, **b**; overly, **b**; overt, **b**; overtone, **a**; oxymoron, **c**.

QUICKPICK: SPOT THE MISFITS. clear; obligate; assist; observe; include; tenant; opaque; intolerant; rarely.

P

CHOOSE THE CORRECT MEANINGS. pacifist, **b**; paediatrician, **b**; palaver, **a**; palimpsest, **a**; palliative, **b**; palpable, **a**; palpitate, **b**; panacea, **b**; panache, **a**; panegyric, **b**; panjandrum, **b**; pantheism, **a**; paparazzi, **b**; paradigm, **a**; paragon, **b**; paramour, **b**; paranoia, **b**; paraphrase, **a**; pariah, **b**; pari mutuel, **b**; parity, **a**; parlance, **b**; parlous, **b**; parodic, **a**; paroxysm, **b**; parsimonious, **a**; partiality, **a**; partisan, **b**; parvenu, **a**; passé, **b**; pastiche, **a**; paterfamilias, **a**; pathogenic, **b**; patina, **b**; patisserie, **a**; patois, **b**; patrial, **a**; patrician, **b**; Pauline, **b**; Pecksniffian, **b**.

WORDS IN USE: RIGHT OR WRONG? 1. right; 2. right; 3. wrong – a pedagogue is not an enthusiastic traveller but a teacher or educator – see peripatetic; 4. wrong – pedantic means to be excessively concerned with details; 5. wrong – a woman's peignoir is her dressing gown; 6. right; 7. right; 8. wrong – to have a penchant is to have a taste or liking for something; 9. wrong – the penumbra is the vague area of shadow between light and dark; 10. right.

CHOOSE THE CORRECT MEANINGS. peregrination, **a**; peremptory, **b**; perennial, **b**; perfunctory, **a**; peripatetic, **b**; periphrasis, **a**; permeate, **a**; pernicious, **b**; peroration, **b**; perquisite, **a**; persiflage, **a**; perspicacious, **b**; pertinacious, **b**; pervasive, **b**; philanderer, **a**; philippic, **b**; philanthropist, **a**; Philistine, **a**; phlegmatic, **b**; physiognomy, **b**; picaresque, **a**; picayune, **a**; pied-à-terre, **a**; pinchbeck, **b**; pinnate, **b**; piquant, **a**; piqûe, **a**; pixilated, **a**; placate, **b**; placebo, **a**; plagiarism, **b**; plangent, **a**; Platonic, **b**; plebeian, **b**; plenary, **a**; plethora, **a**; podiatry, **b**; poetaster, **b**; pogrom, **a**; poignant, **b**.

COMPLETE THE SENTENCE. 1. potable; 2. portentous; 3. poltergeist; 4. polymath; 5. polemic; 6. polyglot; 7. predatory; 8. preclude; 9. precocious; 10. pragmatic.

CHOOSE THE CORRECT MEANINGS. predicate, **a**; predilection, **b**; prehensile, **b**; preponderance, **b**; prerogative, **a**; prescient, **a**; pretentious, **b**; prevaricate, **a**; prima facie, **b**; primordial, **b**; probity, **b**; proclivity, **a**; procrastinate, **b**; profligate, **a**; prognosis, **b**; prolapse, **b**; prolix, **a**; propensity, **b**; prophylactic, **b**; propinquity, **b**; propitious, **b**; prosaic, **a**; proscribe, **a**; proselytise, **b**; prosthesis, **a**; protean, **a**; protégé, **b**; provenance, **b**; proviso, **b**; prurient, **b**; psychosomatic, **a**; puerile, **a**; puissant, **b**; pulchritude, **b**; pullulate, **b**; punctilious, **a**; purlieus, **b**; pusillanimous, **b**; putative, **a**; Pyrrhic victory, **a**.

QUICKPICK: ADD THE FINAL LETTERS. 1. papyrus; 2. perceive; 3. perforate; 4. populace; 5. psychiatry; 6. pugilism; 7. premiere; 8. plethora; 9. persuade; 10. promenade.

Q

SELECT THE CORRECT USAGE. qualm, **a**; quandary, **a**; quango, **a**; quantum, **b**; quasar, **b**; querulous, **a**; quiddity, **b**; quidnunc, **b**; quiescent, **a**; quietus, **b**; quintessence, **a**; quisling, **b**; quixotic, **b**; quoin, **a**; quondam, **b**; quorum, **b**; quotidian, **a**.

QUICKPICK: QUESTIONS! QUESTIONS! 1. papillote; 2. loupe; 3. cattery; 4. topiary; 5. perforations; 6. risers; 7. spittoon; 8. font; 9. plectrum; 10. steel.

R

POP THE WORD IN PLACE. 1. rancour; 2. rara avis; 3. Rabelaisian; 4. rapprochement; 5. raconteur; 6. raison d'étre; 7. ratiocination; 8. raffish; 9. raillery; 10. rapport.

COMPLETE THE WORDS. raucous; reactionary; rebarbative; recalcitrant; recant; recapitulate; recherché; recidivism; recipient; reciprocate; recrimination; recondite, recrudescent; rectitude; recurrent; redolent; redoubtable; referendum; refractory; refulgent; refute; regimen; reiterate; remiss; remonstrate; remuneration; rendezvous; renege; reparation; repartee.

CHOOSE THE CORRECT USAGE. repertoire, **a**; replicate, **b**; reprehensible, **b**; reprobate, **b**; repudiate, **a**; repugnant, **b**; rescind, **a**; resonant, **a**; respite, **b**; resplendent, **a**; resurgent, **b**; reticent, **a**; retrench, **a**; retrograde, **b**; retroussé, **b**; reverberate, **a**; reverie, **b**; rhetorical, **b**; rictus, **b**; riparian, **a**; riposte, **b**; risible, **a**; rococo, **b**; roué, **b**; rubicund, **a**; rumbustious, **a**; ruminate, **a**; rusticate, **b**.

QUICKPICK: SPOT THE MISPRINTS. 1. racy; 2. resit; 3. rump steak; 4. Rip Van Winkle; 5. relaid; 6. rates; 7. rear admiral; 8. rites; 9. runway; 10. role.

S

WHAT'S THE CORRECT MEANING? sacrilegious, **a**; sacrosanct, **b**; sagacious, **b**; salacious, **a**; salient, **a**; salubrious, **b**; salutary, **a**; sanctimonious, **b**; sang-froid, **a**; sanguine, **b**; sardonic, **a**; sartorial, **b**; Sassenach, **b**; saturnine, **b**; savoir-faire, **b**; scatology, **b**; sceptic, **b**; schadenfreude, **a**; schism, **a**; scintilla, **b**; scion, **a**; scrupulous, **b**; scurrilous, **a**; sebaceous, **b**; secular, **b**; sedentary, **a**; sedulous, **a**; semantics, **b**; semiotics, **a**; senescent, **b**.

WORDS INTO SPACES. 1. simian; 2. similitude; 3. sidereal; 4. sententious; 5. serpentine; 6. shibboleths; 7. sequestered; 8. servile; 9. serrated; 10. serendipitous; 11. simulacrum; 12. sibilant.

CHOOSE THE CORRECT MEANING. sinecure, **a**; sinistral, **b**; Sisyphean, **b**; skulk, **a**; slander, **a**; sobriety, **b**; sobriquet, **b**; sodality, **b**; soi-disant, **b**; soignée, **a**; soiree, **a**; solecism, **b**; solicitous, **b**; soliloquy, **a**; solipsism, **a**; sommelier, **b**; somnambulism, **b**; somnolent, **b**; sonorous, **a**; sophistry, **a**; soporific, **b**; sotto voce, **b**; soupçon, **b**; spasmodic, **a**; spatial, **a**; spavined, **a**; specious, **b**; splenetic, **b**; spoonerism, **b**; sporadic, **b**; spurious, **a**; staccato, **a**; stasis, **a**; statutory, **b**; stentorian, **b**; stigmatise, **a**; stoical, **a**; stolid, **b**; stringent, **b**; stultify, **a**; Stygian, **b**; subjugate, **a**; sublimate, **b**; subliminal, **a**; subservient, **a**; substantiate, **b**; subsume, **a**; subterfuge, **b**; succinct, **b**; supercilious, **b**; superfluity, **a**; supernumerary, **b**; supplant, **a**; suppurate, **b**; surrogate, **a**.

WORDS IN USE: RIGHT OR WRONG? 1. right; 2. right; 3. right; 4. wrong – a sycophantic lawyer would use fawning and flattery to win his case; 5. right; 6. right; 7. wrong – synchronous means 'occurring at the same time'; 8. right; 9. right; 10. wrong – the laboratory would have been asked to analyse the substance – that is to break it down into components to find out what it is; to synthesise is to combine substances to form something more complex.

QUICKPICK: COMPLETE THE SIMILE. 1. cucumber; 2. button; 3. bone; 4. parrot/dog; 5. sheet; 6. mouse; 7. judge; 8. peacock; 9. beetroot; 10. ditchwater.

T

COMPLETE THE WORD. tachometer; tacit; taciturn; tactile; talisman; tangibl; tantamount; taupe; tautological; telekinesis; temerity; temporal; temporise; tendentious; tenet; tenuous; tercentenary; terrestrial; tertiary; tessellated; testator; testosterone; téte-à-téte; theism; therapeutic; thespian; thrall; timorous; tinnitus; tocsin.

WHAT'S THE CORRECT MEANING? torpid, **a**; tort, **b**; tortuous, **b**; touché, **a**; tractable, **c**; traduce, **a**; tranche, **b**; transcend, **b**; transient, **b**; translucent, **a**; traumatic, **a**; travail, **b**; travesty, **b**; tremulous, **c**; trenchant, **a**; trepidation, **c**; trichology, **c**; tridactyl, **b**; triptych, **a**; triumvirate, **b**; troglodyte, **c**; trompe l'oeil, **b**; trope, **a**; truculent, **b**; truism, **b**; truncate, **a**; tsunami, **c**; tumescent, **c**; turbid, **a**; turgid, **b**; turpitude, **a**; tyrannise, **b**; tyro, **c**.

QUICKPICK: COMPLETE THE SIMILE. 1. lord; 2. eel; 3. pancake; 4. bat; 5. old boots; 6. post; 7. hatter; 8. toast; 9. mustard; 10. daisy.

U

SELECT THE CORRECT USAGE. ubiquitous, **a**; ullage, **b**; ululation, **b**; umbrage, **a**; unanimity, **b**; unconscionable, **a**; unctuous, **b**; unequivocal, **a**; unguent, **b**; unilateral, **b**; uninhibited, **a**; unison, **a**; unmitigated, **a**; unprecedented, **b**; unreconstructed, **a**; unseemly, **b**; untenable, **a**; untoward, **b**; unwonted, **a**; urbane, **a**; usurious, **b**; usurp, **a**; utilitarian, **a**; Utopian, **b**.

QUICKPICK: DEFUSING CONFUSABLES. 1. adopt; 2. razed; 3. flair; 4. bated; 5. passed; 6. sceptic; 7. duel; 8. geyser; 9. whetted; 10. hale.

V

CHOOSE THE CORRECT MEANING. vacillate, **a**; vacuous, **b**; vagary, **b**; vainglorious, **a**; valedictory, **b**; valetudinarian, **a**; vanguard, **a**; vapid, **a**; variegated, **b**; vegetate, **b**; vehement, **a**; venal, **a**; vendetta, **b**; veracity, **b**; verbatim, **a**; verbose, **b**; verisimilitude, **a**; vernacular, **b**; vernal, **a**; vertiginous, **b**.

COMPLETE THE SENTENCE. 1. vis-à-vis; 2. virago; 3. virtu; 4. viable; 5. vicissitudes; 6. vindictive; 7. vilify; 8. virulent; 9. vicarious; 10. vindicate.

IDENTIFY THE WORD. visceral; viscous; vitiate; vitreous; vitriolic; vituperation; vivacious; vivisection; vociferous; volition; volte-face; voluptuary; vortex; votary; vouchsafe; vox populi; voyeur; vulpine; vulturine.

QUICKPICK: ODD MAN OUT. 1. occupied; 2. velocity; 3. barren; 4. satisfied; 5. vicious; 6. satisfied; 7. dreary; 8. authorise; 9. careless; 10. vulgar.

THE PENULTIMATE REVISION. As noted at the end of the exercise, all eight usages are wrong. Check the definitions of those that tripped you up!

WXYZ

CHOOSE THE CORRECT MEANING. wagon-lit, **b**; waive, **a**; wanton, **c**; whet, **b**; winsome, **b**; wizened, **b**; wraith, **c**; wunderkind, **a**; xanthic, **a**; Xanthippe, **b**; xenophobic, **a**; yahoo, **a**; yashmak, **b**; yclept, **a**; zealot, **a**; zeitgeist, **a**; zenith, **c**; zwieback, **b**; zygote, **a**; zymotic, **b**.

QUICKPICK: X-QUIZ. 1. 'In Xanadu did Kubla Khan / A stately pleasure-dome decree: / Where Alph, the sacred river, ran / Through caverns measureless to man / Down to a sunless sea.' 2. Socrates. 3. Xerox. 4. 1895. 5. a rare gas. 6. South Africa. 7. wood. 8. Christ.

Collins Wordpower

English is the most widely used language in the world, yet it is also one of the easiest languages to be misunderstood in. The Collins Wordpower series is the ultimate in user-friendliness for all who have wished for an authoritative, comprehensive yet accessible range of guides through the maze of English usage. Designed for ease of use and illustrated by top cartoonists, these books will enrich your powers of communication – whether in speech, writing, comprehension or general knowledge – and they are fun to use!

PUNCTUATION
0 00 472373 2
How to handle the "nuts and bolts" of English prose £5.99

GOOD GRAMMAR
0 00 472374 0
How to break down the barriers between you and clear communication £5.99

SUPER SPELLER
0 00 472371 6
How to master the most difficult-to-spell words and names in the English language £5.99

GOOD WRITING
0 00 472381 3
How to write clear and grammatically correct English £5.99

VOCABULARY EXPANDER
0 00 472382 1
How to dramatically increase your word power £5.99

ABBREVIATIONS
0 00 472389 9
The complete guide to abbreviations and acronyms £5.99

FOREIGN PHRASES
0 00 472388 0
The most commonly used foreign words in the English language £5.99

WORD CHECK
0 00 472378 3
How to deal with difficult and confusable words £5.99